DATE DUE

# Critical Essays on
# Edgar Allan Poe

# Critical Essays on Edgar Allan Poe

## Eric W. Carlson

**G. K. Hall & Co.** • **Boston, Massachusetts**

Copyright © 1987 by Eric W. Carlson

All Rights Reserved

Library of Congress Cataloging in Publication Data

Critical essays on Edgar Allan Poe.

(Critical essays on American literature)
Includes index.
1. Poe, Edgar Allan, 1809–1849—Criticism and
interpretation.   I. Carlson, Eric W.   II. Title.
III. Series.
PS2638.C75   1987        818′.309        87–18
ISBN  0–8161–8878–5

This publication is printed on permanent/durable acid-free paper
MANUFACTURED IN THE UNITED STATES OF AMERICA

# CRITICAL ESSAYS ON AMERICAN LITERATURE

This series seeks to anthologize the most important criticism on a wide variety of topics and writers in American literature. Our readers will find in various volumes not only a generous selection of reprinted articles and reviews but original essays, bibliographies, manuscript sections, and other materials brought to public attention for the first time. This volume is a collection of 30 reviews and essays tracing the critical reputation of Edgar Allan Poe's career. Among the reprinted materials in this volume are reviews and comments by Margaret Fuller, Rufus Wilmot Griswold, Henry James, Walt Whitman, D. H. Lawrence, Edmund Wilson, G. R. Thompson, and Donald Barlow Stauffer. In addition to an original introduction by Eric W. Carlson, there are new essays by Roger Forclaz, Claude Richard, and Eric W. Carlson written especially for inclusion in the collection. We are confident that this book will make a permanent and significant contribution to American literary study.

James Nagel, GENERAL EDITOR

Northeastern University

# CONTENTS

# INTRODUCTION

The title of this volume points up its primary purpose: to offer essays of truly critical interest for their analytical, interpretive, or evaluative content. Strictly defined, "critical essays" here excludes biographical, textual, and source studies. This introduction is of necessity limited to highlighting those essays that seem original, influential, or historically important. The collection is intended as a companion to, rather than a revised edition of, my earlier *The Recognition of Edgar Allan Poe: Selected Criticism since 1829* (1966).[1]

## 1829-1909

### Poe's Contemporaries

The early reviews set the stage for the unfolding drama of how Poe's life and work would be received and understood in future years. That criticism had not yet developed into an aesthetic discipline may be seen in the frequent reliance on generalization, description, synopsis, or paraphrase rather than conclusions drawn from analysis and specific examples. As Emerson noted in 1846, "criticism is in its infancy. The anatomy of genius it has not unfolded."[2]

Among the earliest responses to Poe's first two volumes of poetry, the comments of John Neal, the Maine-born editor of the *Yankee and Boston Literary Gazette*, were rather typical. "Fairy-Land" he termed "nonsense, rather exquisite nonsense," adding the hope that Poe "might make a beautiful and perhaps a magnificent poem." The 1831 *Poems* were noticed as "a strange mixture of genius and nonsense," of imagination and obscurity.[3] The publication of *The Narrative of Arthur Gordon Pym* in 1838 brought forth thirty-odd notices praising "the skillful air of reality" and the "ingenious mystification" but more often condemning it as "a willful hoax" because of its incredible and shocking episodes.[4] When *Tales of the Grotesque and the Arabesque* (1840) appeared, a fine paragraph notice by the abolitionist Louis Fitzgerald Tasistro (re-

1

printed here) eloquently summed up the high qualities of intellect, imagination, and style of this collection.

Next came the judgments of four prominent New England writers. In reply to Poe's request for a contribution on 19 May 1841, Longfellow noted that "all that I have read from your pen has inspired me with a high idea of your power; and I think you are destined to stand among the first romance-writers of the country, if such be your aim." Five years later he again expressed his admiration for the "force and originality" of Poe's tales.[5] The first full-length critique of the time was James Russell Lowell's in *Graham's Magazine*, February 1845. "A monomania he paints with great power," Lowell wrote. Though he admired the poems and "Usher," he reserved his highest compliment for Poe's criticism: "Mr. Poe is at once the most discriminating, philosophical, and fearless critic upon imaginative works who has written in America."[6] In her two reviews, reprinted here, Margaret Fuller sensed that the tales were the product not only of "genuine observations and experience, combined with an invention which is not 'making up' . . . but a penetration into the causes of things. . . ." Yet she wished that he would "enter the higher walk of the metaphysical novel and . . . give us a deeper and longer acquaintance with its life. . . ." Except for "The Raven" the poems struck her as no better than "fragments—fyttes upon the lyre."

In 1846, E.-D. Forgues, the French literary critic and translator, found the 1845 *Tales* to have "an evident kinship with the serious work of the learned Marquis [Laplace]" in that logic, "the cause and the effect," dominates the narrative action as Poe weighs the probabilities by intuition. Two years later P. Pendleton Cooke offered a "sequel" to Lowell's memoir. Extolling the poems and the science fiction tales, Cooke also singled out "Ligeia" and "Usher" as examples of a wild and poetic imagination. Like Neal and Margaret Fuller, he asked Poe to attempt "one cheerful book made by his invention . . . full of homely doings . . . a book healthy and happy throughout, and with no poetry in it at all."[7] Of the score of reviews of *Eureka*, two were especially noteworthy. One, in the *Evening Express*, reprinted here, probably by John H. Hopkins, Jr., recommended Poe's "extraordinary essay" for its novelty, its logical acumen—equal to that of Isaac Newton—and its "speculative force." A week later it was definitely Hopkins (identified by Poe as the "Student of Theology") whose much longer review complained of Poe's reliance on intuitive guesses, and of his impiety and imbecility of intolerable polytheism.[8]

Dominated by "The Griswold Controversy," this period (1849–60) saw the hardening of opposed attitudes toward Poe. Rufus Wilmot Griswold (1815–57), of course, played the main role. Most accounts have dealt with Griswold's vindictive animosity, his falsification of letters, and his defamation of Poe's character.[9] But here the focus is on Griswold's literary criticism of Poe. It is well to recall T. O. Mabbott's cautionary note regarding Giswold: "Although his tampering with the texts of Poe's letters cannot be excused, he did so many fine things that he must not be regarded as the complete villain some of Poe's later biographers have thought him."[10]

Of the two direct attacks on Poe by Griswold, the "Ludwig" article, the obituary letter printed in the *New York Daily Tribune* of 9 October 1849, is the more familiar and available. In it Poe's writings received scant attention compared to the characterization of Poe as one who had "few or no friends" and one whose "harsh experience deprived him of all faith in man or woman," and so forth. On 2 September 1850, volume 3 of the Griswold (Redfield) edition, complete with the "Memoir," came off the press. Because the "Memoir" appeared in every successive Griswold edition it reached many more readers than any other "authoritative" document on Poe. Today, no longer reprinted and not always available even in research libraries, it remains largely unread. The excerpts here selected represent Griswold's criticism, both objective and biased. The most eloquent and penetrating defense undoubtedly was Sarah Helen Whitman's *Edgar Poe and His Critics* (1860). In her view Poe did not repudiate moral values: the themes of conscience and remorse are present, as in "William Wilson" and "The Man of the Crowd." From her appreciation of "Ligeia," "Morella," and "Eleonora" it is clear that her interest in spiritualism did not distort her judgment. In *Eureka*, however, she found only "a form of unbelief far more appalling than that expressed in the gloomy Pantheism of India."[11]

### Creative Writers on Poe

Almost simultaneously in France a new appreciation of Poe began to take shape with the translation of seven Poe tales between 1845 and 1848. On discovering Poe's writings Charles Baudelaire felt "a strange commotion" or "unbelievable sympathy." Unable to obtain a copy of the Griswold edition, Baudelaire managed to borrow enough to write a two-part essay of forty pages for the *Revue de Paris* in 1852. Revised in 1856, according to W. T. Bandy "it has probably been read by more people in more different countries than anything ever written on Poe. It certainly had a major part in shaping the European view of Poe."[12] Essentially Baudelaire saw Poe as the alienated artist—*le poète maudit*—which became the central image of Poe among artists and creative writers, especially in Europe.

The 1857 essay is reprinted here in Professor Alfred Engstrom's translation, livelier and more idomatic than the Hyslop version. Poe's poetry Baudelaire described as "something deep and shining like a dream, something mysterious and perfect like crystal." Through Baude-laire's insights into Poe's aesthetics and poetics, Poe became the major influence on the Parnassians, the Symbolistes, and Modern Poetry.

In 1861 the forty-year-old Dostoevski published a translation of three Poe tales in his magazine *Wremia*. In his preface he referred to Poe as "a strange, though enormously talented writer," with a "capri-cious" imagination and "amazing realism." Typical of the poets' response was Algernon Swinburne's 1872 observation that out of American poetry in general there sounded "one pure note of original song . . . neither wide nor deep, but utterly true, rich, clear and native to the singer; the short exquisite music, subtle and simple and sombre and sweet, of Edgar Poe." But if Poe was a great genius and poet, he was also "one of the worst critics that ever existed."[13] In 1875, Able Reid composed "words of answering rebuke" to the moralists and aesthetes who failed to under-stand that Poe's art is linked with "the circles of the universe, . . . the song of eternities, . . . the ear of God." Reid's is but one of many such for-gotten poems—over 300 since 1830—that represent particular imaginative responses to Poe's image or work.[14] In reviewing the Ingram edition of 1874, Robert Louis Stevenson praised Poe's brilliant workmanship and his "almost incredible insight into the debatable region between sanity and madness." Yet, Stevenson added, one wearies of such ingenuity and "begins to marvel at the absence of the good homespun motives and sentiments." And the "ghastly" tales at the end of volume two left Steven-son overcome by "loathing and horror . . . He who could write 'King Pest' had ceased to be a human being." But in "The Pit and the Pendu-lum" and "Hans Pfaal" Poe "cheats us with gusto."[15]

In 1876 Stéphane Mallarmé composed his famous sonnet for the dedication of Poe's tomb in Baltimore. (The improved 1883 version is reprinted here.)[16] Thus in the most eloquent poetic tribute to Poe ever, the purity and power of his poetry became both the theme and the reply and challenge to his detractors, past and future.

Despite a boyhood enthusiasm for Poe's tales and poems, in 1876 Henry James made a notoriously negative comment, reprinted here, on Poe's poetry and intellect, while in the same breath speaking of Poe's "very original genius." This form of criticism by paradox or ambiva-lence also marked the longer statement on Poe as a critic in James's *Hawthorne* (1879). In *The Golden Bowl* James referred to *Pym* as "a wonderful tale . . . which was a thing to show, by the way, what imagina-tion Americans could have."

Thomas Wentworth Higginson's account of Poe's lecture-reading at the Boston Lyceum in 1845 is one of the most vivid and revealing recol-lections of Poe as reader of his own poems. He described Poe's impressive face, then his voice—at first "thin, tremulous, hardly musical," later "attentuated tò the finest golden thread; the audience became hushed, and, as it were, breathless; there seemd no life in the hall but his; and every syllable was accentuated with such delicacy, and sustained with such sweetness as I never heard equaled by other lips." The remarks by Higginson on Poe's poems are discriminating enough, but the severely negative judgments on Poe's *Eureka*, the fiction and the criticism illustrate again how moralistic preconceptions interfered with aesthetic appreciation.[17] As Walt Whitman noted in his *Specimen Days* journal for 1880, he too had his difficulties with Poe's works. But by patient rereading of Poe's poems, he was able to see through the Gothic and demonic to the "the tally-marks of the time."

The 1889 essay by Ola Hansson, the Swedish author and critic, now deservingly regarded as "Poe's first major psychological critic," has only recently been translated into English by Carl Anderson.[18] Poe was seen as anticipating modern mental pathology and psychiatric research in his studies of hypnotism, the loss of consciousness, criminal psychology, and personality doubling. Hansson also applied Carl Du Prel's monistic theory of personality, which posited a "transcendental" nucleus of organic wholeness not unlike the concept of the Unconscious.

Among young creative writers, Willa Cather responded to Poe's life and works with a remarkably eloquent appreciation in a talk to the literary societies at the University of Nebraska in June 1895, the end of her senior year. Identifying deeply with Poe the artistic genius who was misunderstood, friendless, and plagued by hunger, not alcoholism, she saw Poe as, except for Hawthorne and James, "our only master of pure prose"; except for Lowell, "our only great poet. . . . He first gave the short story purpose, method, and artistic form." Similarly, in 1896 Ruben Darío (1867–1916), a young Nicaraguan poet and essayist, composed a romantic, rhetorical tribute in which he viewed Poe as an Ariel, with an innate mythological gift rich in religious and philosophical convictions and speculations.[19]

In France, Remy de Gourmont in his "Marginalia on Edgar Poe and Baudelaire" (1904), devoted numbers 18 and 19, reprinted here, to "The Philosophy of Composition" as a "paradox" in its absurd claim to know what "takes place in the impenetrable night of the subconscious." J. Brander Matthews's essay on "Poe and the Detective Story" significantly defined and illustrated the difference between the "mystery-mongering" of such writers as Dickens and Balzac, on the one hand, and Poe's shift to a "new key" in the portrayal of character—"the recognition of the unsuspected capabilities of the human brain."[20]

As a British centenary tribute to Poe the London *Nation* on 16 January 1909 ran a brilliant essay by George Bernard Shaw, included here. Condemning both America and England for their materialism and sensuality, Shaw proclaimed that "Poe remains homeless." Yet he became "the most legitimate, the most classical, of modern writers, . . . the greatest journalistic critic of his time," and the author of "exquisitely refined" poetry. "'Ligeia' is unparalleled and unapproached." Another major centenary tribute came from Edmund Gosse, who took up the dismissal of Poe by Leslie Stephens and Henry James by admitting that the "value" of Poe's verses lay not in their moral truth or ideas but in an "indefinite and indeed indefinable delight," in "language so definite and pure that when he succeeds it is with a cool fulness . . . that clear sound of a wave breaking on the twilight sands. . . ." He was the earliest modern poet to employ symbolism "by drawing over a subject veil after veil of suggestion." By insisting on mystery and symbol and restoring to poetry a "primitive faculty," Poe became "the discoverer and founder of Symbolism."[21]

## 1910-1949

The original version (April 1919) of D. H. Lawrence's famous essay, reprinted here, remains relatively unknown in comparison with the 1923 version, which added only some humorous comments and some views on love and on the Holy Ghost (as a metaphor). The theme of intellectual domination or spiritual vampirism was central to both versions and influential on Poe criticism, especially Allen Tate's. But the 1923 edition omitted the opening pages of the earlier version, which presented the metaphor of the tree dying down to its elemental state in winter. Lawrence viewed Poe's tales as "science" rather than art because "they reveal the workings of the great inorganic forces, disruptive within the organic psyche," as in the central stories, "Ligeia" and "Usher."

Paul Valéry's "On Poe's *Eureka*" is offered here in the recent translation by Malcolm Cowley and James Lawler. Though Valéry wrote this preface to Baudelaire's translation of *Eureka* of 1921, it was thirty years earlier that Valéry had discovered this "poème cosmogonique moderne," one of the oldest forms of myth literature. His later view here is colored by a sense of irony and scepticism as to Poe's concepts of causality, finalism, and consciousness inherent in matter. Despite this ambivalence, Valéry saw Poe as anticipating modern science.

In 1925 William Carlos Williams published a landmark essay on Poe in his *In the American Grain*. As if replying to Shaw's and Eliot's view that Poe's work placed him in the European or English tradition, Williams held that Poe's sense of an American locality represented "a reawakened genius of place," an authentic "provincialism." In Poe's tales the feeling of locality is not one of sentiment or mood, nor of trees and Indians, but a feeling that is "the hidden, under, unapparent part," which gives a quality of "luminosity" to his imaginative prose. Poe was American, a product of American experience—truculent, hot, angry. "In him American literature is anchored, in him alone, on solid ground."[22]

The following year, Edmund Wilson set forth his views in "Poe at Home and Abroad," another milestone in the history of Poe criticism. Wilson blamed a faulty historical sense for the prevailing belief that Poe had no connection with his time or with "reality." To Wilson, Poe was a "thorough romantic" and a "bridge" between Romanticism and later nineteenth-century Symbolism.[23]

Howard P. Lovecraft became famous for his 1927 essay on "The Supernatural Horror in Literature" in which he gave Poe "a permanent place as deity and fountain-head of all modern diabolic fiction." Poe was also credited for his "impersonal and artistic intent . . . aided by a scientific attitude not often found before; whereby Poe studied the human mind rather than the usages of Gothic fiction." Malcolm Cowley in "The Edgar Allan Poe Tradition" expressed a characteristic stance of the journalistic appreciation of Poe when he wrote that Poe has been "curiously misjudged . . . by professors of literature, by philosophers, and by critics in general." Summarizing the findings of the psychological critics, Cowley concluded that, though "the causal critics have no real standards of judgment, . . . the bent of Poe's genius was certainly influenced by his physical and psychical infirmities, but his genius, in the strict sense, was produced by more complicated forces which can probably never be determined." Poe was "probably the most important American man of letters" whose effect on literature here, in England and on the Continent, has been "greater than that of any other American author."[24] The view that Poe was steeped in the Western intellectual tradition received further support in *Biblical Allusions in Poe* by William Mentzel Forrest, professor of Biblical History and Literature at the University of Virginia. Despite its overly narrow title, this scholarly work is one of the most comprehensive studies of the religious and philosophical roots of Poe's ideas.[25]

Poe's achievement as a critic was appraised in a chapter of *American Criticism: A Study of Literary Theory from Poe to the Present* (1928) by Norman Foerster, one of the leading neo-Humanists of the time. Poe's alleged failure to fuse the moral and the aesthetic in art as in life was blamed on his deficient ethical development and his "lack of interest in humanity." He was "unmoral and unphilosophical in his poems and tales because he was himself unmoral and unphilosophical. . . ." Poe was also charged with a "diffused romanticism," Shelleyan, not Platonic; with a notion of "strangeness" that is infernal, not supernal; and with a theory of art that is conscious and rational, not organic. In her classic essay, "The Omnibus of Crime" (1928), Dorothy L. Sayers credited Poe with "the formula of the eccentric and brilliant private detective" and with the basic plot elements in the detective story, especially in "Rue Morgue."[26]

"The Facts in the Case of Monsieur Poe," another long and notorious attempt at an expose, appeared in *Contemporaries and Snobs* (1928) by Laura Riding. Without the slightest sympathy and without any evidence of interpretive understanding of the writings, Riding's attack is easily the most contemptuous of the three major destructive essays on Poe. "The mystery is not Poe, but how Poe ... ever came to be a legitimate subject at all with serious readers and still more serious critics.... The only explanation, indeed, for Poe is that nobody has ever read him." Meanwhile, Aldous Huxley had published his "Vulgarity in Literature." Poe, he maintained, is not a major poet; for the English reader "a taint of vulgarity" spoils all but two or three of the poems—"the marvellous 'City in the Sea' and 'To Helen,' for example, whose beauty and crystal perfection make us realize, as we read them, what a very great artist perished on most of the occasions when Poe wrote verse." That "Diamond rings on every finger proclaim the parvenu" Huxley illustrated by two stanzas from "Ulalume." In so doing, however, he failed to sense the hypnotic function of Poe's sound effects.[27]

In direct contrast to Huxley's in both content and form, Floyd Stovall's three fine essays in *University of Texas Studies in English* (Nos. 9, 10, 11 in 1929–31) dealt with the very elements missing in Huxley's essay—with the philosophical ideas in "Al Aaraaf," with Poe's debt to Coleridge and Schlegel, and with Poe as "a poet of ideas."[28]

In 1931 Poe's humor was the subject of two studies: James S. Wilson's "The Devil Was in It" on Poe's burlesquing the style of several popular authors of his time; and Constance M. Rourke's pages on Poe in *American Humor: A Study of the National Character*, in which the romantic tradition of the American comic tale is credited as the primary source of Poe's use of the burlesque, the hoax, the comic fantasy, and the dramatization of subconscious conflict in the first person, as in "William Wilson."[29]

Marie Bonaparte's famous three-volume study first appeared in French as *Edgar Poe: Sa vie, son oeuvre—Étude psychanalytique* (Paris: Demoel et Steele, 1933), subsequently translated into German, Italian, and by John Rodker into English as *The Life and Works of Edgar Allan Poe: A Psycho-Analytic Interpretation* (1949). Despite its doctrinaire extremism, it has become recognized as the classic Freudian opus on Poe. His "grim contribution," Bonaparte claimed, is the "immense cathartic value" of his work in helping men to adapt to "the universal misery," "the ill-chance," through "sadism" or "erotic aggression against that first of all victims, the mother—woman."[30] In the name of such a pessimistic "realism," Freud's doctrines and special terminology were applied in an inconsistent yet unsparing way, as Roger Forclaz so tellingly points out in his essay on "Poe and Psychoanalysis." At the same time, Killis Campbell in *The Mind of Poe and Other Studies* applied his scholarship to probe mind and meaning without benefit of Freud. Ernest Marchand's

"Poe as a Social Critic" also has held up these past fifty years as a defini-tive study of Poe's views on democracy, progress, and social reform.[31]

In his chapter on Poe in *American Prosody* (1935), Gay Wilson Allen credited Poe for being "the first American author to publish a real treatise on English and American prosody," which remains "little studied, and still less understood." After an analysis of *The Rationale of Verse* came an exposition of Poe's prosodic theory, the problem posed by Poe's revisions, and the characteristics of Poe's rimes, consonants, and metrics. Two years later Yvor Winters in his "Edgar Allan Poe: A Crisis in the History of American Obscurantism" expressed violent disagreement with "the impressive body of scholarship" from Harrison, Woodberry, and Stedman down to such writers as Campbell and Stovall. The central problem in Poe criticism was identified as "the late romantic theory and practice" of which Poe was seen as both an extreme and typical example. He is therefore "a bad influence" as well as "an explicit obscurantist."[32]

Another notable event was the publication of Arthur H. Quinn's *Edgar Allan Poe: A Critical Biography* (1941). Here, at long last, Poe critics had a fully documented, scholarly biography free of psychologiz-ing or other speculation about the nature of Poe's personality. To this day it remains the most reliable traditional Poe life-and-letters.[33] In his *Murder for Pleasure: The Life and Times of the Detective Story*, Howard Haycraft described in detail how Poe's three Dupin tales set the pattern for "the entire evolution of the detective romance as a literary form" by identifying and illustrating ten contributions by Poe to the internal structure of the genre.[34] "Poe as a Literary Critic," a second important essay on Poe by Edmund Wilson, appeared in the *Nation* on 31 October 1942. Comparing Poe's achievement as a critic in his day to Shaw's and Eliot's in theirs, Wilson disposed of Henry James's provincialism charge: "Intellectually he [Poe] stands on higher ground than any other American writer of his time." Wilson offered his own evaluation of Poe as a critic in these often-quoted words: "His literary articles and lectures, in fact, surely constitute the most remarkable body of criticism ever produced in the United States."[35]

There was a certain poetic justice in the fact that Poe, like Whitman, ignored by the New Critics as too romantic to be worthy of attention, should be declared by George Snell to be "The First of the New Critics." Poe's advocacy of objective analysis of "the poem per se" in all its complexity and subtlety was seen as marking the beginning of modern-day textual criticism.[36] Matthiessen in his long essay in the *Sewanee Review* (1946), later reprinted in *The Literary History of the United States* (1: 321–42), also credited Poe with insisting on "the importance, not of the artist, but of the created work of art. He stands as one of the very few great innovators in American literature. Like Henry James and T. S. Eliot, he took his place, almost from the start, in international culture as an original creative force in contrast to the more superficial international vogue of Cooper and Irving." In 1949, N. Bryllion Fagin published *The Histrionic Mr. Poe*, which remains the only detailed study that has traced and analyzed the dramatic elements in Poe's writings.[37]

In "From Poe to Valéry," T. S. Eliot described the influence of Poe on French poets as both "immense" and "puzzling." Holding that Poe's writing does not stand up to close analysis, that his ideas are provincial and his poetic diction faulty, Eliot nevertheless was convinced that by reading Poe through the eyes of Baudelaire, Mallarmé, and Valéry, we too would discover the importance of Poe's work as a whole. Three generations of French poets had "seen something in Poe that English-speaking readers have missed." Echoing Shaw, Eliot placed Poe as "a kind of displaced European . . . a wanderer with no fixed abode." More surprising was Eliot's belief that Poe lacked a coherent and consistent view of life, for a familiarity with Poe's work as a whole would reveal the opposite to be true. For English and American readers "The Philosophy of Composition" is "either a hoax, or a piece of self-deception. . . ."[38]

"Our Cousin, Mr. Poe," the first of two major Poe essays by Allen Tate, echoed D. H. Lawrence by elaborating on Poe's "vision of dehumanized man" and the theme of "spiritual vampirism." In sharp contrast to "the American case" against Poe before the First World War—a case that rested on Poe's alleged indifference to moral values—Tate maintained that "there is no indifference; there is rather a compulsive, even a profound, interest in a moral problem of universal concern." Impressed by Poe's brilliant art as an anticipation of Kafka without the latter's obscurities, Darrel Abel analyzed the subtleties of the setting in "Usher" as both descriptive (of mood) and symbolic (the house, tarn). The matter-of-fact, sceptical narrator was seen as gradually becoming convinced of supernatural causation, and Roderick, suffering from introverted vitality and hypochondria, was understood to be wracked by a conflict between Life-Reason and Death-Madness, his final shriek of "Madman" marking his loss of sanity.[39]

## 1950-1969

*Modern Criticism*

The outpouring of major essays before and after 1949, the centennial year, has come to be recognized as one of several significant breakthroughs in Poe criticism. In his introduction to the 1950 Rinehart edition of Poe's works,[40] W. H. Auden praised *Pym* as "one of the finest adventure stories ever written." Auden agreed with Valéry that the remarkable intuitive predictions in *Eureka* have been confirmed and that this lucid prose-poem combined most of Poe's obsessions—his passions for unity and logic. Because characters like William Wilson "cannot exist except operatically" Poe's "operatic" style and decor are dramatically right. In "The Raven" the thematic and the prosodic interests often conflict. Similarly, "Ulalume," an interesting experiment in diction, sacrifices sense to the vowel sounds, Auden held.

In a landmark lecture on "The Angelic Imagination" Allen Tate attempted to define "what I think I have seen that nobody else has seen," namely the "philosophic perspective" implicit in the three angelic colloquies and in *Eureka*. But when Tate found only the unity of a silent God, an abyss of nothingness, a zero, he overlooked the closing theme of "Life—Life—Life within Life . . . and all within the Spirit Divine." And when he again called Poe "the transitional figure in modern literature because he discovered our great subject, the disintegration of personality," Tate missed the positive countertheme—the reintegration of the divided self.[41]

In "Poe's Imaginary Voyage," the first full critique of *The Narrative of Arthur Gordon Pym*, Patrick Quinn found this novel to be a true voyage of the mind bringing to the surface the submerged emotional life. Despite its obvious flaws, *Pym* has coherence of structure and theme in its pattern of recurrent revolt and deception. In "A Reinterpretation of 'The Fall of the House of Usher,'" Leo Spitzer centered on the incestuous, sterile love of the Ushers. Madeline resists the curse and later frees herself from the tomb, "the true male and last hero of the House of Usher" in her will to live.[42]

In the mid-1950s William Whipple published two pioneering analyses: "Poe's Two-Edged Satiric Tale," on "The System of Doctor Tarr and Professor Fether" as a satire of the "moral treatment" at insane asylums of the day; the other, "Poe's Political Satire," on "The Man That Was Used Up."[43] Poe as a Southerner was the subject of several studies by Jay B. Hubbell, first in *The South in American Literature, 1607–1900* (1954), in a chapter on Poe's conservative views of society, women, literature, New England, and its attitudes. In an essay on "Poe and the Southern Literary Tradition,"[44] Hubbell concluded that Poe was Southern in his literary formality, classicism, and stylistic excesses.

Also in 1954 Clark Griffith in "Poe's 'Ligeia' and the English Romantics"[45] read this serious take as a burlesque and a satire. It was published in the same year as "How to Write a Blackwood Article" and soon after "Silence," both of which Griffith regarded as satires of Transcendentalism. "Silence" is "a ruthless parody of Transcendentalism," he flatly stated, without the slightest evidence, noting only "its Gothic background plus its inarguable irony" and "its lush prose." Contrary to Griffith's view, only one-tenth of "How to Write a Blackwood Article," concerns itself with Transcendentalism. That "Blackwood" is a satire does not make "Ligeia" a sequel. And, out of context, the verbal echoes of "Silence" prove nothing. Griffiths was most inaccurate when he said that "the narrator [in 'Ligeia'] is pictured as a psychopath" and that Poe is "slyly mocking Ligeia's spiritual depths" when he compares them to "an assortment of oddly incongruous details," the circle of analogies. Those analogies function as positive symbols, not "oddly incongruous details."

Edmund Wilson revised his earlier "Poe as a Literary Critic" (1942) for *The Shock of Recognition* (1955, 1969), coming to Poe's defense by describing his critical prose as "sharp and precise: our only first-rate classical prose of this period. There is no other such critical survey in our literature." In strong disagreement with W. H. Auden's introduction to Poe, Howard Mumford Jones defended "The Raven" in "Poe, 'The Raven,' and the Anonymous Young Man," filling out the character of the persona as credible, and justifying the prosodic interest as "one and indissoluble" with the theme.[46]

In 1957 two excellent studies enriched the field of Poe criticism. Edward H. Davidson's *Poe: A Critical Study* developed the thesis that Poe tried to solve the problem of Cartesian dualism by renouncing the real world and reconstructing through artistic experience the mind's unity with the world. If Davidson failed to demonstrate his claim that Poe attempted to invent a new symbolism, a new use of language for new poetic meaning, his keen analysis of *Pym* as consistent with Poe's other work was convincing. Patrick Quinn's *The French Face of Edgar Poe* contained five chapters on the French response to Poe, the earlier essay on *Pym*, and analyses of the double in "William Wilson," "The Man of the Crowd," and the detective stories. The final chapter examined the themes of death, death as metamorphosis, the fusion and continuity of life and death, of dream and fact, the double, etc., as these express "the life of a great ontological imagination." In Harry Levin's *The Power of Blackness: Hawthorne, Poe, and Melville*, chapter 4, "Journey to the End of Night," concentrated on *Pym* as the first novel of American innocence and individuation. Chapter 5, "Notes from Underground," discussed Poe's tales, concluding that "Poe's cult of blackness is a bold attempt to face the true darkness . . . the narrowing yet bottomless abyss that underlies the human condition."[47]

During 1959 the first two of Richard Wilbur's Poe essays were published: the Introduction to the Dell Laurel *Poe* in March and "The House of Poe," the Library of Congress lecture, on 4 May 1959. The former concentrated on the themes of psychic integrity and visionary self-sufficiency, as in "Eleonora," "Morella," "Ligeia," and the dream journeys of "Arnheim" and "Usher." "The best of Poe's stories . . . are masterly and trailblazing realizations of psychic life." But most of the poems are obscurantist in their "indefinitiveness," a withholding of meaning. "The House of Poe" has been widely read and admired. Restating his conception of Poe's transcendental art as a "deliberate and often brilliant allegory"

Wilbur again defined the poet's psychic conflict that drives him into the hypnagogic dream state, symbolized by the motifs of enclosure or circumscription. Despite Poe's "insane" belief that art should repudiate everything earthly and human, "Poe is a great artist, and I would rest my case for him on his prose allegories of psychic conflict. In them, Poe broke wholly new ground, and they remain the best things of their kind in our literature."[48]

In 1960 three new essays applied entirely different approaches to *Pym*. "The Troubled Sleep of Arthur Gordon Pym" by Walter E. Bezanson developed earlier readings of the dream symbolism, holding that *Pym*, being implausible on the surface, can only be taken seriously on the apocalyptic level. Leslie Fiedler in "The Blackness of Darkness: E. A. Poe and the Development of the Gothic," maintained that this novel is "not a trivial hoax but the archetypal American story." The quest for innocence turns into a gothic nightmare, ending in "death without resurrection, a sterile, white womb. . . ." Moreover, "the proper subject for American gothic is the black man," the American dilemma. In his introduction to the American Century Series edition of *Pym*, Sidney Kaplan speculated that in the concluding portion of the novel, with its "chiaroscuro arabesque" of black and white symbolism, the blacks on the island of Tsalal have Hebrew names and speak a kind of Hebrew; the words on the chasm walls are Ethiopian, Arabic, and Egyptian. Pym, frightened by the blackness around him, flees into "the embracing arms of the comforting White," a revelation that Kaplan attributes to Poe's Biblical fundamentalism and his belief in Negro slavery. "It was the 'will of God' that Poe tried to present in his allegory of black and white at the end of *Pym*."[49]

In 1961–62 Stephen L. Mooney published three notable essays, the first, "Comic Intent in Poe's Tales: Five Criteria," suggesting five "rough rules for classification": ascending or descending motion, group-action, machine-motions, the devil as a character. In "The Comic in Poe's Fiction" Mooney charted a comic progression for a group of selected tales: from disguise, to action, to error, to the comic revelation and result—their common quality being "charades played by marionettes" revealing the deadness and the pretensions of society and, by implication, affirming "the superiority of the solitary man." In his next, a landmark essay, "Poe's Gothic Waste Land," Mooney held that from the conventions of Gothic fiction "Poe fashioned ironic images of man in a nineteenth century age of anxiety which . . . forecast the twentieth century waste land as a theme for literature." Poe's Gothic is a "heightening of sense perception, sublimity of mind; secrecy; terror of soul." "Metzengerstein" and "Usher" are Gothic parables, "fatal dramas of cognition" climaxing in "one symbolic action, a psycho-architectural or psychosomatic gesture, in which mind and body, dying together, become one."[50]

One of the few essays on Poe from the perspective of the American cultural historian was Charles L. Sanford's "Edgar Allan Poe: A Blight upon the Landscape." Poe was viewed in the context of the American Adam's quest for paradise and the American belief in spiritual rebirth and social re-formation, which for Poe meant the extinction of industrialism—the blight on the landscape—and the embracing of poetry as realization of transcendent ideality.[51]

James Gargano's "The Question of Poe's Narrators" became a basic point of reference on the Poe narrator as a dramatic persona defined by the psychology, structure, and purpose of the tale. Whereas "his narrators are often febrile or demented, Poe is conspicuously 'sane'. . . mature and lucid."[52] "Symbol and Sense in Poe's 'Ulalume'" by Eric W. Carlson saw this poem as a problem in criticism because of the readings by Winters, Huxley, Brooks and Warren, James Miller, Jr., and Roy Basler. A detailed analysis of the dramatic structure, conflict, theme, and the entirely functional use of tone, repetition, and sound values, was followed by a stanza-by-stanza interpretation of the conflict between sensuality (Astarte) and spiritual integrity (Psyche).[53] Floyd Stovall added to his impressive list of Poe studies "The Conscious Art of Edgar Allan Poe,"[54] a reply to Eliot, Huxley, Winters, Lawrence, Krutch, and Bonaparte. In a by-now rare yet plausible Gothic reading of "Usher," J. O. Bailey described in detail Roderick's struggle against a power that he feels to be spiritual or psychic vampirism, and that the narrator regards as natural. "The House as a psychic sponge drains Roderick's vitality through his hair and lives on it," Bailey observed.[55]

During 1964 the one Poe book of note was Edd Winfield Parks's *Edgar Allan Poe as Literary Critic* (Athens: University of Georgia Press). Beginning with "Poe as a Magazine Critic," Parks sought to show that Poe's critical theory was narrow, reflecting the emergence of the magazine, and yet independent, analytical, and aesthetic. In his lucid, concise *Edgar Allan Poe* (1965) Geoffrey Rans first established biographical and metaphysical frames of reference, the ideas in *Eureka* being "crucial to an understanding of the underlying patterns of Poe's tales and poems." Then Poe's symbolic, visionary, intuitive art was clarified by incisive comments on "Ulalume" and the ending of *Pym*. An unusual concluding chapter offered a selective survey of Poe criticism from the 1920s to 1960.[56]

Poe's significant anticipations of modern impressionism became fully evident in two original analytical essays by Donald Barlow Stauffer: "Style and Meaning in 'Ligeia' and 'William Wilson,'" reprinted here, and "The Two Styles of 'MS. Found in a Bottle.'" Stauffer analyzed the function of stylistic elements, scanned the rhythmic pattern and noted the symbolic use of words in "Ligeia," etc. In his second essay, Stauffer distinguished the "plausible" style of verisimilitude from the "arabesque" style. In 1970 his third essay dealt with "Poe's Views on the Nature and Function of Style."[57]

After the initial half dozen major essays on *Pym* in the 1950s and early 60s, another six appeared within three years. In "Chartless Voyage: The Many Narratives of Arthur Gordon Pym" (1966), J. V. Ridgely and Iola S. Haverstick responded to this quickening interpretive interest in *Pym* with a line-by-line analysis of the basic texts, reaching the conclusion that *Pym* lacks unity, controlling theme, and serious meaning. "For what *Pym* finally offers us is not mystery but mystification, not a problem for serious explication but an unsolvable puzzle, not complexity of meaning but meaningless complication." The next year Sidney P. Moss added fuel to the debate by basing his case for "the fallacy of thematic interpretation" on the lack of unity of theme and structure.[58] But these efforts to stem, or at least channel, the tide were largely ignored.

In "The Pit and the Apocalypse" David H. Hirsch interpreted Poe's tale as a dream vision of Judgment Day. Using Kierkegaard as a gloss, Hirsch elicited the Existentialist themes of dread and absurdist freedom. In the allusion to Revelation, he found undertones of transcendental meaning, apocalyptic patterns, and a final salvation that is "an absurd leap into transcendence." Georges Poulet, the distinguished French critic, devoted a chapter to Poe in *The Metamorphosis of the Circle* (1967). Poe's "poetry of memory," he maintained, disintegrates into a circle of confused memories, of emptiness and death. Then there comes an awakening, a surging consciousness, an effort "to understand where one is in one's life." That horror is followed by the horror of knowing that life, like a whirlpool, is a closed cycle of existence. In "The Comic Masks of Edgar Allan Poe" Robert Kiely saw Poe as "a fabricator and fantasist" whose peculiar humor functioned as a mask of rationality to preserve sanity, often ending in terror, and hiding Poe's anger toward society and toward God for his indifference to man.[59]

Three critical studies in 1967–68 threw new light on Poe's detective stories. A review by Richard Wilbur entitled "The Poe Mystery Case" analyzed in detail Dupin's two modes of thought and two voices, along with other double motifs, in "Rue Morgue." Given the "allegorical stratum" of this tale, Wilbur interpreted the three fourth-floor apartments as becoming a single structure signifying Dupin's "reintegrated" consciousness as he uses his genius "to detect and restrain the brute in himself, thus exorcising the fiend." In a piece of detective work of his own, John Walsh in *Poe the Detective: The Curious Circumstances Behind "The Mystery of Marie Roget"* (1968) studied the real case on which Poe based his tale and proved that Poe had made insertions, deletions, and footnotes in an effort to match his account with developments in the case, developments different from the facts and conclusions he had imagined. Another fine corrective essay, "The Mystery of Marie Roget"—A Defense" (1969) by Richard P. Benton, related this story to a form known as the "anatomy" or colloquy, a mixed form with elements of both the tale and the essay. It is also a satire of the Jacksonian common man. In brief, it is "the most genuine piece of detective fiction Poe wrote." Another mystery was solved by John E. Reilly in "The Lesser Death-Watch and 'The Tell-Tale Heart.'" The narrator was seen as a victim of paranoid schizophrenia when the volume and tempo of the insect sound is mistaken for the beating heart of the old man—an example of the "enlarging of the psychological dimension of Poe's fiction."[60]

Poe's views of transcendentalism and the New England Transcendentalists were examined in scholarly detail by Ottavio M. Casale in "Poe's Transcendentalism." Surveying Poe's response to Kant, Coleridge, and Emerson, Casale found that Poe objected more to their style, "cant," and "mysticism" than their "substance"—that, in fact, he praised transcendentalism as "an ennobling philosophy," including the idea of an immanent God and the primacy of intuition. In one of the most integrative and challenging analyses of the decade, Joseph J. Moldenhauer clarified Poe's unitary theory of art, mind, nature, and metaphysics in "Murder as a Fine Art: Basic Connections between Poe's Aesthetics, Psychology, and Moral Vision."[61]

In *The Romance in America* (1969) Joel Porte focused on three tales, "The Raven," and *Pym*. "Usher" is a dream allegory of incest, "Ligeia" a "dark erotic fantasy," and *Pym* the ultimate romance, "a journey that ends ... in an apocalypse of cosmic mystery." In his long chapter on "The Death of the Present: Edgar Allan Poe" John F. Lynen argued, in overabstract fashion, that Poe's poems and tales depicted experience consonant with Poe's ontology and cosmogony in *Eureka*. Differing with Wilbur's view that Poe's characters represent states of mind, Lynen saw "a certain relevance today" in the driving compulsion of the Poe protagonist to achieve unity and beauty beyond time and experience to the point of losing his identity as he becomes one with God or the universe.[62]

Also in 1969 four new books on Poe appeared. Floyd Stovall's *Edgar Poe the Poet: Essays New and Old on the Man and His Work* has already been noted for its individual essays as they originally came into print. In his *Poe: Journalist and Critic* Jacobs investigated thoroughly the origins and tenets of Poe's aesthetic, epistemology, and rhetoric, and in the final two chapters defined Poe's perspective in terms of pantheism, a transcendental World Spirit or Life Force, gradation as the order of nature, man's power of unmediated cognition, and his visionary capacity. Louis Broussard in *The Measure of Poe* attempted "to assign a renewed emphasis ... to Poe's work as allegory and symbolism" by examining *Eureka*, the colloquies, "The Raven" and the tales, concluding that Poe's aesthetic and philosophy were one, and that *Eureka* reached beyond dissolution and death to a romantic vision of unity of life. For all its undue emphasis on the influence of *Blackwood's* on Poe's writing, Michael Allen's *Poe and the British Magazine Tradition* has become a point of reference for the "two-audience" theory that a "quality-popularity" readership of the elite "few" and the gullible "many" caused Poe to adapt his work to certain British magazine conventions.[63]

## 1970-1985

The new decade began auspiciously with notable essays and two new volumes. Robert A. W. Lowndes's "The Contributions of Edgar Allan Poe" in *The Mystery Writer's Art* included thirty-two contributions in all, and discussions of three Dupin tales. In "Hawthorne's 'Plagiary': Poe's Duplicity," Robert Regan suggested calling Poe "the Captain Kidd of Literature" because of the number of "treasure-maps" he left to decoders of his "duplicity." Thus Regan read "The Mask of the Red Death" as "a colossal spoof" that delights because "it raises us above less perceptive readers."[64]

Especially noteworthy were two highly original essays by Barton Levi St. Armand: "Poe's 'Sober Mystification': The Uses of Alchemy in 'The Gold Bug,'" an analysis of Poe's use of alchemical materials and the process of transmutation, though "Legrand depends as much upon the unmediated grace of unknown powers as upon his innate ingenuity." "Usher Unveiled: Poe and the Metaphysic of Gnosticism" disclosed a whole pattern of gnostic, hermetic, and alchemical symbols and ideas in "The Fall of the House of Usher." In the next issue of *Poe Studies* Alexander Hammond summarized his extensive research in "A Reconstruction of Poe's 1833 Tales of the Folio Club: Preliminary Notes." Although he failed to question whether four of the eleven tales are satires, he perhaps justly concluded that the loss of this "major" satiric project "significantly distorted Poe's literary reputation." The same question carried over into "Splitting Poe's 'Epicurean Atoms': Further Speculations on the Literary Satire of *Eureka*," by Harriet R. Holman, who found that Poe used the discredited Epicurean atomic theory as "an elaborate and protracted conceit" in his war against the Boston transcendentalists.[65]

In *Edgar Poe: Seer and Craftsman* (1972) Stuart Levine focused on selected tales in which he noted a consistent pattern of "transcendental philosophy," with its source in Concord. *Eureka* has a "purely occult thesis . . . the interconnectedness of all things" and Dupin is a Transcendental artist hero who "creates a beautiful pattern . . . in the act of perceiving." *Pym* is hack work, "a very bad book . . . a cliff hanger." In the same year another, more informal, personal appreciation of Poe was published: Daniel Hoffman's *Poe Poe Poe Poe Poe Poe Poe*. A flip, at times flippant, challenge to academic treatises, this idiosyncratic account of the author's experience with Poe's work had a serious purpose in studying the seven faces of Poe, with a separate chapter each on *Pym* and "Usher."[66]

*Papers on Poe: Papers in Honor of John Ward Ostrom* (1972), ed. Richard P. Veler,[67] contained seventeen articles representating a variety of critical perspectives. Among the more philosophical was Sidney Moss's "Poe's Apocalyptic Vision," which held that Poe's existentialist view of man and nature is universal in history and literature. In an excellent brief essay on "Poe and the Gothic,"—without the slightest allusion to his earlier view of "Ligeia" as a satiric parody—Clark Griffith joined the symbolist critics by extolling Poe as the writer of "a genuinely new Gothic."

*Papers* also contained Eric W. Carlson's "Poe's Vision of Man," questioning the view that death, annihilation, and disintegration are central to Poe's outlook on life. For Carlson the controlling theme, often indirectly suggested, was rather "the spiritual rebirth or rediscovery of the lost psychal power essential to every man and artist seeking his fullest self-realization." Poe's psycho-transcendentalism was further developed in Carlson's Baltimore lecture, "Poe on the Soul of Man" (1973).

In his contribution, "Poe and 'Romantic Irony,'" G. R. Thompson proposed a reading of Poe's Gothic tales on three levels: supernatural-istic, psychological, and absurdist. Although Poe's favorite German writers—Tieck and A. W. Schlegel—believed in "the idealistic 'transcendence' of earthly limitations through the Godlike immanence and detachment of the artistic mind," Thompson saw them as concerned mainly with the comic, the ironic, and the absurd, that is, with "Romantic Irony." With the publication of *Poe's Fiction: Romantic Irony in the Gothic Tales* (1973)[68] it became clear that Thompson had re-enforced rather than changed or modified this view of Poe. His call for "a new way of reading Poe" to supersede "the traditional Gothicist view"—as if no other existed—in effect dismissed fifty years of significant scholarship and criticism. For at least that long, new symbolic dimensions in Poe's writings had been the subject of study by distinguished Poe specialists—none of them "Gothicist critics." Nor was the case for irony enhanced by claiming that "almost everything that Poe wrote is qualified by, indeed controlled by, a prevailing duplicity or irony in which the artist presents us with slyly insinuated mockery of both ourselves as readers and himself as writer." Incredibly, *Eureka* was said to be "Poe's most colossal hoax" and "Mesmeric Revelation" "a parody on the beatitudes of the psychal mystics." In the non-Gothic fiction, however, elements of irony and satire were justifiably noted, especially social and political satire.

The year 1973 was especially rich in new Poe offerings. In a twenty-page introduction to the Godine edition of *Pym*, Richard Wilbur developed an interpretation of Poe's novel as a dream allegory of regeneration that moves through death and rebirth, hope and despair, perdition and deliverance to final "reunion of the voyager's soul with God or—what is the same thing—with the divinity in himself."[69] By close readings of several tales, Paul John Eakin clarified "Poe's Sense of an Ending" in "the root Poe story," the mesmeric tale, and in "Descent," "Ligeia," and *Pym*, where the ending functions as a vision of the "unutterable sublime" in a significant, not an absurdist, universe. Making exemplary use of Poe's philosophic perspective, Richard O. Finholt in "The Vision at the Brink of the Abyss: 'The Descent into the Maelstrom' in the Light of Poe's Cosmology" drew upon *Eureka* and "Mesmeric Revelation" to show how this tale transforms terror into a lucid cosmic vision of reunification with the Unity (God) toward which all matter tends.[70]

The first comprehensive application to Poe of phenomenology as critical method was David Halliburton's *Edgar Allan Poe: A Phenomenological View*. The "one big thing" that formed the basis of Poe's "system" and cosmogony Halliburton found to be the unity and the deliverance of being, a monistic "plenitude." *Eureka* is Poe's cosmic vision, his essay on the sublime, not a hoax perpetrated on gullible readers. Long chapters on the poems and the tales supported this view of Poe's vision as affirmative and transcendental, in which the heroines embody the theme of ontological power. Pym is seen as "a kind of existentially displaced-person" with a tendency to perverseness. The looming white figure at the end is Poe's attempt to render "pure transcendence." J. V. Ridgely reported on his survey of the criticism of *Pym* in "Tragical-Mythical-Satirical-Hoaxical: Problems of Genre in *Pym*," concluding with six aspects of the novel that needed study.[71]

Roger Forclaz's *Le Monde d'Edgar Poe* (1974) offered an encyclopedic survey of Poe biography, social and intellectual contexts, influences, and artistic theories. With more attention to the tales than the poems, Forclaz found the larger values in Poe's work to be unity, American pragmatism and idealism, dark Romanticism, and a mystical cosmic vision. In Claude Richard's *Edgar Allan Poe: Journaliste et Critique*, the main text of 600 pages was divided into four chapters on Poe as critic and editor, the temptations of an American journalist, Poe's literary tastes in prose and poetry, and his poetics. In his discussion of Poe's aesthetic, Richard saw "The Philosophy of Composition" as a serious, even prophetic essay in Poe's transcendental "poétique théologique."[72]

Although the year 1975 had no magnum opus to its credit, it did produce essays of good to high quality. Eleven interpretive articles appeared in *Poe as Literary Cosmologer: Studies on "Eureka." A Symposium*, edited by Richard P. Benton. Several essays took a new direction by describing Poe's purpose as therapeutic healing through the rhetoric of strengthening, calming, and renewing (John P. Hussey), the attempt to present "wholeness" (Julia W. Mazow), and "a breath-taking leap into self-unification and self-healing" (William Drake). In "Poe and the Sublime: His Two Short Sea Tales in the Context of an Aesthetic Tradition," Kent Ljungquist traced the development of the sublime in nature and in "Ideality" as manifested in "MS." and "Descent," and the movement away from it in "Arnheim," with *Eureka* as the culminating revelation of "the sublimity of the universe."[73]

At least twenty-five good essays on *Pym* appeared in the 1970s. In 1974 J. V. Ridgely, struck by the lack of agreement concerning genre, theme, and meaning in *Pym*, made another attempt to give direction to future criticism by defining six problem areas: the genre of true voyage narratives; Poe's use of sources; the way the text was composed; consideration of the whole text; the hoaxing tone—real or imagined?; and the danger of overingenuity on the part of the critic. Harold Beaver's introduction to the 1975 Penguin edition of *Pym* dwelt not only on the reversals in plot and character, the elements of hoax and deception, but also on Poe's Southern fantasies and Biblical racism in the treatment of Tsalal as an "inverted Eden," with its Hamitic language and symbolism. For Beaver the ending represented Pym's transformation from a passive innocence to a spiritual "rebirth" or revelation that "acknowledges all life."[74]

Despite differences of approach, two fine essays on "Morella" reached surprisingly similar conclusions. James Gargano read the tale in terms of death, but in his concluding paragraph stated forcefully and well the positive main theme of Morella's "trans-human vitality." In "Animatopoeia: Morella as a Siren of the Self," Martin Bickman applied Jungian concepts to arrive at the themes of psychic identity, individuation, and creative mysticism. Edward W. Pitcher in "The Arnheim Trilogy: Cosmic Landscapes in the Shadow of Poe's *Eureka*" discussed the three landscapes as symbolizing the continuity of the earthly and the celestial, the dreams of youth and the complexities of adulthood, and the cosmological universals of *Eureka*. In 1976 Pitcher's "Poe's *Eureka* as a Prose Poem" was one of the few good explications of its ontological and aesthetic implications.[75]

The year 1976 was also made memorable by the publication of Harold Beaver's Penguin edition of *The Science Fiction of Edgar Allan Poe*, fleshed out by the inclusion of the angelic colloquies, the two sea tales, and *Eureka*. The editor's introductory essay, one of the best, carefully established the period interest in electromagnetism, animal magnetism, and "every form of transcendentalism," especially among the French, who were the first to salute Poe as "le créateur du roman merveilleux-scientifique." But if Poe became a dupe of his own hoaxing, as Beaver concluded, then how doubly duped must be those critics who theorized that Poe's gulling of the average reader actually worked by what they call Poe's "duplicity," "sly-foxery," and "self-parody." A new example came to hand in "Poe's 'Tarr and Fether': Hoaxing in the Blackwood Mode," in which Benjamin Franklin Fisher IV argued that textual parallels with "Masque" and "Usher" made these three tales a chain of burlesques. That such was Poe's intention seems highly unlikely. By contrast, Fisher's earlier "Poe's 'Metzengerstein': Not a Hoax" was an admirably straightforward analysis of the lack of comic or burlesque qualities in this tale, with the added note that "No contemporary of Poe's seems to have noticed comic elements in "Metzengerstein.' "[76]

In "Poe's 'Murders in the Rue Morgue': The Ingenious Web Unravelled," Burton R. Pollin attributed the numerous errors and inconsistencies of scene and action to Poe's whimsy and caprice in amusing the reader, quoting Poe on his "method and air of method" and the "purely imaginary" nature of the incidents. Richard P. Benton edited another symposium of varied critical approaches: *Journey into the Center—Studies in Poe's "Pym."* In replies to Ridgely and Haverstick's 1966 article, David Ketterer held that *Pym* has unity and structure, and Alexander Hammond questioned their view of its composition. Leonard Engel related the crises of "enclosure" to the pattern of terror, death, and rebirth, and Barton Levi St. Armand invoked the mythical uroboros and dragon figures for interpretation, especially of the ending. By 1981 Frederick S. Frank in his "Polarized Gothic: An Annotated Bibliography of Poe's *Narrative of Arthur Gordon Pym*" had listed over one hundred studies, chiefly in English, evidence that even if the continuing debate over unity of form or the lack thereof has "fractured *Pym* scholarship into several factions" Poe's novel "is somehow central to an understanding of the total Poe and therefore deserves close reading." The following year Douglas Robinson capped this growing interest with his "Reading Poe's Novel: A Speculative Review of *Pym* Criticism, 1950–1980," the most comprehensive and incisive evaluation of recent years. Noting the lack of consensus, Robinson outlined six key critical issues, including "the text's relation to the author's experiential universe." After his survey of the critical applications of textual and source analysis, psychology, philosophy (especially existentialism), social mythography, satire, irony, and deconstructionist theory, Robinson expressed his personal preference for the "visionary reading" as being "methodologically the most fruitful and descriptively the most accurate." The visionary critics—only a few of which were identified—were praised for "bringing all the accumulated interpretive detail from three decades of close reading to a new perspective on the text-author relation."[77]

The special edition of "Eleonora" for the Print Club of Cleveland was enriched by Richard Wilbur's introduction (reprinted here), which related the tale to the gnostic pattern of life and the arabesque style. In *The Rationale of Deception in Poe*, David Ketterer succeeded in tracing the "full design" of the suggestive "arabesque dimension" in Poe's work as a whole, thus adding significantly to the interpretation of Poe as visionary. Chapter 1 treated transcendence as a "fusion" of experience into a new psychal whirl. Chapter 6 on the "Arabesques" provided a structured discussion of ten tales, with "Ligeia" and "Usher" at the center as the most important embodiments of Poe's transcendentalism. In *Edgar Allan Poe: An American Imagination*, Elizabeth Phillips documented the American quality of Poe's imagination as manifest in his poetic landscapes, his use of "mania" as a recognized form of intensified consciousness, and his response to the American cultural value system as presented in de Tocqueville's *Democracy in America.* In "The Secret of Arthur Gordon Pym: The Text and the Source," Richard Kopley attempted, by a rigorous textual analysis, to establish "the material identity" of the "shrouded human figure" at the end of Pym, concluding that it was "the giant wooden penguin, the figurehead on the ship Penguin." In a sequel, "The Hidden Journey of Arthur Gordon Pym," Poe was found to be in search of his brother, Henry, and the two brothers in search of their dead mother. Both essays seemed to be first steps toward determining "the definitive symbolic identity as well," the real hidden secret.[78]

The new decade began with John T. Irwin's *American Hieroglyphics: The Symbol of the Egyptian Hieroglyphics in the American Renaissance*, which included a 200-page analysis of *Eureka*, "Rue Morgue," two balloon hoaxes, two sea tales, and especially *Pym. Pym* was seen as a Platonic journey quest enriched with the themes of rebirth, doubling, the writing self / the written self, among others. In an extended interpretation of the climactic image of the "gigantic white shadow," Irwin draws on Poe's "psychal fancies" and *Eureka* for contextual value and on parallels in Coleridge, Thoreau, and others, especially New Testament passages. Although the "undifferentiated sublime" is glimpsed through the mist, Pym's final vision of a self-projected "God," remains indeterminate as his "quest for fixed certainty" and the primal Oneness of *Eureka* ends as a death wish."[79]

A rare exchange in Poe criticism, reprinted here, occurred in 1981 when Patrick Quinn was invited to respond to G. R. Thompson's interpretation of the "Usher" tale in *Poe's Fiction* (1973). Thompson's argument centered on the idea that everything may be "the fabrication of the completely deranged mind of the narrator." In his response, Patrick Quinn effectively repudiated the argument for an unreliable narrator and an ironical author in discussing the appearance of the house, the narrator's experience, the ending, and the theme. As is usual with collections, the offerings in the *Poe-Purri: Edgar Allan Poe Issue of UMSE*, 1982, New Series vol. 3, varied in content and quality. Among the noteworthy interpretive essays were David Hirsch's on "Metzengerstein";

James Gargano's on "Usher," and Joan C. Dayan's "The Road to 'Landor's Cottage': Poe's Landscape of Effect." Dayan held that Poe's real aim was not to paint a picture but to use the "picturesque" as a linguistic invention for transcending and recreating what we see. Kent Ljungquist made the same point in more conventional terms. With his usual clarity and insight, Richard Wilbur in his "Poe and the Art of Suggestion," reprinted here, applied the method of cross reference to "William Wilson," "Israfel," "Annabel Lee," and "The Masque."

J. A. Leo LeMay analyzed "The Psychology of 'The Murders in the Rue Morgue' " in a detailed but strained application of a sexuality theory reminiscent of Bonaparte. Dupin represents the head, the mind; the orangutan the body or a psychotic sex mania. Thematically, "we all are potential psychotic sex maniacs ... in a non-rational, chaotic world." Kent Ljungquist's 1983 Baltimore Society lecture identified two drives in Poe's treatment of landscape: "the vast, mysterious splendor of nature's grand design and the subtle, elusive beauty of a fair world well-kept." This and other landscape essays were later reprinted under the same title, *The Grand and the Fair: Poe's Landscape Aesthetics and Pictorial Techniques* (1985). In "Phantasms of Death in Poe's Fiction," J. Gerald Kennedy distinguished four kinds of death in Poe's fiction and saw the Poe hero as unable to transcend his physical and earthly limitations through the aesthetic or the occult experience.[80]

*Structuralist and Deconstructionist Essays on Poe*

In 1980 and 1981, Barbara Johnson in "The Frame of Reference: Poe, Lacan, Derrida"[81] looked back to the beginnings of deconstructionist criticism of Poe in 1966. In that year Jacques Lacan published "Le seminaire sur 'La Lettre volée' " in *Écrits* (Paris: Éditions du Seuil), translated by Jeffrey Mehlman as "The Seminar on The Purloined Letter," *Yale French Studies* 48 (1972): 38–72. Jacques Derrida's response, "The Purveyor of Truth," appeared in *YFS* 52 (1975): 31–113, a translation of "Le facteur de la vérité," *Poétique* 21 (1975): 96–147. In this exchange the letter was viewed as signifier, the pattern of scenes and character relations as forms of "doubling," and the main theme as a struggle for power. Derrida complained that Lacan's reading eliminated the frame of the text, "the stratum of narration through which the stories are told," in short, "literature itself." Johnson summed up Derrida's analysis as not an interpretation but as an act of "untying the knot"—the letter is not a thing nor a word but a knot in a symbolic structure—thus enacting "the impossibility of any ultimate analytical metalanguage, the eternal oscillation between unequivocal undecidability and ambiguous uncertainty."

Also in response to Lacan's seminar, Shoshana Felman pointed out that the "impressive bulk of Poe scholarship, the very quantity of the critical literature to which Poe's poetry has given rise, is itself an indication of its effective poetic power." According to Felman, Lacan's approach, "unprecedented in the whole history of literary criticism," is superior because it concerns itself with "not just meaning, but the lack of meaning" and the disruption of consciousness.[82] Equally revealing was Claude Richard's commentary on the Lacan-Derrida exchange after his lecture at the University of Iowa on 6 December 1980. Richard noted that "Neither Derrida nor Lacan, nor practically any of the modern French critics, is interested in the writer he talks about. That is to say Poe is not the case in point. Literature of text becomes a pretext for philosophy . . . Derrida doesn't know anything about Poe. . . ."[83]

The political consciousness of the Poe "text" and its status as a critical asset also defined the point of departure in "Poe's Secret Autobiography" by Louis A. Renza, who claimed that "Francophile criticism has again purloined the Poe oeuvre from the archives of American literary history right before the eyes of the latter's self-consciously nationalistic guardians." Renza viewed the tales as secretly autobiographical in that Poe imagined their being misread by others; through verbal jokes, puns, anagrams, and so forth, Poe is said to have mocked his readers' attempts to fathom meaning where none exists. Renza (cf. Ricardou) likened Poe to the white figure at the end of *Pym*—Poe's autobiographical ghost fading into the blank margins of the text. It would seem that, apart from his influence, the "value of Poe" escapes the deconstructionist net, thus underscoring the dependence of interpretive criticism on ideatics as well as semiotics,—on the very "original American ideological setting" that Renza dismissed as of little consequence.[84]

Among the earliest structuralists writing on Poe were Jean Ricardou and Roland Barthes. The former's two Poe essays of 1967–1968 were translated into English as "The Singular Character of the Water" [in *Pym*] and "Gold in the Bug."[85] Although praised for his close, creative reading of the text, Ricardou in his exegesis suffered from the same excess of connotation as did Barthes. Barthes's "Textual Analysis of a Tale by Edgar Poe" dealt with "The Facts in the Case of M. Valdemar."[86] Barthes's foreword explained the theory of textual analysis as not a form of literary criticism seeking "to find the sense, nor even a sense of the text" but a playful reader-response guided by working procedures called "codes": the "actional" code (plot), code of the "Enigma" (reader interest), symbolic overtones, "cultural code," and "code of communication" (relation of narrator to reader). No attempt was made to integrate these codes into a unified interpretation.

Recently reprinted from the mid-seventies is John Carlos Rowe's "Writing and Truth in Poe's *The Narrative of Arthur Gordon Pym*,"[87] one of the more lucid of the early Derridean critiques. Regarding *Pym* as a marginal, problematic text in the Poe canon, Rowe viewed the textual inconsistencies as intentionally disruptive of the novel's coherence until Pym's experiences were transformed into a "true journey" symbolic of the writing experience itself. In "Recovering the Purloined Letter: Reading as a Personal Transaction" (1980) Norman Holland applied his concept of "transactive criticism" as a form of reader-response theory. The outcome seemed indistinguishable from subjectivism, however.[88]

*The Naiad Voice: Essays on Poe's Satiric Hoaxing* (1983), ed. Dennis W. Eddings, a reprinting of essays (1954 to 1977) by James Cox, Fisher, Ljungquist, Griffith, Gargano, Regan, and others. Reflecting the contradictory title (naiad hoaxing?), some of the essayists found "duplicity," others unity or harmony. The editor, unlike the contributors, candidly admitted that "many Poe scholars are not convinced by this reading [of Poe as a hoaxer].... If such a tale as 'Ligeia,' for instance, is a satiric hoax, how then are we to account for the obvious seriousness of its development of theme? How, in other words, can Poe be guilty of ridiculing that which he presents seriously?" One answer was provided by Patrick Quinn in his review of *The Naiad Voice.* As no reader with "elitist" credentials had been identified by the advocates of the "two-audience" theory, Quinn, with the help of Allen Nevins, located such a reader, only to discover that this had been his response to *Pym*: "I suppose Poe may be called an artist in putrefaction...."[89]

In his 1983 Baltimore lecture, "Circumscribed Eden of Dreams: Dreamvision and Nightmare in Poe's Early Poetry," G. Richard Thompson seemed to have abandoned his earlier doctrine of "romantic irony," not previously applied to Poe's poetry. Here Poe's transcendental poetics of pure Beauty was set forth in great detail in the context of Platonism as "the shaping matrix of Poe's aesthetics and metaphysics." And *Eureka* was seen not as a hoax but as having a monistic basis for integrating the poetics and the metaphysics. Part two dealt with the *Tamerlane* poems and "Al Aaraaf" as examples of the circumscribed power of the poetic vision.

In the 1970s most of the published works on fantasy literature omitted Poe, and disagreed on how to define "fantasy." Tzvetan Todorov's basic study, *The Fantastic* (1975), devoted three pages only to the uncanny and the marvellous in "Usher," nothing to the fantastic. The chapter on Poe in Brian Attebery's *The Fantasy Tradition in American Literature* (1980) was little better. In the two volumes of selected essays from the First International Conference on the Fantastic in Literature and Film (1980), neither of the two articles on Poe dealt specifically with elements of fantasy. As of 1983 the only study (in English) of any merit was Kent Ljungquist's "The Short Fiction of Poe" in *Survey of Modern Fantasy Literature* (1983), which *Survey* also contained Richard Kopley's summary listing of critical approaches to *Pym*.[90]

In "Inescapable Poe," intended as a major Poe essay for the *New York Review of Books*, 11 October 1984, Harold Bloom tried to deflate what he regarded as the critical myth of "the French Poe" (Poe as "misread" and "overvalued" by Baudelaire and Valéry) and to set forth his view of Poe's "mythopoeic" power and significance. Quoting a "dreadful stanza" from "For Annie," and invoking Aldous Huxley's 1930 attack on "Ulalume," Bloom dismissed the poems as of little or no value. Poe's applied criticism received the same short shrift: "There are no critical insights, no original perceptions, no accurate or illuminating juxtapositions or historical placements," and one negative example: Poe's mistaken praise of Tennyson's "The Lady of Shalott" for its "indefinitiveness" and "vague" spiritual effect. The tales fare better: they have a permanent place in our literary culture, witness "William Wilson" which, despite its "awful diction," survives by virtue of its "psychological dynamics and mythic reverberations." It is Poe's "mythical power that makes him inescapable . . . at once the Narcissus and the Prometheus of American literature." That power derives from Poe's "own difficult sense that the ego is always a bodily ego" (as Freud labeled the instinctive drives), embodied in *Eureka*, where the ego and the cosmos become one; in *Pym*, where "the giant white shadow" represents a magnified projection of Pym, the Gnostic self, the original bodily ego, "the American triumph of the will"; and in "Ligeia," where the daemon of will defines the theme of character as destiny. In mythopoeic terms, Bloom found Poe to be "central to the American canon, both for us and the rest of the world" and all his work to be a "hymn to negativity" in opposition to "the affirmative force of Emersonian America" and its "pragmatic vision of American Self-Reliance."[91]

Another overrated reader-response critique, "Poe: The Captain Regrets" by Judith L. Sutherland, treated *Pym* as a "problematic" fiction on "the borderline between romance and an absurd self-parody." Apparently unfamiliar with much of Poe criticism, Sutherland complained that "there is no key to Poe's own work" and that thematic criticism offers no solution—there is no "overriding theme." Failing to define Poe's philosophic and aesthetic perspective, she too readily settled for humor, irony, a "deep ambivalence," and deception as the keys to *Pym*. The result is an odd patchwork of views borrowed from Irwin, Thompson, Wilbur, Casale, Davidson, and reader-response theory. Poe was "the transcendentalist par excellence," but his vision is impossible and abstract, with a unity that is dangerous; the transcendental self was undermined by Poe's idea of perversity, and that self, in turn, "undermines and destroys the dangerously solipsistic self . . . the soul's doppelganger." Forced back on the distinction between the narrative voice and the authorial voice, Sutherland found Pym's, the emerging voice, to be obtuse, lacking humor and control, and Peters' to be controlled and ironic, while the reader frees himself from Pym but not from Poe.[92]

Evan Carton's *The Rhetoric of American Romance: Dialectic and Identity in Emerson, Dickinson, Poe, and Hawthorne* (1985), obviously indebted to Moldenhauer, Lynen, et al., correlated key passages in *Eureka* and "Psychal Fancies" (*Marginalia*) with selected tales so as to illuminate several basic themes—death and "the ultimate life," double identity, the paradox of the lost self through the process of "reunification" or "intense identification with the universe." Taking John Irwin's *American Hieroglyphics* as his model, Douglas Robinson in *American Apocalypses: The Image of the End of the World in American Literature* claimed Poe and Emerson as "our seminal apocalyptists," thereby placing Poe in "his most significant context." In *Pym* the series of image motifs were held to develop by a process of intensification to a powerful but ambiguous ending: the New Testament "white shadow" that reflectively projects human beings into the transfigured beyond.[93]

Two new essays by Joan Dayan appeared in 1984–85. In the first, "The Identity of Berenice, Poe's Idol of the Mind,"[94] the protagonist gives way to an obsessive quest for identity, purity, and self-renewal. The second essay, "The Analytic of the Dash: Poe's *Eureka*," adapted for this volume, is rich with insights into Poe's various uses of the dash: to define, deflect, suspend, and goad along the path of reflection. In *Eureka* its most significant function is to emend or to present a second thought as part of realization-in-process—"to keep things pending, to make us know uncertainty while imposing bounds on any thought," while tending toward designed idea.

In "Psychoanalysis and Edgar Allan Poe" [A Critique of the Bonaparte Thesis] by Roger Forclaz, Bonaparte's Freudian concepts of necrophilism, sexual impotence, and sadism are exposed as inadequate and fallacious when applied to Poe's writings. Another rewarding essay is Claude Richard's "The Heart of Poe and the Rhythmics of the Poems," which develops step by step the thesis that fundamental to Poe's poetry is the contrast between the cadence of "The Raven," and "the rhythmical creation of beauty" in "Israfel" and "For Annie." So too in "The Sleeper" and "To Helen" (1848) as examples of woman's poetic function as "a luminous center." In "Al Aaraaf," the true poetic voice of Ligeia expresses the universal rhythm or harmony: the ray of light, unheard rhythms, silence, even the sacred number of Being itself, Being as rhythm. "Frames of Reference for Poe's Symbolic Language" by Eric W. Carlson attempts to define the confusing situation in Poe criticism today and to suggest a way out in terms of Allen Tate's concept of "philosophic perspective," Barbara Johnson's "frame of reference" and Carlson's own "parallactic method." Two semantic clusters of key terms are established as frames of reference for Poe criticism, one as defining his epistemology, the other his ontology and cosmogony. Thus a base line is laid for interpreting the symbolic language in, for example, "Usher" and "Ligeia" (especially the symbolic use of *wild*). In conclusion Carlson suggests that if the interpretive Poe community is to reestablish a sound center it must build on such an approach and on the consensus that has developed over the years within the mainstream of Poe criticism.

## Notes

1. Eric W. Carlson, *The Recognition of Edgar Allan Poe* . . . (Ann Arbor: University of Michigan Press, 1966). Hereafter *REAP*.

2. *The Journals and Miscellaneous Notebooks of Ralph Waldo Emerson*, vol. 9 (Cambridge: Harvard University Press, 1960– ), 440.

3. See Burton R. Pollin's "Poe 'Viewed and Reviewed': An Annotated Checklist of Contemporaneous Notices," *Poe Studies* 13 (December 1980): 18–34. Another invaluable documentary source is Part 1 of Dudley Robert Hutcherson's dissertation (University of Virginia, 1936), "One Hundred Years of Poe: A Study of Edgar Allan Poe in American and English Criticism, 1827–1927."

4. Pollin, "Checklist," 21–22.

5. Quoted by Arthur H. Quinn, *Edgar Allan Poe, A Critical Biography* (New York: D. Appleton-Century, 1941), 317. Letter of 17 June 1846 is quoted on p. 511.

6. James Russell Lowell, "Edgar Allan Poe," *Graham's Magazine* 27 (February 1845): 44–53.

7. P. Pendleton Cooke, "Edgar A. Poe," *Southern Literary Messenger* 14 (January 1848): 34–38. Reprint, James A. Harrison, ed., *Complete Works of Edgar Poe*, 17 vols. (New York: Thomas Y. Crowell, 1902), 1:383–92. Also in *REAP*, 21–28.

8. *Evening Express* 12 (12 July 1848): 1. John H. Hopkins, Jr., *The Literary World* 3 (29 July 1848): 502.

9. For the most detailed report, see Quinn, *Poe*, 446–50, 668–76 (Memoir), and reactions by various of Poe's friends and enemies, 677–81.

10. Thomas O. Mabbott, *The Collected Works of Edgar Allan Poe*, vol. 1 (Cambridge: Harvard University Press, 1969), 551.

11. The "Ludwig" article is reprinted in *REAP*, 28–35. For Griswold "Memoir" and Whitman *Poe*, see source notes on respective selections.

12. See W. T. Bandy, *Edgar Allan Poe: sa vie et ses ouvrages* (University of Toronto Press, 1973), xxxi, xxix–xlii, ix.

13. Sir Edmund Gosse and Thomas James Wise, eds., *The Complete Works of Algernon Charles Swinburne* (New York: G. Wells, 1925–27) 20 vols. Cited are *Works* 16:418–19; *Works* 18:384: letter to Paul Hamilton Hayne, 4 July 1884.

14. I am indebted to Professor John E. Reilly for this information.

15. Robert Louis Stevenson, "The Works of Edgar Allan Poe," *Academy*, n.s., 7 (January 1875): 1–2. Reprinted in *The Works of Robert Louis Stevenson*, vol. 11 (New York: The Davos Press, 1906), 255–62.

16. Various translations in prose and verse have been made by Sarah Helen Whitman, Geoffrey Brereton, Roger Fry, Anthony Hartley, Mary Caws, and Mallarmé himself. In the original 1876 version, line 9 read "Du sol et de l'ether hostiles, o grief!" Mallarmé translated that line as "Of the soil and the ether, (which are) enemies, O struggle!" Brereton holds that Mallarmé mistranslated "grief" as "struggle"; usually it means "grievance" or "complaint." Mary Caws and C. F. Mac-

Intyre translate it as "alas." W. T. Bandy has pointed out that "Mallarmé often used words in an etymological sense, or what he considered the etymological sense" and that "line 9 contains an inversion; the logical order should be: 'O grief du sol et la nue hostiles!' If you translate 'grief' as 'alas' the syntax of lines 9–10 is understandably odd" (Letter to the editor, 1 April 1985). Mallarmé's translation, with his notes, may be found in Caroline Ticknor's *Poe's Helen* (New York: Charles Scribner's Sons, 1916), 268–69.

17. Thomas Wentworth Higginson, "Edgar Allan Poe," 10 *Literary World*, (15 March 1879): 89–90. *REAP*, 67–75.

18. See Carl L. Anderson, *Poe in Northlight* (Durham: Duke University Press, 1973), 167–217 for the essay text, chapter 4 for the discussion of Hansson, and pp. 71–72 on the psychologists mentioned.

19. William M. Curtin, ed., *The World and the Parish: Willa Cather's Articles and Reviews 1893–1902* (Lincoln: University of Nebraska Press, 1970), 157–63, 349. Darío's essay, in *Los Raros* and reprinted by Educa, 1972, pp. 7–21. No English translation seems to exist.

20. J. Brander Matthews, *Scribner's* 42 (September 1907):287–93. *REAP*, 81–94.

21. Edmund Gosse, "The Centenary of Edgar Allan Poe," *Contemporary Review* 95 (February 1909): 1–8.

22. William Carlos Williams, *In the American Grain* (Norfolk: New Directions, 1925), 216–33. *REAP*, 127–42.

23. Edmund Wilson, "Poe at Home and Abroad," *New Republic* 49 (8 December 1926):77–80. *REAP*, 142–52.

24. Howard P. Lovecraft, *The Supernatural Horror in Literature* (New York: B. Abramson, 1945), 52–59. Originally published in *The Recluse* (Athol, Mass.: Ben Abramson, 1927). Malcolm Cowley, "The Edgar Allan Poe Tradition," *Outlook* 149 (23 July 1928):497–99, 511.

25. William M. Forrest, *Biblical Allusions in Poe* (New York: Macmillan, 1928).

26. Norman Foerster, *American Criticism* (New York: Houghton Mifflin, 1928), 1–52. Dorothy Sayers, reprinted in *The Art of the Mystery Story* (New York: Simon and Schuster, 1946), 71–109.

27. Laura Riding, *Contemporaries and Snobs* (Garden City, N.Y.: Doubleday Doran & Co., 1928), 201–55. Aldous Huxley, "Vulgarity in Literature," *Saturday Review of Literature* 7 (27 September 1930):158–59; *REAP*, 160–67.

28. These essays, with others, were collected in Stovall's *Edgar Poe the Poet* (Charlottesville, University Press of Virginia, 1969).

29. James S. Wilson, "The Devil Was in It," *American Mercury* 24 (October 1931):215–20. Constance Rourke, *American Humor* (New York: Harcourt Brace, 1931), 179–86.

30. John Rodker, trans., *The Life and Works of Edgar Allan Poe: A Psycho-Analytic Interpretation* (London: The Hogarth Press); also (London: Imago Publishing Co., 1949); and (New York: Humanities Press, 1971), 666–68, 696–97.

31. Killis Campbell, *The Mind of Poe* (Cambridge: Harvard University Press, 1933). Ernest Marchand, "Poe as a Social Critic," *American Literature* 6 (March 1934): 28–43.

32. Gay Wilson Allen, *American Prosody* (New York: American Book Co., 1935). Yvor Winters, "Edgar Allan Poe," *AL* 8 (January 1937):379–401.

33. A. H. Quinn, *Edgar Allan Poe* (New York: Appleton-Century, 1941).

34. Howard Haycraft, *Murder for Pleasure* (New York: Appleton, 1941). The chapter on Poe is reprinted in Haycraft, ed., *The Art of the Mystery Story* (New York: Simon and Schuster, 1946), 158–77.

35. Edmund Wilson, "Poe as a Literary Critic," *Nation* 155 (31 October 1942): 452–53. The later version will be found in this volume under the year 1955.

36. George Snell, "The First of the New Critics," *Quarterly Review of Literature* 2 (1945):333–40.

37. F. O. Matthiessen, "Poe," *Sewanee Review* 54 (Spring 1946):175–205; N. B. Fagin, *The Histrionic Mr. Poe* (Baltimore: Johns Hopkins University Press, 1949).

38. T. S. Eliot's lecture was delivered at the Library of Congress, 19 November 1948, then published in *Hudson Review* 2 (Autumn 1949):327–42.

39. Allen Tate, "Our Cousin, Mr. Poe," *Partisan Review* 16 (December 1949): 1207–19; Darrel Abel, "A Key to the House of Usher," *University of Toronto Quarterly* 18 (January 1949):176–85.

40. *Edgar Allan Poe: Selected Prose and Poetry*, edited with an introduction by W. H. Auden (New York: Rinehart & Co., 1950).

41. Allen Tate, "The Angelic Imagination," lecture delivered at Boston College, February 1951; reprinted in *Kenyon Review* 14 (Summer 1952):455–75.

42. Patrick Quinn, "Poe's Imaginary Voyage," *Hudson Review* 4 (Winter 1952):562–85; Leo Spitzer, "A Reinterpretation of 'The Fall of the House of Usher,'" *Comparative Literature* 4 (Fall 1952):351–63.

43. William Whipple, "Poe's Two-Edged Satiric Tale" *NCF* 9 (September 1954):121–33. "Poe's Political Satire," *UTSE*, no. 35 (1956):81–95.

44. Jay B. Hubbell, "Edgar Allan Poe," *The South in American Literature, 1607–1900* (Durham, N. C.: Duke University Press, 1954), 528–50. "Poe and the Southern Literary Tradition," *TSLL* 2 (Summer 1960):151–75; revised as "Edgar Allan Poe and the South" in *South and Southwest* (Durham, N.C.: Duke University Press, 1965):100–22.

45. Clark Griffith, "Poe's 'Ligeia' and the English Romantics," *University Toronto Q* 14 (October 1954):8–25.

46. Edmund Wilson's 1955 revision of "Poe as a Literary Critic": see source note in text. Howard Mumford Jones, "Poe, 'The Raven'. . ." *Western Humanities Review* 9 (Spring 1955):127–38.

47. Elward H. Davidson, *Poe: A Critical Study* (Cambridge: Harvard University Press, 1957); Patrick Quinn, *The French Face of Edgar Poe* (Carbondale: Southern Illinois University Press, 1957). Harry Levin, *The Power of Blackness* (New York. Knopf, 1958).

48. *Poe: Complete Poems* (New York, Dell Publishing Co., 1959), ed. with introduction by Richard Wilbur, 7–40. For another long Wilbur essay on Poe, see *Major Writers in America*, vol. 1 (New York: Harcourt Brace, 1962), 369–82, reprinted in Wilbur's *Responses* (1976):39–66.

49. Walter E. Bezanson, in R. Kirk and C. F. Main, eds., *Essays in Literary History, Presented to J. Milton French* (New Brunswick: Rutgers University Press, 1960), 149–75. Leslie Fiedler, "The Blackness of Darkness," chapter 11 of *Love and Death in the American Novel* (New York: Hill and Wang, 1960; rev. 1966), 391–400. Sidney Kaplan, ed., *The Narrative of Arthur Gordon Pym* (New York: Hill and Wang, 1960).

50. Stephen L. Mooney, "Comic Intent," *MLN* 76 (May 1961):432–34; "The Comic," *AL* 33 (January 1962):433–41; "Waste Land," *SR* 70 (January–March 1962):261–83, reprinted in *REAP*.

51. Charles L. Sanford, "Edgar Allan Poe," *Rives* (Paris) 18 (Spring 1962): 1–19. *REAP*, 297–307. This essay was revised and expanded for later publication in *American Quarterly* 20 (Spring 1968):54–66.

52. James Gargano, "The Question of Poe's Narrators," *College English* 25 (February 1963):177–81.

53. Eric W. Carlson, "Symbol and Sense in Poe's 'Ulalume,'" *AL* 35 (March 1963):22–37.

54. Floyd Stovall, "The Conscious Art of Edgar Allan Poe," *College English* 24 (March 1963):417–25.

55. J. O. Bailey, "What Happens in 'The Fall of the House of Usher,'" *AL* 35 (January 1964):445–66.

56. Geoffrey Rans, *Edgar Allan Poe* (London: Oliver and Boyd, Ltd., 1965).

57. Donald Stauffer, "The Two Styles...." *Style* 1 (1967):107–20; "Poe's Views...," *ESQ* 60 (Spring 1970):Supplement, part 1, 23–30.

58. J. V. Ridgely and Iola S. Haverstick, "Chartless Voyage," *TSLL* 7 (Spring 1966):63–80. Sidney P. Moss, "Arthur Gordon Pym, or the Fallacy of Thematic Interpretation," *University Review* 33 (1967):299–306.

59. David Hirsch, "The Pit and the Apocalypse," *SR* 76 (October–December 1968):632–52; Georges Poulet, "Edgar Poe," in *The Metamorphoses of the Circle* (Baltimore: J. H. Press, 1967), 182–202, translated by Elliott Coleman; Robert Kiely, "The Comic Masks of Edgar Allan Poe," *Unamesimo* 1 (1967):31–41.

60. Richard Wilbur, in the *New York Review of Books* 10 (13 July 1967):16, 25–28; reprinted in Wilbur's *Responses* (1976), 127–38. John Walsh, *Poe the Detective* (New Brunswick: Rutgers University Press, 1968). Richard P. Benton, "The Mystery of Marie Roget" *SSF* 6 (Winter 1969):144–51. John E. Reilly, "The Lesser Death Watch," *ATQ*, no. 2 (2d Quarter, 1969):3–12.

61. Ottavio M. Casale, "Poe's Transcendentalism," *ESQ* 50 (1st Quarter, 1968): 85–97. Joseph J. Moldenhauer, "Murder as a Fine Art," *PMLA* 83 (May 1968): 284–97.

62. Joel Porte, *The Romance in America* (Middletown: Wesleyan University Press, 1969):53–94. John F. Lynen, *The Design of the Present: Essays on Time and Form in American Literature* (New Haven: Yale University Press, 1969):205–71.

63. Robert D. Jacobs, *Poe: Journalist and Critic* (Baton Rouge: Louisiana State University Press, 1969). Louis Broussard, *The Measure of Poe* (Norman: University of Oklahoma Press, 1969). Michael Allen, *Poe and the British Magazine Tradition* (New York: Oxford University Press, 1969).

64. A. W. Lowndes, in Francis M. Nevins, ed., *The Mystery Writer's Art* (Bowling Green, Ohio: Bowling Green University Popular Press, 1970), 1–17. Robert Regan, "Hawthorne's 'Plagiary': Poe's Duplicity," *NCF* 25 (December 1970):281–98.

65. Barton Levi St. Armand, "Poe's 'Sober Mystification,'" *Poe Studies* 4 (June 1972):1–7; "Usher Unveiled," *PoeS* 5 (June 1972):1–8; Alexander Hammond, *PoeS* 5 (December 1972):25–32; Harriet R. Holman, "Splitting Poe's 'Epicurean Atoms,'" *PoeS* 5 (December 1972):33–37; the first of Holman's articles was entitled "Hog, Bacon, Ram, and Other 'Savans' in *Eureka*: Notes toward Decoding Poe's Encyclopedic Satire," *PoeS* 2 (October 1969):49–55.

66. Stuart Levine, *Edgar Poe: Seer and Craftsman* (Deland: Everett / Edwards, 1972), 158, 167–68, 263. Daniel Hoffman, *Poe, Poe, Poe, Poe, Poe, Poe, Poe* (New York: Doubleday & Co., 1972).

67. Richard P. Veler, ed., *Papers on Poe* (Springfield, Ohio: Chantry Music Press, 1972).

68. G. R. Thompson, *Poe's Fiction: Romantic Irony in the Gothic Tales.* (Madison: University of Wisconsin Press, 1973).

69. *The Narrative of Arthur Gordon Pym*, with introduction by Richard Wilbur (Boston: David Godine, 1973), vii–xxv. Reprinted in Wilbur, *Responses*, 194–214.

70. Paul John Eakin, "Poe's Sense of an Ending," *AL* 45 (March 1973):1–22. Richard D. Finholt, "The Vision at the Brink of the Abyss," *Georgia Review* 27 (Fall 1973):356–66.

71. David Halliburton, *Edgar Allan Poe: A Phenomenological View* (Princeton: Princeton University Press, 1973). J. V. Ridgely, "Tragical-Mythical-Satirical-Hoaxical," *ATQ* 24 (Fall 1974):4–9.

72. Roger Forclaz, *Le monde d'Edgar Poe* (Berne: Herbert Lang, 1974). Claude Richard, *Edgar Allan Poe: Journaliste et critique* (Paris: Klincksieck Press, 1974, 1978).

73. Richard P. Benton, *Poe as Literary Cosmologer: Studies in Eureka* (Hartford: Transcendental Books, 1975). For an excellent review, see Patrick Quinn's "A Potpourri on *Eureka*," *Poe Studies* 9 (June 1976), 29–31. Kent Ljungquist, "Poe on the Sublime," *Criticism* 17 (Spring 1975):131–51.

74. J. V. Ridgely, "Tragical-Mythical-Satirical-Hoaxical: Problems of Genre in *Pym*," *ATQ* 24 (Fall 1974):4–9. *The Narrative of Arthur Gordon Pym of Nantucket*, ed. with an introduction by Harold Beaver (Baltimore: Penguin Books, 1975), 7–30.

75. James Gargano, "Poe's 'Morella': A Note on Her Name," *AL* 47 (May 1975):259–64. Martin Bickman, "Animatopoeia: Morella as a Siren of the Self," *Poe Studies* 8 (December 1975):29–32. Edward W. Pitcher, "Arnheim," *Canadian Review of American Studies* 6 (Spring 1975):17–25; "Poe's *Eureka* as a Prose Poem" *ATQ* 29 (Winter 1976):61–71.

76. *The Science Fiction of Edgar Allan Poe*, ed. with an introduction by Harold Beaver (New York: Penguin Books, 1976), xvii. Benjamin F. Fisher, "Poe's 'Tarr and Feather': Hoaxing in the Blackwood Mode," *Topic* 31 (1977):29–40. "Poe's 'Metzengerstein': Not a Hoax," *AL* 42 (January 1971):487–94.

77. Burton R. Pollin, "Poe's 'Murders in the Rue Morgue,'" *Studies in the American Renaissance: 1977* (Boston: Twayne Publishers, 1977):235–79; Richard P. Benton, "Journey into the Center—Studies in Poe's *Pym*," *ATQ* 37 (Winter 1978): 1–115; Frederick S. Frank, "Polarized Gothic: An Annotated Bibliography of Poe's *Narrative of Arthur Gordon Pym*," *Bulletin of Bibliography* 38 (1981):117–27; Douglas Robinson, "Reading Poe's Novel: A Speculative Review of *Pym* Criticism, 1950–1980," *PoeS* 15 (December 1982):47–54.

78. David Ketterer, *The Rationale of Deception in Poe* (Baton Rouge: Louisiana State University Press, 1979). See pp. 255–57 for a cogent application of Poe's perspective, and p. 274 (note) for Ketterer's rejection of Harriet Holman on *Eureka* as satire. For a more detailed review, see E. W. Carlson, "Poe: Visionary in a Deceptive World," *PoeS* (June 1980):10–12. Elizabeth Phillips, *Edgar Allan Poe: An American Imagination* (Port Washington, N. Y.: Kennikat Press, 1979). Richard

Kopley, "The Secret of Arthur Gordon Pym," *Studies in American Fiction* 8 (1980): 203–18; "The Hidden Journey of Arthur Gordon Pym," *SAR* (1982), 29–51.

79. John T. Irwin, *American Hieroglyphics* (New Haven: Yale University Press, 1980).

80. J. A. Leo LeMay, "The Psychology of 'The Murders in the Rue Morgue,'" *AL* 54 (May 1982):165–88. Kent Ljungquist, *The Grand and the Fair* (Potomac, Md.: Scripta Humanistica, 1985). J. Gerald Kennedy, "Phantasms of Death in Poe's Fiction," *The Haunted Dusk: American Supernatural Fiction, 1820–1920* (Athens, Georgia: University of Georgia Press, 1983).

81. Johnson's paper was first published in *Psychology and the Question of the Text: Selected Papers from the English Institute, 1976–77*, New Series, no. 2, ed. Geoffrey Hartman (Baltimore: Johns Hopkins University Press, 1978), 149–71.

82. Shoshana Felman, "On Reading Poetry: Reflections on the Limits and Possibilities of Psychoanalytical Approaches," *Psychiatry and the Humanities*, vol. 4 (*The Literary Freud: Mechanisms of Defense and the Poetic Will*), ed. Joseph H. Smith (New Haven, Yale University Press, 1980), 119–48.

83. See "Destin, Design, Dasein: Lacan, Derrida and 'The Purloined Letter,'" *Iowa Review* 12 (1981):1–11; interview 12–32. Citations are from pp. 12, 15–16, 19–20.

84. Louis A. Renza, "Poe's Secret Autobiography," *The American Renaissance Reconsidered: Selected Papers from the English Institute, 1982–83*, n.s., no. 9, ed. Walter Benn Michaels and Donald E. Pease, 1985, pp. 58–89.

85. Jean Ricardou, "The Singular Character of the Water," *Poe Studies* 9 (June 1976):1–6; "Gold in the Bug," *PoeS* 9 (December 1976):33–39.

86. Roland Barthes, "Textual Analysis of a Tale by Edgar Poe," trans. Donald G. Marshall, *Poe Studies* 10 (June 1977):1–12; the original in *Semiotique Narrative et Textuelle* (Paris, 1973). Barthes's codes are fully presented in his *S/Z* (Paris, 1970; New York, 1974):260–68.

87. John Carlos Rowe, "Writing and Truth in Poe's *The Narrative of Arthur Gordon Pym*," *Glyph* 2 (1975–76):101–21; reprinted in *Through the Custom House: Nineteenth-Century American Fiction and Modern Theory*, by John Carlos Rowe (Baltimore: Johns Hopkins University Press, 1982), 91–110.

88. See Susan R. Suleiman and Inge Crosman, eds., *The Reader in the Text: Essays on Audience and Interpretation* (Princeton: Princeton University Press, 1980), 350–70.

89. Dennis Eddings, *The Naiad Voice: Essays on Poe's Satiric Hoaxing* (Port Washington, N. Y.: Associated Faculty Press, 1983), ix–x, 155–65. See also Patrick Quinn, "Poe's Other Audience," *PoeS* 18 (June 1985):13–14.

90. Tzvetan Todorov, *The Fantastic* (Ithaca: Cornell University Press, 1975). Brian Attebery, *The Fantasy Tradition in American Literary Tradition* (Bloomington: Indiana University Press, 1980), 37–41. Robert A. Collins and Howard D. Pearce, eds., *The Scope of the Fantastic—Theory, Technique, Major Authors* and *The Scope of the Fantastic—Culture, Biography, Themes, Children's Literature* (Westport: Greenwood Press, 1985). The second volume contains Richard Kopley's "Early Illustrations of Pym's 'Shrouded Human Figure,'" 155–70. Kent Ljungquist, "The Short Fiction of Poe," *Survey of Modern Fantasy Literature*, vol. 4 (Englewood Cliffs, N. J.: Salem Press, 1983), 1665–78.

91. Harold Bloom, "Inescapable Poe," *New York Review of Books* 31 (11 October 1984):23–26, 35–37, reprinted under the title "Americanizing the Abyss"

(147) as the introduction to Harold Bloom, ed., *Edgar Allan Poe*, Modern Critical Views (New York: Chelsea House Publishers, 1985), 1–14. This selection consists of five familiar essays from 1921–54 and three less known from 1972–80.

92. Judith L. Sutherland, "The Captain Regrets," in *The Problematic Fictions of Poe, James & Hawthorne* (Columbia: University of Missouri Press, 1984), 13–37.

93. Evan Carton, *The Rhetoric of American Romance: Dialectic and Identity in Emerson, Dickinson, Poe, and Hawthorne* (Baltimore: Johns Hopkins University Press, 1985). Douglas Robinson, *American Apocalypses: The Image of the End of the World in American Literature* (Baltimore: Johns Hopkins University Press, 1985).

94. Joan Dayan, "The Identity of Berenice, Poe's Idol of the Mind," *Studies in Romanticism* 23 (Winter 1984):489–511; reprinted in Dayan, *Fables of Mind: An Inquiry into Poe's Fiction* (New York: Oxford University Press, 1987).

# Poe's Contemporaries

## Comments on Poe's Poems
John Neal*

If E. A. P. of Baltimore—whose lines about "Heaven," though he professes to regard them as altogether superior to anything in the whole range of American poetry, save two or three trifles referred to, are, though nonsense, rather exquisite nonsense—would but do himself justice [he] might make a beautiful and perhaps a magnificent poem. There is a good deal here to justify such a hope.

> [Here a dozen lines were quoted from "Fairyland."]
> Poe later described Neal's response as "The very first words of encouragement I ever remember to have heard."
> In the November *American Monthly Magazine* (1:586–87), N. P. Willis rejected "Fairyland," describing the poem as "these sickly rhymes." In the *Yankee*'s December issue, Neal prefaced a letter from Poe (containing excerpts from "Al Aaraaf," "Tamerlane," and "To − −") with a paragraph of praise and advice.

The following passages are from the manuscript works of a young author, about to be published in Baltimore. He is entirely a stranger to us, but with all their faults, if the remainder of "Al Aaraaf" and "Tamerlane" are as good as the body of the extracts here given, to say nothing of the more extraordinary parts, he will deserve to stand high—very high—in the estimation of the shining brotherhood. Whether he *will* do so, however, must depend, not so much upon his worth in mere poetry, as upon his worth hereafter in something loftier and more generous—we allude to the stronger properties of the mind, to the magnanimous determination that enables a youth to endure the present, whatever the present may be, in the hope, or rather in the belief, the fixed unwavering belief, that in the future he will find his reward.

*Reprinted from *Yankee and Boston Literary Gazette* 3 (September 1829):168; NS 2 (December 1829):295–98.

[Here Neal quoted Poe's letter and the extracts of his poems and adds the following statement:]

Having allowed our youthful writer to be heard in his own behalf,—what more could we do for lovers of genuine poetry? Nothing. They who are judges will not need more; and they who are not— why waste words upon them? We shall not.

## A Notice of Poe's Tales    Louis Fitzgerald Tasistro*

Had Mr. Poe written nothing else but "Morella," "William Wilson," "The House of Usher," and the "MS Found in a Bottle," he would deserve a high place among imaginative writers, for there is fine poetic feeling, much brightness of fancy, an excellent taste, a ready eye for the picturesque, much quickness of observation, and great truth of sentiment and character in all of these works. But there is scarcely one of the tales published in the two volumes before us, in which we do not find the development of great intellectual capacity, with a power for vivid description, an opulence of imagination, a fecundity of invention, and a command over the elegance of diction which have seldom been displayed, even by writers who have acquired the greatest distinction in the republic of letters.

*From New York *Mirror* 17 (28 December 1839):215.

## [Review of *Tales* (1845) by Edgar A. Poe]    Margaret Fuller*

Mr. Poe's tales need no aid of newspaper comment to give them popularity; they have secured it. We are glad to see them given to the public in this neat form, so that thousands more may be entertained by them without injury to their eyesight.

No form of literary activity has so terribly degenerated among us as the tale. Now that everybody who wants a new hat or bonnet takes this way to earn one from the magazines or annuals, we are inundated with the very flimsiest fabrics ever spun by mortal brain. Almost every person of feeling or fancy could supply a few agreeable

*Reprinted from the *New York Daily Tribune*, 11 July 1845.

and natural narratives, but when instead of using their materials spontaneously they set to work with geography in hand to find unexplored nooks of wild scenery in which to locate their Indians or interesting farmers' daughters, or with some abridgment of history to hunt monarchs or heroes yet unused to become the subjects of their crude coloring, the sale-work produced is a sad affair indeed and "gluts the market" to the sorrow both of buyers and lookers-on.

In such a state of things the writings of Mr. Poe are a refreshment, for they are the fruit of genuine observations and experience, combined with an invention which is not "making up," as children call their way of contriving stories, but a penetration into the causes of things which leads to original but credible results. His narrative proceeds with vigor, his colors are applied with discrimination, and where the effects are fantastic they are not unmeaningly so.

The "Murders in the Rue Morgue" especially made a great impression upon those who did not know its author and were not familiar with his mode of treatment. Several of his stories make us wish he would enter the higher walk of the metaphysical novel and, taking a mind of the self-possessed and deeply marked sort that suits him, give us a deeper and longer acquaintance with its life and the springs of its life than is possible in the compass of these tales.

As Mr. Poe is a professed critic and of all the band the most unsparing to others, we are surprised to find some inaccuracies in the use of words, such as these: "he had with him many books, but rarely *employed* them."—"His results have, in truth, the *whole air* of intuition."

The degree of skill shown in the management of revolting or terrible circumstances makes the pieces that have such subjects more interesting than the others. Even the failures are those of an intellect of strong fiber and well-chosen aim.

# [Review of *The Raven and Other Poems* (1845) by Edgar A. Poe]    Margaret Fuller*

Mr. Poe throws down the gauntlet in his preface by what he says of the "paltry compensations or more paltry commendations of mankind." Some champion might be expected to start up from the "somewhat sizable" class embraced, or more properly speaking, boxed on the ear by this defiance, who might try whether the sting of criticism was as indifferent to this knight of the pen as he professes its honey to be.

Were there such a champion, gifted with acumen to dissect and a swift glancing wit to enliven the operation, he could find no more legitimate subject, no fairer game than Mr. Poe, who has wielded the weapons of criticism without relenting, whether with the dagger he rent and tore the garment in which some favored Joseph had pranked himself, secure of honor in the sight of all men, or whether with uplifted tomahawk he rushed upon the new-born children of some helpless genius who had fancied and persuaded his friends to fancy that they were beautiful and worthy a long and honored life. A large band of these offended dignitaries and aggrieved parents must be on the watch for a volume of poems by Edgar A. Poe, ready to cut, rend, and slash in turn, and hoping to see his own Raven left alone to prey upon the slaughter of which it is the herald.

Such joust and tournament we look to see, and indeed have some stake in the matter so far as we have friends whose wrongs cry aloud for the avenger. Nevertheless, we could not take part in the melee, except to join the crowd of lookers-on in the cry. Heaven speed the right!

Early we read that fable of Apollo who rewarded the critic, who had painfully winnowed the wheat, with the chaff for his pains. We joined the gentle affirmative school, and have confidence that if we indulge ourselves chiefly with the appreciation of good qualities, Time will take care of the faults. For Time holds a strainer like that used in the diamond mines; have but patience and the water and gravel will all pass through and only the precious stones be left. Yet we are not blind to the uses of severe criticism, especially in a time and place so degraded by venial and indiscriminate praise as the present. That unholy alliance, that shameless sham whose motto is "Caw me, And I'll caw thee," that system of mutual adulation and organized puff which was carried to such perfection in the time and may be seen drawn to the life in the correspondence of Miss Hannah More, is fully represented in our day and generation. We see that it meets a counter

*Reprinted from the *New York Daily Tribune,* 26 November 1845.

agency from the league of Truth-tellers, few, but each of them mighty as Fingal or any other hero of the sort. Let such tell the whole truth, as well as nothing but the truth, but let their sternness be in the spirit of love. Let them seek to understand the purpose and scope of an author, his capacity as well as fulfillments, and how his faults are made to grow by the same sunshine that acts upon his virtues, for this is the case with talents no less than with character. The rich field requires frequent and careful weeding; frequent lest the weeds exhaust the soil; careful lest the flowers and grain be pulled up along with the weeds.

Well, to return to Mr. Poe, we are not unwilling that cavil should do her worst on his book because both by act and word he has challenged it, but as this is no office for us, we shall merely indicate in our usual slight way what naturally and unsought has struck ourselves in the reading of these verses.

It has often been our case to share the mistake of Gil Blas with regard to the Archbishop. We have taken people at their word, and while rejoicing that women could bear neglect without feeling mean pique, and that authors, rising above self-love, could show candor about their works and magnanimously meet both justice and injustice, we have been rudely awakened from our dream, and found that Chanticleer who crowed so bravely showed himself at last but a dunghill fowl. Yet Heaven grant we never become too worldly wise to trust a generous word, and we surely are not so yet, for we believe Mr. Poe to be sincere when he says:

"In defense of my own taste, it is incumbent upon me to say that I think nothing in this volume of much value to the public or very creditable to myself. Events not to be controlled have prevented me from making at any time any serious effort in what under happier circumstances would have been the field of my choice."

We believe Mr. Poe to be sincere in this declaration; if he is, we respect him; if otherwise, we do not. Such things should never be said unless in hearty earnest. If in earnest, they are honorable pledges; if not, a pitiful fence and foil of vanity. Earnest or not, the words are thus far true: the productions in this volume indicate a power to do something far better. With the exception of "The Raven," which seems intended chiefly to show the writer's artistic skill, and is in its way a rare and finished specimen, they are all fragments—*fyttes* upon the lyre, almost all of which leave us something to desire or demand. This is not the case, however, with these lines: ["To One in Paradise" is quoted in full.]

The poems breathe a passionate sadness, relieved sometimes by touches very lovely and tender:

> Amid the earnest woes
> That crowd around my earthly path

> (Drear path, alas! where grows
> Not even one lovely rose).

> For her, the fair and debonair, that now so lowly lies,
> The life upon her yellow hair, but not within her eyes—
> The life still there, upon her hair—the death upon her eyes.

This kind of beauty is especially conspicuous, then rising into dignity, in the poem called "The Haunted Palace."

The imagination of this writer rarely expresses itself in pronounced forms, but rather in a sweep of images thronging and distant like a procession of moonlight clouds on the horizon, but like them characteristic and harmonious one with another according to their office.

The descriptive power is greatest when it takes a shape not unlike an incantation, as in the first part of "The Sleeper," where

> I stand beneath the mystic moon,
> An opiate vapor, dewy, dim,
> Exhales from out a golden rim,
> And, softly dripping, drop by drop,
> Upon the quiet mountain top,
> Steals drowsily and musically
> Into the Universal valley.

Why "Universal"?—"resolve me that, Master Moth."

And farther on, "the lily *lolls* upon the wave"

This word "lolls," often made use of in these poems, presents a vulgar image to our thought; we know not how it is to that of others.

The lines which follow about the open window are highly poetical. So is the "Bridal Ballad" in its power of suggesting a whole tribe and train of thoughts and pictures by few and simple touches.

The poems written in youth, written indeed, we understand, in childhood before the author was ten years old, are a great psychological curiosity. Is it the delirium of a prematurely excited brain that causes such a rapture of words? What is to be gathered from seeing the future so fully anticipated in the germ? The passions are not unfrequently felt in their full shock, if not in their intensity, at eight or nine years old, but here they are reflected upon:

> Sweet was their death—with them to die was rife
> With the last ecstasy of satiate life.

The scenes from Politian are done with clear sharp strokes; the power is rather metaphysical than dramatic. We must repeat what we have heretofore said, that we could wish to see Mr. Poe engaged in a metaphysical romance. He needs a sustained flight and a fair range to show what his powers really are. Let us have from him the analysis of the Passions, with their appropriate Fates; let us have his speculations clarified; let him intersperse dialogue or poems as the occasion prompts, and give us something really good and strong, firmly wrought and fairly blazoned. Such would be better employment than detecting literary larcenies not worth pointing out if they exist. Such employment is quite unworthy of one who dares vie with the Angel. ["Israfel" is here printed in full.]

## The Tales of Edgar A. Poe                    E.-D. Forgues*

[The curious reader will want to read Forgues's critique of Poe, a condensed translation of which is made available below. A twenty-page article in the prestigious *Revue des deux Mondes*, it represents the first discussion of Poe to be published in France and, owing to its perspicacity and judgment, provides a very sharp contrast with Poe's general literary reputation at home. Hardly the least of its value was that it brought Poe to the attention of other French critics, translators, and literary figures, the most important of whom was, of course, Charles Baudelaire.

The chief talent of Forgues, who had abandoned law for belles lettres, lay in discovering, translating, and discussing literary works that would interest his French public. Though he concentrated on English authors such as Thackeray, Dickens, and George Eliot, he devoted critiques to Holmes, Melville, and Hawthorne, among others, and even translated *The Scarlet Letter*, *The House of the Seven Gables*, and *Uncle Tom's Cabin*.

Forgues rendered Poe the ultimate critical courtesy by treating him as a serious writer. He knew Poe only through the *Tales* of 1845, however; he did not know that Poe was also a poet and, like himself, a journalist and critic. What especially impressed him about the handful of stories was Poe's powers as a probabilist, powers, he felt, Poe was using "to explore the most difficult problems of speculative philosophy," and he paid him the highest compliment by placing him in the French mathematical tradition represented by Blaise Pascal, Pierre Fermat, and the Marquis de Laplace. Probability theory was first developed by Pascal (1623–1662) and Fermat (1601–1665) to analyze games of

*This preface (in brackets) and translation, both by Sidney P. Moss, are reprinted with his permission from *Poe's Major Crisis* (Durham, N. C.: Duke, 1970), 143–54, omitting the first four paragraphs of the Forgues text and his notes. This translation, about a third of the original, also appeared in *ESQ*, no. 60 (Fall 1970). For the original review, see "Les Contes d'Edgar Allan Poe," *Revue des Deux Mondes* 16 (15 October 1846):341–66, reprinted by Claude Richard in *Cahier: Edgar Allan Poe* (Paris, 1974).

chance, and it remained limited to such amusements until Laplace (1749–1827), not to mention Karl Friedrich Gauss (1777–1855), discovered that the theory had wider application. Laplace saw no essential difference between calling observable outcomes "heads or tails" and calling them "life or death," from which observation emerged actuarial science and demography. By like logic Mendel's study of the "toss-ups" of genes in garden peas enabled him to formulate his famous laws concerning hereditary phenomena.

Forgues (1813–1889), whose full given name was Paul Emile Daurand, was no trained probabilist and his firsthand knowledge of Laplace seems limited to his *Essai philosophique sur les Probabilités*, a short popular version of his great *Théorie analytique des Probabilités*. For this reason he discussed probability in nonmathematical terms easily understood by the uninitiated. If Poe could have foreseen his French reception on these grounds, he might not have complained so often that Duyckinck's selection for the volume was too one-sided. "Duyckinck," he wrote to Philip Cooke on 9 August 1846, "has what he thinks [is] a taste for ratiocination, and has accordingly made up the book mostly of analytic stories," though he had about seventy to choose from. "But this is not *representing* my mind in its various phases" (Ostrom, II, 328).

Forgues considered all the stories in the *Tales* except two. His neglect of "Lionizing" is understandable; his disregard of "The Fall of the House of Usher" is puzzling.]

Exactly what was Laplace looking for in his analysis of chance and Buffon in his political arithmetic? Each of them ... wanted to subdue an obstinate unknown quantity by the power of induction, to neutralize the resistance it offers to reason, and to gain mathematical certainty in regard to moral problems. For this reason Laplace weighs in the same balance the periodical reappearance of a comet, the chances of a lottery ticket, and the value of historical testimony. The same power of reasoning serves to assure him that the action of the moon on the ocean is more than twice as powerful as that of the sun, and that Pascal's niece, the young Perrier, was not cured of her fistula by the direct and miraculous intervention of divine Providence.[1] Thus whether in respect to the past, the present, or the future, he lays down a system of principles and establishes the general laws of probability.

In his own unique way, Mr. Poe is also concerned with probabilities, but he does not weigh them by rules but by intuition. ... The fundamental idea of his tales seems to be borrowed from the first adventures of Zadig in which the young ... philosopher displays marvelous perspicacity. The eccentric character who is Mr. Poe's favorite protagonist and whose subtle intelligence he puts to such difficult tests would also have inferred by merely inspecting their tracks that the Queen of Babylon's spaniel had just had a litter of puppies and that the King's horse...had twenty-three-caret gold bosses on his bit.[2] This protagonist is really Mr. Poe who hardly troubles to conceal himself, and in those tales in which he does not have a surrogate Mr. Poe appears in his own person.

Who other than this searcher after problems to solve would have imposed on himself the task of imagining what the posthumous sensations of a man, or rather of a body, might be stretched out first on the funeral bed, then in a coffin under the damp earth, listening to himself dissolve and watching himself rot? To whose mind would it have occurred to relate in such a convincing way the final catastrophe which must reduce this terrestrial globe to nothingness? To touch on these great secrets of human and plantary death seems the business of the profoundest thinkers, the longest studies, and the most complete systems. For Mr. Poe it is only a question of assuming a hypothesis, of establishing a starting point, and letting the tale develop in the most plausible way among all its probable and possible consequences.

Monos has died. Una, his adored mistress, has followed him into the somber kingdom of death. They meet. Una wants to know of her beloved what he felt a while ago when, desolate, she contemplated him immobile, cold, disfigured, marked by the supreme wound. Had all thought disappeared with life? Is the divorce of soul and body so abrupt,...so complete, that with the last death-rattle the soul escapes entirely, leaving behind it only an inert lump? The common man answers yes. Hardly afraid of shocking everyone's judgment, our author denies the validity of this unprovable assumption and, supporting his denial by logic, he erects his narrative from beyond the grave.

It is not, to tell the truth, the first time that imagination has gone beyond the limits of life, those limits impassable to reason and before which all philosophy lowers its eyes, humbled; but I do not think that anyone has ever before in fiction given to the *recollections of a dead person* this character of exact definition and reasoned conviction. It is not a question here of fantastic adventures, of arbitrary complications, of dialogues...filled with fancy, but rather the matter of a veritable monograph patiently and methodically developed which seems to aspire to take its place among the other documents of humane philosophy. Mr. Poe has deduced from the phenomena of the dream the phenomena of the sensibility of the corpse; he has taken seriously the brotherhood of sleep and death of which so many poets have sung; and from this philosophical doctrine he has applied himself to drawing all the truths he could derive from it. One will agree that such work is not hackneyed. [Here follows a long quotation from "The Colloquy of Monos and Una" in which Monos describes his postmortem sensations.]

We shall not prolong this singular quotation which is indispensable for justifying what we said above of the unique character of Mr. Poe's work—in this instance, that of a dead man analyzing his posthumous sensations.

The final ruin of the globe, the destruction of our planet, is as methodically treated in the conversation of Eiros and Charmion as is the decomposition of the human being in that of Monos and Una. The principle is presented in the same way. Given the elementary fact that the breathable air is composed of twenty-one parts oxygen and seventy-nine parts nitrogen, . . . as well as the fact that the earth is surrounded by a thick atmosphere of nearly fifteen leagues, what would happen if the elliptical course around the sun taken by a comet led that comet into contact with the terrestrial globe? This is exactly the supposition Trissotin makes in *The Learned Ladies*,[3] but Mr. Poe does not adopt his way of viewing the problem. He sees the comet not as a massive and heavy body but as a whirlwind of impalpable material whose nucleus is of a density much less than that of our lightest gases. The imminent meeting does not present the same kind of danger as that of two locomotives rushing toward each other on the same rails; indeed, it even seems probable that the earth might pass through this enemy comet without difficulty. But what is likely to happen to us while we are in this peculiar situation? Oxygen, the principle of combustion, would become a hostile force, for nitrogen would be completely drawn out of our earthly atmosphere. And what would be the result of this double phenomenon? An irresistible combustion would devour all, would prevail over all. . . . On this fundamental idea, once conceded, the story develops with implacable logic, with inevitable deductions, with pitiless consequences. Challenge if you wish the major and minor premises which are the points of departure; the remainder is strictly unassailable.

[Here follows a detailed retelling of "The Conversation of Eiros and Charmion."]

You see, then, that this extraordinary story, this unprecedented freak of an imagination which nothing stops, has all the appearance, if not all the reality, of a severe logic. Few people will deny that a comet and the earth can meet in space. Granting this, one must recognize that the possibility of this conflagration of gas, this combustion of the atmosphere, and this horrible end of the entire human race, all of whom are reduced to breathing only fire, is at least very probable.

Having approached such problems, one takes pleasure in examining all those that philosophy seems eternally condemned to deny us the solution, reserved as they are to God. Mr. Poe is thus led to look for a plausible explanation of the human soul and of divinity. This is the subject of a third story entitled *Mesmeric Revelation*. The author imagines himself at the bedside of a skeptic who, arrived at the final stage of a fatal illness, has himself treated by mesmerism. Mr. Vankirk has all his life doubted the immortality of the soul. Now, troubled by the vague recollections that mesmeric trances have induced in him, he wonders if in this strange state a series of well-directed questions might not clarify ... those metaphysical truths which philosophy has guessed but has badly explained because of the inadequacy of our ordinary resources. Indeed, granting that mesmeric action permits man to compensate for the imperfection of his finite organs and enables him while endowed with miraculous clairvoyance to be transported to that domain of creation which is beyond the senses, does it not follow that the mesmerized person is better qualified than others to explain to us the hidden realities of the invisible world? This prime point granted, do you trust the storyteller to give you by questions and answers a very probable theory of all that which is related to the division of soul and body, with the essence that constitutes ... the superior order known under the name of God. ..? It goes without saying that we do not take it upon ourselves to guarantee ... the system expounded by the American storyteller. ... [Here is explained Poe's conception of the unparticled materiality of God, to be found in "Mesmeric Revelation."]

We will not pursue this purely hypothetical revelation that reminds us of the inspirations or aspirations of those fiction writers of fourteen or fifteen years ago who found it fascinating to put into "madrigals" the visions of Jacob Boehm, of Saint Martin, of Swedenborg, and even of Mme Guyon. It must be said, however, that Mr. Poe's logic has a much more precise character. It is much more tenacious. ... It is not satisfied with vague, grandiloquent words and with impenetrable formulas rendered with feigned rigor. Once the principles are posed, his logic deviates only rarely; it is always clear, always intelligible, and it takes possession of the reader in spite of himself.

It is time to return to earth and ... follow this inexorable logic. ...

In *The Gold-Bug* we can see all the ratiocinative faculties of man at grips with an apparently impenetrable cipher, upon the solution of which depends a rich pirate's treasure. ... Later, in *A Descent into the Maelström*, Mr. Poe will tell us how a sound observation, a well-followed argument, will deliver safe and sound from the bottom of a Norwegian gulf an unfortunate fisherman carried away by a devouring whirlpool. We do not insist that ordinary verisimilitude be completely respected here—that a theory of gravity could be improvised by an uneducated countryman in a situation that would arrest the mental faculties...; but if everything that is rigorously and strictly possible in the situation is conceived by the human mind, one must admit the possibility that extreme peril might induce in a man ... a peculiar lucidity of intellect, a miraculous power of observation, and that is enough to make this story captivate you, as do the Anacandaïa[?] of ["Monk"] Lewis or the novel of *Frankenstein*, both of which are certainly not very probable.

Here is something easier to believe. [The power of Auguste Dupin is recounted, that of a man who is "first rate in all games in which success depends on the exact valuation of chances" and who is able to read his companion's mind from a few clues.]

Apply this astonishing perspicacity, the result of almost superhuman concentration of the mind and of a marvelous intuition, to a police operation and you have . . . an investigator whom nothing escapes. . . . Mr. Poe fastens upon this situation and with completely American tenacity develops the extraordinary events to their extreme limits.

Three or four stories rest on this very simple contrivance with very telling effect. We regret only that the foreign storyteller has thought to enhance the interest of these tales by locating them in Paris, of which he has not the least idea, and in our contemporary society, which is very badly known in the United States. . . . Mr. Poe was . . . not . . . unwise in removing his scenes to a distance in order to conceal the artifices of his painting and lend to it all the semblance of truth, but he should have foreseen that French readers, pausing before these canvases, would be astounded to find the capital of France completely overturned, the main quarters very suddenly dislodged—an Impasse Lamartine in the neighborhood of the Palais-Royal, a Rue Morgue in the Saint-Roch quarter, and the Barrière du Roule at the edge of the Seine "on the shore opposite the Rue Pavée-Saint–André." Neither should he have applied the ideas of a much more democratic country to our social structure by supposing that the prefect of police, at his wit's end and not knowing which way to turn to recover a mysterious letter. . . , would come one evening familiarly to smoke one or two cigars with the young observer of whom we have spoken, to ask his advice, to express his doubts, and to make a wager on the success of the measures proposed by this obliging counselor. Yet we do not cite all the blunders nor the most egregious ones that our red pencil has noted in the margin of these curious little fictions. These blunders are explained not only by their foreign origin but also by the method that the author adopts of transporting to our country some real chronicles chosen from among the crimes which have occupied the magistrates of New York or Boston. The story of Marie Roget . . . is a famous American case; the names alone have been changed to French ones; the incidents could not be. The Hudson becomes the Seine; Weehawken the Barrière du Roule: Nassau Street, the Rue Pavée-Saint-André, and so forth. Likewise, Marie Roget, the supposed young Parisian grisette, is no other than Mary Cecilia Rogers, the cigar girl whose mysterious murder terrified a few years ago the people of New York. Let us first tell the event as it was related in the *New York Mercury* or in

*Brother Jonathan.* We will return to the fiction when we have an exact idea of the reality.

[Here is summarized the murder mystery of Mary Rogers as it was reported in the newspapers.]

Mr. Poe seizes upon this story in his turn and sets in the midst of all these conflicting newspaper accounts his unique character, this living syllogism of whom we have spoken. The Chevalier Dunin—such is the name he has fabricated for him, a truly characteristic name that has a very remarkable improbability and strangeness—the Chevalier Dupin, attentive to all the contradictory versions, discusses them rigorously and submits them to mathematical analysis. One sees that he has read in Laplace's *Philosophical Essay* the chapter devoted to *The Probability of the Judgments of Tribunals.* . . . His calculations of probability are striking and curious. That is all one must ask of them.

Novalis has this passage in his *Moral Ansichten:* "There are ideal series of events which run parallel with the real ones. They rarely coincide. Men and circumstances generally modify the ideal train of events, so that it seems imperfect, and its consequences are equally imperfect. Thus with the Reformation; instead of Protestantism came Lutheranism." In choosing this passage as the epigraph of his story, the American author explains to us his metaphysical design. When he exhibits the various hypotheses of the French (which is to say, American) journals on the subject of the murder committed in New York, when he exposes the gross errors of common logic, improvised as fodder for the unintelligent masses, his purpose is to prove that by virtue of certain principles an ideal series—one that is purely logical and consisting of mutually related facts—must lead, by an accumulation of mutually corroborative suppositions, to the nearest point of the real series or the truth. By an inexorable dialectic he thus destroys the false systems and, having thoroughly cleared the terrain, constructs a new edifice with all the pieces in place.

In the eyes of this remarkable thinker, the practice of the courts which restricts the admission of evidence to a few crucial facts is extremely erroneous. Modern science, which very often depends on the unexpected and proves the known by the unknown, understands better than the courts the importance of secondary incidents, of collateral evidence, which, above all, must be taken into consideration. There are seemingly inessential facts, apparent fortuities, which have become the foundation of the most complete and best-established systems. . . .

This principle once granted, the consequences are self-evident. By abandoning the main fact in order to concentrate on the details which seem insignificant, the Chevalier succeeds in establishing a number of circumstances that eventually serve to clarify the mystery.

[Here follows a retelling of "The Mystery of Marie Roget" which emphasizes Poe's power of logic. ]

We do not give you—notice this well—a twentieth part of the reasonings which directly or indirectly corroborate this inference. . . .

Now that you have an idea of the American author in his favorite aspect, we should try to see him under another one. We have studied him as a logician, as a pursuer of abstract truths, and as a lover of the most eccentric hypotheses and the most difficult calculations. Now we should see him as a poet, as an inventor of objectless fantasies, of purely literary whims. We will confine ourselves to two tales we have expressly reserved for this purpose, *The Black Cat* and *The Man of the Crowd*.

*The Black Cat* reminds us of the gloomiest inspirations of Theodore Hoffmann. Never did the Sérapion Club listen to anything more fantastic than the story of this man, this unfortunate maniac, who harbors in his liquor-burned brain a monstrous hatred, the hatred of his poor cat. [Here follows a retelling of the story.]

*The Man of the Crowd* is not a story; it is a study, a simple idea vigorously rendered. [Here the tale is retold.]

We have already compared the talent of Mr. Poe with that of Washington Irving, the latter more cheerful, more varied, less ambitious, as well as to that of William Godwin, whose "sombre and unwholesome popularity" was so severely censured by Hazlitt. One must, however, recognize in the author of *St. Leon* and *Caleb Williams* more true philosophy and a tendency less pronounced toward purely literary paradox. If one wanted to show in America itself a predecessor of Mr. Edgar Poe, one could . . . compare him to Charles Brockden Brown who also searched in good faith, even in his most frivolous fictions, for the solution of some intellectual problem, taking pleasure as Mr. Poe does in describing those interior tortures, those obsessions of the soul, those maladies of the mind which offer so vast a field for observation and so many curious phenomena to the thoughtful makers of metaphysical systems.

Brockden Brown, it is true, wrote novels and we know of Poe only by very brief short stories, some no more than six to ten pages, but it would be unwise, it seems to us, to classify compositions of this genre by length. It is so easy to protract indefinitely a series of facts and so difficult, on the other hand, to condense . . . in the form of a tale a whole abstract theory with all the elements of an original concept. Today when the least scribbler appears with a melodrama in ten or twenty volumes, Richardson himself, if he returned to the world, would be . . . obliged to trim his characterizations, curtail his interminable dialogues, and reduce to finely wrought medallions the numerous figures of his vast canvases. Yesterday the victory was to large battalions; tomorrow it will belong to elite troops. From the great novels . . . one came to the stories of Voltaire and Diderot. . . . Tales like these of Mr. Poe's offer more substance to the mind, open newer horizons to the imagination, than twenty volumes like those of Courtilz de Sandras, de Baculard D'Arnaud, and de Lussan, precursors and prototypes of many contemporary story writers. . . .[4] Between such writers and the American author we will refrain from making comparisons. It will be opportune and useful to compare them when time has established the nascent reputation of the foreign storyteller and—who knows?—has shaken a little that of our prolific novelists.

Notes

1. Mlle Perrier had suffered for more than three years from a lachrymal fistula. When she touched her afflicted eye with a relic supposed to be one of the thorns on Christ's crown, she recovered instantaneously. Doctors attested to the remarkable cure and declared it was wrought supernaturally. This "miracle" occurred in 1656 and made a great sensation. See chap. xi of the *Essay on Probabilities* for Laplace's discussion of this event.

2. Zadig's inferences concerning the queen's spaniel and the king's horse are recounted in chap. iii of Voltaire's *Zadig*.

3. Trissotin in Molière's play, *Les Femmes savantes*, remarks: "Last night we had the narrowest escape! / A world passed just beside us, fell across / Our vortex; if in passing it had struck us, / We had been dashed to pieces just like glass." This allusion to Trissotin is odd, for Trissotin, meaning Triple Fool, is the name under which Molière satirized the Abbé Charles Cotin. A poet and member of the French Academy, Cotin had published a work entitled *Gallant Dissertation upon the Comet Which Appeared in December 1664 and January 1665*.

4. Gaiten Courtilz de Sandras (1644–1712) spent nine years in the Bastille for writing scandalous novels; Françoise-Thomas de Baculard D'Arnaud (1718–1803) and Marguerite de Lussan (1682–1758) were once popular novelists.

## *Eureka: A Prose Poem* by Edgar A. Poe

Anonymous*

A most extraordinary essay upon the Material and Spiritual Universe,—but one to which we are at this moment unable to do anything like adequate justice,—the work itself having barely made its appearance from the press of Mr. Putnam. Those of our readers who remember a report of Mr. Poe's Lecture at the Society Library, a few months ago, which appeared in this journal at the time, may gather some idea of the work before us from the fact that that lecture has been expanded, with really consummate art—but this was to be expected from the ad-

*Reprinted from the *New York Evening Express* 12 (12 July 1848). On question of authorship, see Ostrom, *Letters*, 365, 379–82.

mitted genius of its author—into an elegant volume of nearly 150 pages, in which the ideas which were then set forth with such novelty and effect, have been carefully arranged in a more elaborate form for the public eye. We shall be greatly surprised if this work does not create a most profound sensation among the literary and scientific classes all over the union—displaying as it does a reasoning power and grasp of thought which cannot possibly fail to excite the "Special Wonder" of even the most careless reader. In respect of novelty, Mr. Poe's new theory of the Universe will certainly attract universal attention, in as much as it is demonstrated, so to speak, with a degree of logical acumen which has certainly not been equalled since the days of Sir Isaac Newton, and can hardly be said to have been excelled even by that great philosopher. But we must bring a brief notice of this extraordinary book to a hurried close here—earnestly recommending it to everyone of our readers as one that can in no event fail to shed unfailing lustre upon the American name, as a work of almost unequalled power in respect of philosophical research and speculative force. Mr. Poe has appropriately dedicated it, "with very profound respect," to Alexander Von Humboldt, whose well known "Cosmos" he very justly ranks higher than any other work upon the subject.

# [Review of *The Works of the Late Edgar Allan Poe* (1850 Griswold Edition)]    Evert Augustus Duyckinck*

From the announcement we expected a somewhat fuller account of the life of Mr. Poe than is furnished in the few pages prefixed to this collection of his writings. If we had considered carefully the character of the man's talent this expectation would have been found to be ill-founded. Poe was strictly impersonal; as greatly so as any man whose acquaintance we have enjoyed. In a knowledge of him extending through several years, and frequent opportunities, we can scarcely remember to have had from him any single disclosure or trait of personal character; anything which marked him as a mover or observer among men. Although he had traveled in distant countries, sojourned in cities of our own country, and had, at different times, under favorable opportunities, been brought into contact with life and character of many phases, he had no anecdote to tell, no description of objects, dress or appearance. Nothing, in a word, to say of things. Briefly, he was what Napoleon named

*Reprinted from the *Literary World* 6 (26 January 1850):81.

an ideologist—a man of ideas. He lived entirely apart from the solidities and realities of life: was an abstraction; thought, wrote, and dealt solely in abstractions. It is this which gives their peculiar feature to his writings. They have no color, but are in pure outline, delicately and accurately drawn, but altogether without the glow and pulse of humanity. His genius was mathematical, rather than pictorial or poetical. He demonstrates instead of painting. Selecting some quaint and abstruse theme, he proceeded to unfold it with the closeness, care, and demonstrative method of Euclid; and you have, to change the illustration, fireworks for fire; the appearance of water for water; and a great shadow in the place of an actual, moist, and thunder-bearing sky. His indifference to living, flesh and blood subjects, explains his fondness for the mechanism and music of verse, without reference to the thought of feeling. He is therefore a greater favorite with scholars than with the people; and would be (as a matter of course) eagerly followed by a train of poetastering imitators, who, to do them justice in a familiar image, "hear the bell ring and don't know where the clapper hangs." Poe is an object of considerable, or more than considerable size; but the imitation of Poe is a shadow indescribably small and attenuated. We can get along, for a while, on a diet of common air—but the exhausted receiver of the air-pump is another thing! The method and management of many of Mr. Poe's tales and poems are admirable, exhibiting a wonderful ingenuity, and completely proving him master of the weapon he had chosen for his use. He lacks reality, imagination, everyday power, but he is remarkably subtle, acute, and earnest in his own way. His instrument is neither an organ nor a harp; he is neither a King David nor a Beethoven, but rather a Campanologian, a Swiss bell-ringer, who from little contrivances of his own, with an ingeniously devised hammer, strikes a sharp melody, which has all that is delightful and affecting, that is attainable without a soul. We feel greatly obliged to Messrs. Willis, Lowell, and Griswold, for helping to wheel forward into public view this excellent machine; to which Mr. Redfield has furnished an appropriate cloth and cover, with the performer's head, as large and as true as life, stamped on its front, in an excellent daguerreotype portrait.

# [From "Memoir of the Author"]

**Rufus Wilmot Griswold***

He had commenced in the "Literary Messenger," a story of the sea, under the title of "Arthur Gordon Pym,"[1] and upon the recommendation of Mr. Paulding and others, it was printed by the Harpers. It is his longest work, and is not without some sort of merit, but it received little attention. The publishers sent one hundred copies to England, and being mistaken at first for a narrative of real experiences, it was advertised to be reprinted, but a discovery of its character, I believe prevented such a result. An attempt is made in it, by simplicity of style, minuteness of nautical descriptions, and circumstantiality of narration, to give it that air of truth which constitutes the principal attraction of Sir Edward Seaward's Narrative, and Robinson Crusoe; but it has none of the pleasing interests of these tales; it is as full of wonders as Munchausen, has as many atrocities as the Book of Pirates, and as liberal an array of paining and revolting horrors as ever was invented by Anne Radcliffe or George Walker. Thus far a tendency to extravagance had been the most striking infirmity of his genius. He had been more anxious to be intense than to be natural; and some of his *bizarréries* had been mistaken for satire, and admired for that quality. Afterward he was more judicious, and if his outlines were incredible it was commonly forgotten in the simplicity of his details and their cohesive cumulation. . . .

But his more congenial pursuit was tale writing, and he produced about this period some of his most remarkable and characteristic works in a department of imaginative composition in which he was henceforth alone and unapproachable. The "Fall of the House of Usher," and "Ligeia," are the most interesting illustrations of his mental organization—his masterpieces in a peculiar vein of romantic creation. They have the unquestionable stamp of genius. The analyses of the growth of madness in one, and the thrilling revelations of the existence of a first wife in the person of a second, in the other, are made with consummate skill; and the strange and solemn and fascinating beauty which informs the style and invests the circumstances of both, drugs the mind, and makes us forget the improbabilities of their general design. . . .

In New-York Poe entered upon a new sort of life. Heretofore, from the commencement of his literary career, he had resided in provincial

*Reprinted from Rufus Wilmot Griswold, ed., *The Works of Edgar Allan Poe*, 3 vols. (New York: Redfield, 1849, 1855), with "A Memoir by Rufus Wilmot Griswold," 1: xxi–lv. Excerpts reprinted here are from pp. xxxi, xxxi–xxxii, xxxv–xxxvi, xlii–xliii, xlvii, xlviii, xlix, liv–lv.

towns. Now he was in a metropolis, and with a reputation which might have served as a passport to any society he could desire. For the first time he was received into circles capable of both the appreciation and the production of literature. He added to his fame soon after he came to the city by the publication of that remarkable composition "The Raven," of which Mr. Willis has observed that in his opinion "it is the most effective single example of fugitive poetry ever published in this country, and is unsurpassed in English poetry for subtle conception, masterly ingenuity of versification, and consistent sustaining of imaginative lift;" and by that of one of the most extraordinary instances of the naturalness of detail—the verisimilitude of minute narrative—for which he was preëminently distinguished, his "Mesmeric Revelation," purporting to be the last conversation of a somnambule, held just before death with his magnetizer; which was followed by the yet more striking exhibition of abilities in the same way, entitled "The Facts in the Case of M. Valdemar," in which the subject is represented as having been mesmerized in *articulo mortis.* These pieces were reprinted throughout the literary and philosophical world, in nearly all languages, everywhere causing sharp and curious speculation, and where readers could be persuaded that they were fables, challenging a reluctant but genuine admiration. . . .

His first lecture—and only one at this period—was given at the Society Library, in New-York, on the ninth of February, and was upon the Cosmogony of the Universe; it was attended by an eminently intellectual auditory, and the reading of it occupied about two hours and a half; it was what he afterwards published under the title of "Eureka, a Prose Poem."

To the composition of this work he brought his subtlest and highest capacities, in their most perfect development. Denying that the arcana of the universe can be explored by induction, but informing his imagination with the various results of science, he entered with unhesitating boldness, though with no guide but the divinest instinct,—that sense of beauty, in which our great Edwards recognises the flowering of all truth—into the sea of speculation, and there built up of according laws and their phenomena, as under the influence of a scientific inspiration, his theory of Nature. I will not attempt the difficult task of condensing his propositions; to be apprehended they must be studied in his own terse and simple language; but in this we have a summary of that which he regards as fundamental; "The law which we call *Gravity*," he says, "exists on account of matter having been radiated, at its origin, atomically, into a *limited* sphere of space, from one, individual unconditional, irrelative and absolute Particle Proper, by the sole process in which it was possible to satisfy, at the same time, the two conditions, radiation and equable distribution throughout the sphere—that is to say, by a force varying in *direct* proportion with the squares of the distances between the radiated atoms, respectively, and the particular centre of radiation."

Poe was thoroughly persuaded that he had discovered the great secret; that the propositions of "Eureka" were true; and he was wont to talk of the subject with a sublime and electrical enthusiasm which they cannot have forgotten who were familiar with him at the period of its publication. He felt that an author known solely by his adventures in the lighter literature, throwing down the gauntlet to professors of science, could not expect absolute fairness, and he had no hope but in discussions led by wisdom and candor. Meeting me, he said, "Have you read 'Eureka?'" I answered "Not yet: I have just glanced at the notice of it by Willis, who thinks it contains no more fact than fantasy, and I am sorry to see—sorry if it be true—suggests that it corresponds in tone with that gathering of sham and obsolete hypotheses addressed to fanciful tyros, the 'Vestiges of Creation'; and our good and really wise friend Bush, whom you will admit to be of all the professors, in temper one of the most habitually just, thinks that while you may have guessed very shrewdly, it would not be difficult to suggest many difficulties in the way of your doctrine." "It is by no means ingenuous," he replied, "to hint that there are such difficulties, and yet to leave them unsuggested. I challenge the investigation of every point in the book. I deny that there are any difficulties which I have not met and overthrown. Injustice is done me by the application of this word 'guess:' I have assumed *nothing* and proved *all*." In his preface he wrote: "To the few who love me and whom I love; to those who feel rather than to those who think; to the dreamers and those who put faith in dreams as in the only realities— I offer this book of truths, not in the character of Truth-Teller, but for the beauty that abounds in its truth: constituting it true. To these I present the composition as an Art-Product alone:—let us say as a Romance; or, if it be not urging too lofty a claim, as a Poem. What I here propound is true: therefore it cannot die: or if by any means it be now trodden down so that it die, it will rise again to the life everlasting."

When I read "Eureka" I could not help but think it immeasurably superior as an illustration of genuis to the "Vestiges of Creation"; and as I admired the poem, (except the miserable attempt at humor in what purports to be a letter found in a bottle floating on the *Mare tenebrarum*,) so I regretted its pantheism, which is not necessary to its main design. [Here follows Poe's significant letter to C. F. Hoffman of 20 September 1848.]

*De mortuis nil nisi bonum* is a common and an honorable sentiment, but its proper application would lead to the suppression of the histories of half of the most conspicuous of mankind; in this case it is impossible on account of the notoriety of Mr. Poe's faults; and it would be unjust to the living against whom his hands were always raised and who had no resort but in his outlawry from their sympathies. Moreover, his career is full of instruction and warning, and it has always been made a portion of the penalty of wrong that its anatomy should be displayed for the common study and advantage.

The character of Mr. Poe's genius has been so recently and so admirably discussed by Mr. Lowell, with whose opinions on the subject I for the most part agree, that I shall say but little of it here, having already extended this notice beyond the limits at first designed. There is a singular harmony between his personal and his literary qualities. St. Pierre, who seemed to be without any nobility in his own nature, in his writings appeared to be moved only by the finest and highest impulses. Poe exhibits scarcely any virtue in either his life or his writings. Probably there is not another instance in the literature of our language in which so much has been accomplished without a recognition or a manifestation of conscience. Seated behind the intelligence, and directing it, according to its capacities, Conscience is the parent of whatever is absolutely and unquestionably beautiful in art as well as in conduct. It touches the creations of the mind and they have life; without it they have never, in the range of its just action, the truth and naturalness which are approved by universal taste or in enduring reputation. In Poe's works there is constantly displayed the most touching melancholy, the most extreme and terrible despair, but never reverence or remorse. . . .

His realm was on the shadowy confines of human experience, among the abodes of crime, gloom, and horror, and there he delighted to surround himself with images of beauty and of terror, to raise his solemn palaces and towers and spires in a night upon which should rise no sun. His minuteness of detail, refinement of reasoning, and propriety and power of language—the perfect keeping (to borrow a phrase from another domain of art) and apparent good faith with which he managed the evocation and exhibition of his strange and spectral and revolting creations—gave him an astonishing mastery over his readers, so that his books were closed as one would lay aside the nightmare or the spells of opium. The analytical subtlety evinced in his works has frequently been over-estimated, as I have before observed, because it has not been sufficiently considered that his mysteries were composed with the express design of being dissolved. When Poe attempted the illustration of the profounder operations of the mind, as displayed in written reason or in real action, he frequently failed entirely.

In poetry, as in prose, he was eminently successful in the metaphysical treatment of the passions. His poems are constructed with wonderful ingenuity, and finished with consummate art. They display a sombre and weird imagination, and a taste almost faultless in the apprehension of that sort of beauty which was most agreeable to his temper. But they evince little genuine feeling, and less of that spontaneous ecstasy which gives its freedom, smoothness and naturalness to immortal verse. His own account of the composition of "The Raven," discloses his methods—the absence of all impulse, and the absolute control of calculation and mechanism. That curious analysis of the processes by which he wrought would be incredible if from another hand. . . .

In criticism, as Mr. Lowell justly remarks, Mr. Poe had "a scientific precision and coherence of logic"; he had remarkable dexterity in the dissection of sentences; but he rarely ascended from the particular to the general, from subjects to principles: he was familiar with the microscope but never looked through the telescope. His criticisms are of value to the degree in which they are demonstrative, but his unsupported assertions and opinions were so apt to be influenced by friendship or enmity, by the desire to please or the fear to offend, or by his constant ambition to surprise, or produce a sensation, that they should be received in all cases with distrust of their fairness. A volume might be filled with literary judgments by him as antagonistical and inconsistent as the sharpest antitheses. [Several examples of Poe's criticism are quoted here.]

He was at all times a dreamer—dwelling in ideal realms—in heaven or hell—peopled with the creatures and the accidents of his brain. He walked the streets, in madness or melancholy, with lips moving in indistinct curses, or with eyes upturned in passionate prayer, (never for himself, for he felt, or professed to feel, that he was already damned, but) for their happiness who at the moment were objects of his idolatry;— or, with his glances introverted to a heart gnawed with anguish, and with a face shrouded in gloom, he would brave the wildest storms; and all night, with drenched garments and arms beating the winds and rains, would speak as if to spirits that at such times only could be evoked by him from the Aidenn, close by whose portals his disturbed soul sought to forget the ills to which his constitution subjected him— close by the Aidenn where were those he loved—the Aidenn which he might never see, but in fitful glimpses, as its gates opened to receive the less fiery and more happy natures whose destiny to sin did not involve the doom of death.

He seemed, except when some fitful pursuit subjugated his will and engrossed his faculties, always to bear the memory of some controlling sorrow. The remarkable poem of "The Raven" was probably much more nearly than has been supposed, even by those who were very intimate with him, a reflection and an echo of his own history. *He* was that bird's

"————unhappy master whom unmerciful Disaster
Followed fast and followed faster till his songs one burden bore—
Till the dirges of his Hope that melancholy burden bore
                    Of 'Never—never more.' "

Every genuine author, in a greater or less degree, leaves in his works, whatever their design, traces of his personal character: elements of his immortal being, in which the individual survives the person. While we read the pages of the "Fall of the House of Usher," or of "Mesmeric Revelations," we see in the solemn and stately gloom which invests one, and in the subtle metaphysical analysis of both, indications of the idiosyncrasies—of what was most remarkable and peculiar—in the author's intellectual nature. But we see here only the better phases of his nature, only the symbols of his juster action, for his harsh experience had deprived him of all faith, in man or woman. He had made up his mind upon the numberless complexities of the social world, and the whole system with him was an imposture. This conviction gave a direction to his shrewd and naturally unamiable character. Still, though he regarded society as composed altogether of villains, the sharpness of his intellect was not of that kind which enabled him to cope with villainy, while it continually caused him by overshots to fail of the success of honesty. He was in many respects like Francis Vivian, in Bulwer's novel of "The Caxtons."[2] Passion, in him, comprehended many of the worst emotions which militate against human happiness. You could not contradict him, but you raised quick choler; you could not speak of wealth, but his cheek paled with gnawing envy. The astonishing natural advantages of this poor boy—his beauty, his readiness, the daring spirit that breathed around him like a fiery atmosphere—had raised his constitutional self-confidence into an arrogance that turned his very claims to admiration into prejudices against him. Irascible, envious—bad enough, but not the worst, for these salient angles were all varnished over with a cold repellent cynicism, his passions vented themselves in sneers. There seemed to him no moral susceptibility; and, what was more remarkable in a proud nature, little or nothing of the true point of honor. He had, to a morbid excess, that desire to rise which is vulgarly called ambition, but no wish for the esteem or the love of his species; only the hard wish to succeed—not shine, not serve—succeed, that he might have the right to despise a world which galled his self-conceit.

## Notes

1. *The Narrative of Arthur Gordon Pym, of Nantucket;* comprising the Details of a Mutiny and Atrocious Butchery on board the American Brig Grampus, on her way to the South Seas—with an Account of the Re-capture of the vessel by the

Survivors; their Shipwreck, and subsequent Horrible Sufferings from Famine; their Deliverance by means of the British schooner Jane Gray; the brief Cruise of this latter Vessel in the Antarctic Ocean; her Capture, and the Massacre of her Crew among a Group of Islands in the 84th parallel of southern latitude; together with the incredible Adventures and Discoveries still further South, to which that distressing Calamity gave rise.—I vol. 12mo. pp. 198. New-York, Harper & Brothers. 1838.

2. In Griswold's "Ludwig" article (New York *Daily Tribune,* 9 October 1849), the remainder of this paragraph, enclosed in quotation marks, describes Bulwer's Vivian. Here, however, not identified as a quotation, the passage seems to describe Poe's character [—ed. note].

# [From *Edgar Poe and His Critics*]
Sarah Helen Whitman*

A certain class of his writings undeniably exhibits the faculties of ingenuity and invention in a prominent and distinctive light. But it must not be forgotten that there was another phase of his mind—one not less distinctive and characteristic of his genius—which manifested itself in creations of a totally different order and expression. It can hardly have escaped the notice of the most careless reader that certain ideas exercised over him the power of fascination. They return, again and again, in his stories and poems and seem like the utterances of a mind possessed with thoughts, emotions, and images of which the will and the understanding take little cognizance. In the delineation of these, his language often acquires a power and pregnancy eluding all attempts at analysis. It is then that by a few miraculous words he evokes emotional states or commands pictorial effects which live forever in the memory and form a part of its eternal inheritance. No analysis can dissect—no criticism can disenchant them.

As specimens of the class we have indicated read "Ligeia," "Morella," "Eleonora." Observe in them the prevailing and dominant thoughts of his inner life—ideas of "fate and metaphysical aid"—of psychal and spiritual agencies, energies and potences. See in them intimations of mysterious phenomena which, at the time when these fantasies were indited, were regarded as fables and dreams, but which have since (in their phenomenal aspect simply) been recognised as matters of popular experience and scientific research.

*Reprinted from *Edgar Poe and His Critics,* by Sarah Helen Whitman (New York: Gordian Press, 1981), 58–61, 75–82. Original edition was published by Rudd and Carleton (New York, 1860).

In "Ligeia," the sad and stately symmetry of the sentences, their rhythmical cadence, the Moresque sumptuousness of imagery with which the story is invested, and the weird metempsychosis which it records, produce an effect on the reader altogether peculiar in character and, as we think, quite inexplicable without a reference to the supernatural inspiration which seems to pervade them. In the moods of mind and phases of passion which this story represents we have no laboured artistic effects; we look into the haunted chambers of the poet's own mind and see, as through a veil, the strange experiences of his inner life; while, in the dusk magnificence of its imagery, we have the true heraldic blazonry of an imagination royally dowered and descended. In this, as in all that class of stories we have named, the author's mind seems struggling desperately and vainly with the awful mystery of Death.

In "Morella," as in "Ligeia," the parties are occupied with the same mystic philosophies—engrossed in the same recondite questions of "life and death and spiritual unity," questions of "that identity which, at death, is, or is not, lost forever." Each commemorates a psychal attraction which transcends the dissolution of the mortal body and over-sweeps the grave; the passionate soul of the departed transfusing itself through the organism of another to manifest its deathless love. Who does not remember as a strain of Æonian melody the story of "Eleonora"? Who does not lapse into a dream as he remembers the "River of Silence" and "The Valley of the many-colored Grass"?

In this story the purport, though less apparent to the general reader, and differently interpreted by a writer in the *North American Review,* is still the same as in the preceding. Read the closing sentences, so eloquent with a tender and mysterious meaning, which record, after the death of the beloved Eleonora, the appearance "from a far, far distant and unknown land" of the Seraph Ermengarde. Observe, too, in these closing lines the indication, so often manifest in Poe's poems and stories, of a lingering pity and sorrow for the dead;—an ever-recurring pang of remorse in the fear of having grieved them by some involuntary wrong of desertion or forgetfulness.

This haunting remembrance—this sad, remorseful pity for the departed, is everywhere a distinguishing feature in his prose and poetry.

The existence of such a feeling as a prevalent mood of his mind, of which we have abundant evidence, is altogether incompatible with that cold sensualism with which he has been so ignorantly charged.

The unrest and faithlessness of the age culminated in him. Nothing so solitary, nothing so hopeless, nothing so desolate as his spirit in its darker moods has been instanced in the literary history of the nineteenth century.

It has been said that his theory, as expressed in *Eureka,* of the universal diffusion of Deity in and through all things, is identical with the Brahminical faith as expressed in the *Bagvat Gita*. But those who will patiently follow the vast reaches of his thought in this sublime poem of the "Universe" will find that he arrives at a form of unbelief far more appalling than that expressed in the gloomy Pantheism of India, since it assumes that the central, creative Soul is, alternately, not *diffused* only, but merged and *lost* in the universe, and the universe in it: "A new universe swelling into existence or subsiding into nothingness at every throb of the Heart Divine." The creative Energy, therefore, "*now* exists solely in the diffused matter and spirit, of the existing universe." The author assumes, moreover, that each individual soul retains in its youth a dim consciousness of vast dooms and destinies far distant in the bygone time, and infinitely awful; from which inherent consciousness the conventional "World-Reason" at last awakens it as from a dream. "It says you live, and the time was when you lived not. You have been created. An Intelligence exists greater than your own, and it is only through this Intelligence that you live at all." "These things," he says, "*we struggle to comprehend and cannot*: cannot, because being untrue, they are of necessity incomprehensible.

"No thinking man lives who, at some luminous point of his life, has not felt himself lost amid the surges of futile efforts at understanding or believing that anything exists *greater than his own soul*. The intense, overwhelming dissatisfaction and rebellion at the thought, together with the omniprevalent aspirations at perfection, are but the spiritual, coincident with the material, struggles towards the original Unity. The material *and* spiritual God *now* exists solely in the diffused matter and Spirit of the Universe, and the regathering of this diffused Matter and Spirit will be but the reconstitution of the *purely* Spiritual and Individual God."

In a copy of the original edition of *Eureka*, purchased at the recent sale of Dr. Griswold's library, the following note was found inscribed in the handwriting of the author on the half blank page at the end of the volume. It is singularly ingenious and characteristic.

> *Note.*—The pain of the consideration that we shall lose our individual identity, ceases at once when we further reflect that the process, as above described, is neither more nor less than that of the absorption by each individual intelligence, of all other intelligences (that is of the Universe) into its own. That God may be all in all, *each* must become God.

This proud self-assertion betrays a mysterious isolation from the "Heart Divine" which fills us with sadness and awe.

We confess to a half faith in the old superstition of the significance of anagrams when we find, in the transposed letters of Edgar Poe's name, the words *a God-peer*; words which, taken in connexion with his daring speculations, seem to have in them a mocking and malign import "which is not man's nor angel's."

Yet, while the author of *Eureka*, like Lucretius,

——————dropped his plummet down the broad,
Deep Universe and found no God,

his works are, as if unconsciously, filled with an overwhelming sense of the power and majesty of Deity; they are even dark with reverential awe. His proud intellectual assumption of the supremacy of the individual soul *was but an expression of its imperious longings for immortality and its recoil from the haunting phantasms of death and annihilation*; while the theme of all his more imaginative writings is, as we have said, a love that survives the dissolution of the mortal body and oversweeps the grave. His mental and temperamental idiosyncrasies fitted him to come readily into rapport with psychal and spiritual influences. Many of his strange narratives had a degree of truth in them which he was unwilling to avow. In one of this class he makes the narrator say, "I cannot even now regard these experiences as a dream, yet it is difficult to say how otherwise they should be termed. *Let us suppose only that the soul of man, to-day, is on the brink of stupendous psychal discoveries.*"

Dante tells us that

——————minds dreaming near the dawn
Are of the truth presageful.

Edgar Poe's dreams were assuredly often presageful and significant, and while he but dimly apprehended through the higher reason the truths which they foreshadowed, he riveted public attention upon them by the strange fascination of his style, the fine analytical temper of his intellect, and, above all, by the weird splendors of his imagination, compelling men to read and to accredit as *possible truths* his most marvellous conceptions. He often spoke of the imageries and incidents of his inner life as more vivid and veritable than those of his outer experience. We find in some pencilled notes appended to a manuscript copy of one of his later poems the words, "All that I have here expressed was actually present to me. Remember the mental condition which gave rise to 'Ligeia'—recall the passage of which I spoke, and observe the coincidence." With all the fine alchymy of his subtle intellect he sought to analyze the character and conditions of this introverted life. "I regard these visions," he says, "even as they arise, with an awe which in some measure moderates or tranquillizes the ecstacy—I so regard them through a conviction that this ecstacy in itself, is of a character supernal to the human nature—*is a glimpse of the spirit's outer world.*" He had that constitutional determination to reverie which, according to DeQuincey, alone enables a man to dream magnificently, and which, as we have said, made his dreams realities and his life a dream. His mind was indeed a "Haunted Palace," echoing to the footfalls of angels and demons. "No man," he says, "has recorded, no man has dared to record, the wonders of his inner life."

Is there, then, no significance in this "supernatural soliciting"? Is there no evidence of a wise purpose, an epochal fitness, in the appearance, at this precise era, of a mind so rarely gifted, and accessible from peculiarities of psychal and physical organization to the subtle vibrations of an ethereal medium conveying but feeble impressions to the senses of ordinary persons; a mind which, "following darkness like a dream," wandered forever with insatiate curiosity on the confines of that

> ————wild, weird clime, that lieth sublime
> Out of Space, out of Time!
> By each spot the most unholy,
> In each nook most melancholy,

seeking to solve the problem of that phantasmal Shadow-Land, which, through a class of phenomena unprecedented in the world's history, was about to attest itself as an actual plane of conscious and progressive life, the mode and measure of whose relations with our own are already recognised as legitimate objects of scientific research by the most candid and competent thinkers of our time? We assume that, in the abnormal manifestations of a genius so imperative and so controlling, this epochal significance *is* most strikingly apparent. Jean Paul says truly that "there is more poetic fitness, more method, a more intelligible purpose in the biographies which God Almighty writes than in all the inventions of poets and novelists."

# Creative Writers On Poe

## New Notes on Edgar Poe     Charles Pierre Baudelaire*

*Literature of Decadence!* An empty phrase that one often hears
falling, sonorous as a great yawn, from the mouths of those sphinxes
without riddles that guard the sacred portals of classical Esthetics.
Whenever such an irrefutable oracle sounds off, one can be sure that
it is in relation to a work more amusing than the *Iliad*. It clearly concerns a poem or a novel whose every part is skillfully arranged for
surprise, whose style is magnificently ornate, in which an impeccable
hand has employed all the resources of language and versification. When
I hear the roar of anathema—which, let me say in passing, generally
falls on some esteemed poet—I always want to reply: "Do you take me
for a barbarian like yourself, and do you think I can be amused in the
same miserable way as you?" Then grotesque comparisons whirl in
my mind; I have the impression that two women are presented to me;
one is a rustic matron, repugnant in her health and virtue, without
grace and with no charm in her glance, in brief, *one who draws all her
qualities from simple nature*; the other is one of those beauties who
dominate and haunt the memory, one who combines with a profound
and original charm all that is eloquent in dress, who is mistress of her
bearing, thoroughly conscious of her personality and completely self-
possessed—with a voice that speaks like a well-tuned instrument, and
with glances charged with intelligence and employed with perfect control. There would be no doubt as to my choice between these two, and
yet there are pedantic sphinxes that would accuse me of a deficiency in
classical honor. But, to put aside these allegories, I believe I may be
permitted to inquire of these wise men whether they really comprehend
the vanity and uselessness of their wisdom. The phrase *literature of
decadence* implies that there is a series of stages in literatures—a puling

*Reprinted from *Modern Continental Literary Criticism* (New York: Appleton-
Century-Crofts, 1962), 155–73, by permission of O. B. Hardison, Jr., editor, and
Alfred G. Engstrom, translator. The original, "Notes nouvelles sur Edgar Poe,"
appeared as preface to *Nouvelles histoires extraordinaires par Edgar Poe,* 1857.

period of infancy, a period of childhood, an adolescence, etc. I mean that this term presupposes something fatal and providential, like a decree from which there is no appeal. If so, it is completely unjust to reproach us for obeying the dictates of this mysterious law. All that I can make of the academic expression is that it is shameful to get any pleasure out of complying with this law, and that we are guilty if we rejoice in our destiny.—This sun which, a few hours ago, overwhelmed everything under its direct white light, will soon pour waves of varied colors over the western horizon. In the play of this setting sun, certain poetic minds will find new delights; they will find in it dazzling colonnades, cascades of melted metal, fiery paradises, a mournful splendor, the voluptuous pleasure of yearning, all the magical qualities of dream, all that opium brings back of memories. And for them the sunset will in fact appear as the marvelous allegory of a soul burdened with life that sinks behind the horizon, magnificently provided with thoughts and dreams.

But what the avowed professors have not considered is that, in the activity of life, there may arise complications and combinations entirely unanticipated by their scholarly wisdom. And then their inadequate jargon is found wanting, as in the case (which will perhaps recur many times in varying circumstances) of a nation which begins with decadence and thus starts at the point where other nations end.

As new literatures develop amidst the vast colonies of the present age, there will surely be spiritual accidents baffling to the academic mind. Young and old at the same time, America prattles and drivels with an astonishing volubility. Who could number its poets? They are innumerable. Its *blue stockings?* They fill the magazines. Its critics? You may be sure that America has pedants just as insistent as ours in calling the artist back endlessly to the ancient conceptions of beauty and in questioning a poet or a novelist on the morality of his purpose and the quality of his intentions. In America, even more than in this country, there are men of letters who don't know how to write; there is puerile, useless literary work; there are innumerable compilers, those who wearisomely repeat themselves, and those who plagiarize plagiarisms and criticize critics. In this bubbling up of mediocrities in a world dazzled by material improvements (a new kind of scandal that makes one realize the grandeur of peoples who are not doers), in this society that is so eager to be astonished, so in love with life, and especially a life full of excitement, there appeared a man who was great, not only through his metaphysical subtlety, through the sinister or enchanting beauty of his conceptions, through the rigor of his analysis, but great also, and no less great, as a *caricature*.—Here I must explain myself with some care; for recently an imprudent critic, in order to belittle Edgar Poe and to question the sincerity of my admiration, used the word *jongleur* that I had myself applied to the noble poet as a kind of praise.

From the womb of a greedy world hungry for material things, Poe soared into dreams. Stifled as he was by the American atmosphere, he wrote in the front of *Eureka*: "I offer this book to those who have put faith in dreams as the only realities!" It was an admirable protest, and he made it *in his own way*. The author who, in *The Colloquy of Monos and Una*, lets loose torrents of scorn and disgust upon democracy, progress, and civilization, is the same author who, in order to combat the credulousness and the foolishness of his countrymen, proposed most emphatically the idea of the sovereignty of man and ingeniously devised hoaxes most flattering to the pride of *modern man*. Seen in this light, Poe seems to me like a slave seeking to make his master blush. Finally, to express my thought even more precisely, Poe was always great, not only in his noble conceptions, but even when he played the role of buffoon.

## II

For Poe was never a dupe! I do not believe that the man from Virginia who calmly wrote in the full flood of democratic idealism: "The people have nothing to do with laws, except to obey them," has ever been gulled by modern wisdom;—nor has the author of "The nose of a mob is its imagination. By this, at any time, it can be quietly led"— and a hundred other passages in which mockery rains down as thick as grape-shot, but yet remains careless and proud.—The Swedenborgians congratulate him for his *Mesmeric Revelation*, like those innocent Illuminati of another day who looked upon Cazotte's *Diable amoureux* as a revelation of their mysteries; they thank the author for the great truths he has just proclaimed—for they have discovered (O verifiers of what cannot be verified!) that everything he stated is absolutely true— although they admit that at first they suspected it might very well be a mere fiction. Poe answers that, so far as he is concerned, he never had the slightest doubt about it.—Need I cite again this little passage that leaps out at me from the page as, for the hundredth time, I thumb through his amusing *Marginalia*, which seem to reveal the innermost part of his mind: "The enormous multiplication of books in all branches of knowledge is one of the greatest calamities of the present age! for it is one of the most serious obstacles to the acquisition of any positive knowledge." An aristocrat by nature even more than by birth, a Virginian, a man from the South, a Byron who had strayed into a wretched society, Poe always kept his philosophic calm, and whether he was defining the nose of the populace, or mocking those who were inventing religions or making game of libraries, he remained what the true poet was and will always be—a truth in strange garb, an apparent paradox, one who desires no intimacy with the crowd and who runs as far as he can to the east when the fireworks are shot off in the west.

But most important of all: we shall observe that this author, the product of an age infatuated with itself, the child of a nation more infatuated with itself than any other, saw clearly, and imperturbably affirmed, the natural perversity of man. There is in man, he said, a mysterious force which modern philosophy does not want to consider; and yet, without this nameless force, without this primordial inclination, a multitude of human actions will remain unexplained and inexplicable. Such actions are attractive only *because* they are wicked and dangerous; they have the attraction of the abyss. This primitive, irresistible force is natural Perversity, which makes man unceasingly at the same time a killer of others and of himself, a murderer and an executioner;—for, he adds, with a remarkably satanic subtlety, the impossibility of finding a sufficiently reasonable motive for certain bad and dangerous actions could lead us to consider them as the result of suggestions from the Devil, if history and experience did not teach us that God often uses them for the establishment of order and the punishment of rogues;—*after having used these same rogues as his accomplices!* such is the phrase, I admit, that glides into my mind, with an implication as perfidious as it is inevitable. But at present I wish to consider only that great forgotten truth—the primordial perversity of man—and it is not without a certain satisfaction that I see some fragments of ancient wisdom returning to us from a country from which we did not expect them. It is a source of comfort that a few explosions of old truth burst like this in the face of all these flatterers of humanity, of all these coddlers and cajolers who repeat with every possible variation of tone: "I was born good, and you too, and all of us, were born good!" forgetting—no, pretending to forget, these upside-down egalitarians—that we were all born marked for evil!

What illusion could dupe this man who sometimes, under the painful compulsion of his environment, aimed so well against illusions? What scorn he had for pseudo-philosophy in his best days, when he was, as it were, gifted with vision! This poet, several of whose fictions seem wantonly made to confirm the supposed omnipotence of man, wished at times to purge himself. The day on which he wrote: "All certainty is in dreams," he thrust back his own Americanism into the region of inferior things; at other times, entering again into the true way of poets, obedient doubtless to the inevitable truth that haunts us like a demon, he breathed the ardent sighs of *the fallen angel that remembers Heaven*; he mourned for the golden age and the lost Paradise; he wept for all the magnificence of nature, *shrivelling up before the hot blast of fiery furnaces*; and finally he wrote down the admirable pages of *The Colloquy of Monos and Una*, which would have charmed and disconcerted the impeccable Joseph de Maistre.

It is he who said of socialism at a time when the latter did not yet have a name, or when its name at least was not completely popularized: "The world is infested, just now, by a new sect of philosophers, who have not yet suspected themselves of forming a sect, and who, consequently, have adopted no name. They are *the Believers in everything Old.* Their High Priest, in the East, is Charles Fourier—in the West, Horace Greeley; and high priests they are to some purpose. The only common bond among the sect is Credulity:—let us call it Insanity at once, and be done with it. Ask any one of them *why* he believes this or that, and, if he be conscientious (ignorant people usually are), he will make you very much such a reply as Talleyrand made when asked why he believed in the Bible. 'I believe in it first,' said he, 'because I am Bishop of Autun; and secondly *because I know nothing about it at all.'* What these philosophers call *argument* is a way they have *de nier ce qui est et d'expliquer ce qui n'est pas.*"[1]

Progress, that great heresy of decrepitude, could not escape Poe's attention. The reader will see, in various passages, the terms he employed to characterize it. One would truly say, on seeing the ardor of his attack, that he was seeking to avenge himself, as if for some public humiliation or against some common nuisance. How he would have laughed, with that scornful laugh of the poet who is always aloof from the fatuous herd, if, as I did recently, he had come upon this marvelous sentence, which makes one think of buffoons and the wilful absurdities of mountebanks, and which I found perfidiously on display in one of the most solemn journals: *The continuous progress of science has very recently made possible the recovery of the secret lost and so long sought for of . . .*(Greek fire, tempering of brass, whatever else has disappeared), *whose most successful applications date back to a barbarous and very ancient time!!!*— There is a sentence that can be called a real find, a dazzling discovery, even in an age of *continuous progress*; but I believe that Poe's mummy Allamistakeo would not have failed to ask, with the tone, at once gentle and discreet, of one talking to his inferiors, whether it was also thanks to *continuous progress*—to the fatal, irresistible law of progress—that this famous secret had been lost.—Indeed, to abandon the tone of farce in discussing a subject that has about it as much of tears as of laughter, is it not a truly stupefying phenomenon to see a nation—several nations, and soon it will be all humanity—say to its wise men and its wizards: "I shall love you and make you great if you persuade me that we progress involuntarily, inevitably—even in our sleep; free us from responsibility, veil for us the humiliation of comparisons, falsify history, and you can call yourselves the wisest of the wise"? Is it not a source of astonishment that so simple an idea as this does not spring up in all minds: that progress (in so far as there is any) increases suffering in proportion as it refines enjoyment, and that, if the epidermis of the peoples of the earth goes on becoming more delicate, they clearly pursue only a retreating goal—an *Italiam fugientem*—a conquest lost at every moment, a progress that is forever its own negation?

But these illusions, which are, moreover, selfish ones, originate in perversity and falsehood. They are will'-o'-the-wisps that arouse disdain in souls that love the eternal fire, like Edgar Poe, and that stir up hazy intelligences, like Jean-Jacques Rousseau, who, in place of philosophy have an injured sensibility eager for revolt. One cannot deny that Rousseau was right in what he said against the *depraved animal;* but the depraved animal has a right to reproach him for invoking simple nature. Nature creates nothing but monsters, and the whole problem is to come to an understanding of what is meant by *savages.* No philosopher will dare propose as models those corrupt, unhappy hordes, victims of the elements, the prey of wild beasts, creatures as incapable of fashioning arms as they are of conceiving the idea of a supreme spiritual power. But, if one wishes to compare modern, civilized man with man in a state of savagery, or rather a so-called civilized nation with a nation in a savage state, that is to say deprived of all the ingenious inventions that make heroism unnecessary in the individual, who fails to see that all honor is due the savage? By his very nature, by necessity itself, he is encyclopedic, whereas civilized man finds himself confined within the infinitely small areas of his specialty. Civilized man invents the philosophy of progress to console himself for what he has given up and for his lowered state; while man in a state of savagery, feared and respected as a husband, as a warrior under compulsion to be brave, a poet in his hours of melancholy when the setting sun inspires him to sing of the past and his ancestors, approaches much nearer than civilized man to the threshold of the ideal. What shortcoming will we dare accuse him of? He has the priest, the magician, and the doctor. More than that, he has the dandy, the supreme incarnation of the idea of the beautiful carried over into material life, the one who dictates form and gives the rules for manners. His clothing, his ornaments, his arms, his calumet, bear witness to an inventive faculty that civilized men have long since lost. Shall we even think of comparing our dull eyes and our ears that have lost their perception to those keen eyes that pierce the mist, or to those ears *that would hear the grass grow?* And woman in a savage state, with her simple and childlike soul, an obedient wheedling animal, giving herself completely and knowing that she is only half of a destiny—shall we call her inferior to the American lady whom M. Bellegarigue (editor of *The Grocer's Advocate!*) thought to praise by saying that she was the ideal of the "kept woman"? This very woman, whose too-forward manners inspired in Edgar Poe—in Poe, so gallant, so respectful of beauty—the following sad lines:

The frightfully long money-pouches—"like the Cucumber called the Gigantic"—which have come in vogue among our belles—are *not* of Parisian origin, as many suppose, but are strictly indigenous here. The fact is, such a fashion would be quite out of place in Paris, where it is money *only* that women keep in a purse. The purse of an American lady, however, must be large enough to carry both her money and the soul of its owner.[2]

As for religion, I admit shamelessly that I prefer by a great deal the cult of the Celtic god Teutatès to that of Mammon; and the priest who offers to the cruel extortioner of human sacrifices victims who die *honorably*, victims who *want* to die, seems to me a being quite gentle and human in comparison to the man of finance who sacrifices whole populations for no interest but his own. At long intervals these things are still vaguely perceived, and I found once in an article of M. Barbey d'Aurevilly a philosophic exclamation of distress that sums up all that I should like to say on the subject: "Civilized peoples, you who are forever throwing stones at the uncivilized, soon you will not even deserve to be worshipers of idols!"

Such an environment—as I have already said, but cannot resist repeating—is hardly made for poets. What even the most democratic French mind understands by a State would never occur to an American. For any intelligent citizen of the old world, a political State has a center of activity that is its brain and the sun at the center of its system; it has ancient and glorious memories, poetic and military annals that go far back, an aristocracy, to which poverty, the daughter of revolutions, can only add a paradoxical splendor; but *this!* this mob of buyers and sellers, this nameless thing, this headless monster, this phenomenon deported beyond the Ocean, this State!—if a vast tavern, where the drinkers crowd in and discuss business over dirty tables, amidst the noisy babble of vulgar conversation, can be compared to a *salon*, to what we used formerly to call a salon, a republic of the mind presided over by beauty, I wish it well!

The role of man of letters will always be hard to carry out, at once nobly and profitably, without being exposed to defamation, to the slander of the incompetent, to the envy of the rich—that envy which is their punishment!—to vengeful actions of bourgeois mediocrity. But what is difficult enough in a limited monarchy or in a well-ordered republic becomes all but impracticable in a sort of Bedlam where every police officer for public opinion enforces the law for the profit of his personal vices—or of his personal virtues, for it is all the same;—where a poet or a novelist of a region that has slaves is a detestable writer in the eyes of a critic who happens to be an abolitionist; where one cannot tell which is the greater scandal—the indecency of the cynicism or the imperturbable religious hypocrisy. Burning chained Negroes, guilty of having felt their dark cheeks tingle from blushing for their honor's sake; firing off a re-volver in a theatre; establishing polygamy in the paradise of the West, which the savages (the term seems unjust) had not yet soiled with such shameful utopias; advertizing on walls, doubtless to consecrate the princi-ple of limitless liberty, *a cure for nine-month illnesses*—these are some of the salient features, some of the moral examples of the noble country of Franklin, the inventor of sales-counter ethics, the hero of a century de-voted to material things. It is of value to call attention unceasingly to these marvelous examples of brutality, at a time when Americanomania has become almost a fashionable passion, to such a point that an arch-bishop has been able to promise us with a straight face that Providence would soon summon us to the enjoyment of this transatlantic ideal.

### III

Such a social environment of necessity engenders corresponding er-rors in matters of literature. It was against these errors that Pope reacted as often as he could, and with all his strength. We must not be astonished, therefore, that American writers, while recognizing Poe's unusual power as a poet and as a storyteller, always wanted to undermine his reputation as a critic. In a country where the idea of utility, the idea most hostile in the world to the idea of beauty, is pre-eminent and rises above every-thing else, the perfect critic will be the one who is the most *honorable*, that is the one whose tendencies and desires come closest to the ten-dencies and desires of his public—the one who, mixing together all the talents and kinds of literary production, will assign to them all a single aim—the one who will seek in a book of poetry ways to improve the conscience of mankind. Naturally, he will become proportionately less concerned about the beauty of poetry and proportionately less shocked at imperfections and even downright faults in the writer's performance. Edgar Poe, on the contrary, dividing the world of the mind into *pure intellect, taste,* and *moral sense*,[3] applied his criticism according to whether the object of his analysis belonged to one or another of these three divisions. He was before everything else sensitive to the perfection of the over-all plan and to the precision of its execution; dismantling works of literature as if they were defective mechanisms (so far as the aims they sought to attain were concerned), noting carefully the faults of construction; and, when he passed to the detail of the work, to its plastic expression, in a word to its style, examining minutely, and without exception, the faults in prosody, the errors in grammar and all that mass of waste material that scatters its impurities over the best intentions and deforms the noblest conceptions when writers are incapable in their art.

For Poe, imagination is the queen of the faculties; but he means by imagination something greater than what the word signifies for ordinary readers. Imagination is not fantasy; nor is it sensibility, though it is hard to conceive of a man of imagination who would not be sensitive. The imagination is a faculty that is almost divine and that perceives from the very first moment, by ways other than those of the philosopher, the intimate and secret relations between things, their correspondences and analogies. The honors and functions that Poe confers upon the imagination give it so great a value (at least when one has well understood the author's meaning) that a learned man without imagination appears as no more than a pseudo-scholar, or at least as an incomplete one.

Among the literary domains in which imagination can obtain the most curious results and win, not the richest and most precious rewards (for those belong to poetry), but those that are most numerous and most varied, there is one for which Poe had a special preference—the Short Story. This form has the immense advantage over the lengthy novel that its brevity adds to the intensity of its effect. The reading of a Short Story, which can be accomplished at a single sitting, leaves a much more powerful memory in the mind than a reading that is broken up into parts and often interrupted by the turmoil of business and concern for worldly affairs. The unity of impression, the *totality* of effect, is an immense advantage that can give to this kind of composition a superiority all its own, to such an extent that a short story which is too short (though this is clearly a fault) is still better than one which is too long. The artist, if he has any skill, will not adapt his thoughts to the incidents; but, having deliberately conceived at his leisure an effect to be produced, he will invent the incidents and combine the events most suitable to lead to the desired effect. If the first sentence is not written with the object of preparing for this final impression, the work is a failure from the very beginning. There must not slip into the whole composition a single word that was not intended and that does not tend, directly or indirectly, to complete the premeditated design.

There is one particular through which the short story is superior even to the poem. Rhythm is necessary to developing the ideal beauty, which is the greatest and most noble aim of the poem. Now, the artifice of rhythm is an insurmountable obstacle to the minute development of thoughts and expressions which has truth for its object. For truth can often be the goal of the short story, and logical reasoning can be the best tool for construction of a perfect narrative in this form. That is why the short story, which does not have so lofty an elevation as pure poetry, can furnish products more varied and more easily appreciated by ordinary readers. Moreover, the author of a short story has at his disposal a multitude of tones and shades of language—the argumentative tone, the tone of sarcasm, the humorous tone—which poetry rejects, and which are like discords, insulting to the idea of pure beauty. And this is also what causes the author who pursues a simple goal of beauty in a short story to work at a great disadvantage, since he is deprived of rhythm, his most useful instrument. I know that, in all literatures, efforts have been made, and often successfully, to create tales that are purely poetic; Edgar Poe has himself written some very fine ones of this kind. But such efforts and struggles serve only to show the power of the right media adapted to corresponding goals, and I tend to believe that, with some authors, including the greatest that one could select, these heroic efforts arose from despair.

## IV

That poets (using the word comprehensively, as including artists in general) are a *genus irritabile*, is well understood; but the *why* seems not to be commonly seen. An artist *is* an artist only by dint of his exquisite sense of Beauty—a sense affording him rapturous enjoyment, but at the same time implying, or involving, an equally exquisite sense of Deformity or disproportion. Thus a wrong—an injustice—done a poet who is really a poet, excites him to degree which, to ordinary apprehension, appears disproportionate with the wrong. Poets *see* injustice—*never* where it does not exist—but very often where the unpoetical see no injustice whatever. Thus the poetical irritability has no reference to 'temper' in the vulgar sense, but merely to a more than usual clear-sightedness in respect to wrong:—this clear-sightedness being nothing more than a corollary from the vivid perception of right—of justice—of proportion—in a word of *tò kalón*. But one thing is clear—that the man who is *not* "irritable" (to the ordinary apprehension), is *no poet*.[4]

There speaks the poet himself, and thus he prepares an excellent and irrefutable apologia for all those of his race. Poe carried this sensitiveness into literary affairs, and the extreme importance that he attached to poetic matters often led him to adopt a tone of superiority that offended weaklings. I believe I have already remarked that many of the prejudices he had to combat, false ideas, popular judgments that circulated about him, have for a long time now infected the French press. It will not be useless, therefore, to give a brief account of some of his more important opinions on the composition of poetry. The parallel errors in America and in France will make the application of Poe's theories very easy indeed.

But, first of all, I must say that, having made allowance for the natural poet, for innate gifts, Poe provided for knowledge, work, and analysis in a way that seemed exorbitant to arrogant men who had no knowledge. Not only did he expend a great deal of effort to bring under the control of his will the fugitive demon of his happy moments, in order to recall at his pleasure those exquisite sensations, spiritual desires, and conditions of poetic health that are so rare and so precious that one could truly consider them as acts of grace outside of man and as visitations from another world; but he also submitted inspiration to a method and to the

most severe analysis. The choice of a medium! He returns to this unceasingly and insists with learned eloquence upon suiting the medium to
the desired effect, upon the use of rhyme, upon perfecting the refrain, and
upon adapting the rhythm to the sense of the poem. He declared that no
one who cannot grasp the intangible is a poet; that he alone is a poet
who is master of his memory, a sovereign ruler over words, and who keeps
the registry of his own feelings always ready for perusal. Everything for
the dénouement! he says over and over again. Even a sonnet needs a plan;
and construction, the armature, so to speak, is the most important guarantee of the mysterious life of works of the mind.

I turn naturally to the article called *The Poetic Principle*, and I find
there, at the very beginning a vigorous protest against what one could
call, so far as poetry is concerned, the heresy of length or dimension—
the absurd value attributed to long poems. "A long poem does not exist;
the phrase 'a long poem' is simply a flat contradiction in terms." In fact,
a poem deserves its title only in so far as it excites and elevates the soul,
and the positive value of a poem is by reason of this excitement and this
elevation of the soul. But, by a pyschological necessity, all excitations are
fugitive and transitory. This strange condition, into which the reader's
soul has been, so to speak, *drawn* by force, will surely not last throughout
the reading of a poem that exceeds the limits of the human capacity for
enthusiasm.

This is clearly a condemnation of the epic poem. For a work of epic
length cannot be considered poetic except in so far as one sacrifices unity,
which is the vital condition of every work of art; and I do not mean unity
of conception, but unity of impression, of *totality* of effect, as I once stated
in comparing the novel with the short story. The epic poem, then, appears
self-contradictory to us, so far as aesthetics is concerned. It is possible
that former ages produced series of lyric poems that were later bound together by compilers into epics; but every *epic intention* clearly results
from an imperfect sense of art. The time of these artistic anomalies is
past, and it is even very doubtful that a long poem has ever been truly
popular in the complete sense of the word.

We must add that too short a poem, one that fails to supply sufficient
*pabulum* for the excitement that is aroused, and that fails to satisfy the
reader's natural appetite, is also very inadequate. However brilliant and
vivid its effect may be, it will not last; one's memory loses it; it is like a
seal that has been pressed down too lightly and too quickly without having time enough to impress its image upon the wax.

But there is another heresy which, thanks to hypocrisy and the dull-
ness and vulgarity of human minds, is much more to be feared and has
chances of much longer survival—an error that has a tougher vitality—the
heresy of the *didactic*, which includes as inevitable corollaries the here-
sies of *passion, truth,* and *ethics*. Many people imagine that the aim of

poetry is to teach something or other, that it must either strengthen one's conscience, or perfect his behavior, or finally *demonstrate* something useful of any kind whatever. Edgar Poe insists that Americans have been special champions of this heterodox idea; but, unhappily, one does not have to go to Boston to meet this particular heresy. It besets us here at home, and every day batters in upon true poetry. However little one may wish to descend within his consciousness, to question his soul, to recall his memories of exaltation, poetry still has no goal but itself; it can have no other aim, and no poem will be so great, so noble, so truly worthy of being called a poem as the one that its author writes merely for the pleasure of writing it.

Please understand—I do not mean that poetry does not lend nobility to human behavior, or that it does not finally result in elevating man above the level of ordinary concerns; to say that would clearly be absurd. But I do say that if the poet has tried to teach a moral lesson, he has diminished his power as a poet; and it is not imprudent to wager that his work will be bad. Under penalty of collapse or death, poetry cannot be adapted to *science* or to *morality*; it does not have Truth for its object, it has only itself. The modes of demonstrating truth are different and are not found in the realm of art. Truth has nothing to do with song. Everything that makes a poet's song charming, graceful, irresistible, would deprive truth of its authority and its power. Cold, calm, impassive, the mind concerned with the demonstration of truth rebuffs the diamonds and flowers of the Muse; its disposition, then, is the absolute opposite of the poet's.

Pure Intellect has truth as its goal, taste shows us beauty, and the moral sense teaches us the nature of our obligations. It is true that an intermediate sense has intimate connections with the two extremes, and it is separated by so slight a distinction from the moral sense that Aristotle had no qualms about including some of its delicate operations with the virtues. Thus, what especially exasperates the man of taste at the sight of vice is its deformity, its lack of proportion. Vice impairs what is just and what is true, and is revolting to the intellect and the conscience; but, as a violation of harmony, as a dissonance, it will cause particular distress to certain poetic intelligences; and I see no cause for scandal in considering every infraction of superior morality a kind of violation of the rhythm and poetics of the universe.

It is this marvelous and immortal instinct for the beautiful that makes us look upon the earth and what we see of it as a glimpse of something to come, a correspondence linking us to another world. Our insatiable thirst for everything that this life reveals of the beyond is the most enduring proof of our immortality. It is at once by and *through* poetry, by and *through* music, that the soul catches a glimpse of the splendors beyond the grave; and when an exquisite poem brings tears to one's eyes, these tears are not proof of excessive joy but rather indication of an aroused melancholy, a postulation of nerves, a nature exiled in imperfection and desirous of possessing at once, upon this earth, the paradise that it has seen revealed.

Thus, the poetic principle is strictly and simply human aspiration towards a superior beauty, and the manifestation of this principle is seen in an enthusiasm, an excitement of the soul—an enthusiasm that is entirely independent of passion, which is the heart's intoxication, and of truth, which serves as the food of reason. For passion is *natural*, too natural not to introduce an offensive, discordant tone into the domain of pure beauty, too intimate and too violent not to offend the pure desires, gracious melancholies, and noble despairs that dwell in the supernatural regions of poetry.

This extraordinary elevation, this exquisite delicacy, this accent of immortality that Edgar Poe demands of the Muse, far from making him less concerned with the details of execution, impelled him to endless improvement of his technical skill. Many people, especially those who have read the strange poem called *The Raven*, would be shocked if I reviewed the article in which our poet, with apparent candor but with a subtle impertinence for which I cannot blame him, explained in minute detail the method he employed in writing his poem, the adaptation of the rhythm, the choice of a refrain—the shortest one he could find and the one with the most varied applications, and at the same time the one most representative of melancholy and despair, ornamented with the most sonorous of all rhymes (*nevermore*)—the choice of a bird that could imitate the human voice, but a raven—a bird famous in popular imagination for its baneful and fatal character—the choice of the most poetic of all tones, that of melancholy—and of the most poetic of all sentiments, love for a dead woman, etc.[5] "And," said Poe, "I shall not place the hero of my poem in poor surroundings, because poverty is commonplace and contrary to the idea of Beauty...." The reader will discover in several of Poe's short stories curious symptoms of this immoderate taste for beautiful forms, especially for beautiful forms that are unusual, for ornate surroundings and oriental luxury.

I have said that this article seemed to me to show the marks of a subtle impertinence. Those who champion inspiration at all costs would not fail to find blasphemy and profanation in these ideas; but I believe that the article was written especially in their behalf. As insistently as certain writers affect a careless attitude, aiming with their eyes closed at the creation of a masterpiece, full of confidence in their lack of order, and expecting the letters hurled toward the ceiling to fall back on the floor in the shape of a poem, just so insistently Edgar Poe—one of the best inspired men of whom I know—made a point of concealing his spontaneity and of pretending to be completely unmoved and deliberate in his art. "I believe," he said, with an amusing pride that I do not find in bad taste, "that I can boast that no one point in [*The Raven's*] composition is referable either to accident or intuition; that the work proceeded, step by step, to its completion with the precision and rigid consequence of a mathematical problem." And I may say that it is only the fanciers of chance, those who consider inspiration a matter of fate, and the enthusiasts for blank verse, who could find anything strange in these *minutiae*. So far as art is concerned, no details are petty.

On the subject of blank verse, I shall add that Poe attached an extreme importance to rhyme, and that, to his analysis of the mathematical and musical pleasure which the mind draws from rhyme, he brought as much care and subtlety as he brought to all other subjects relating to the poet's craft. Just as he had demonstrated that the refrain can have infinitely varied applications, he sought also to renew, to increase the pleasure of rhyme by adding to it the unexpected element of *strangeness*, which is, as it were, the indispensable seasoning for all beauty. He often employed attractive repetitions of the same verse or of several verses, insistent repetitions of phrases simulating the obsessions of melancholy or of a fixed idea—he used the refrain pure and simple, but brought it into position in several different ways—he employed the variant refrain that gives an impression of indolence and distraction—he employed double and triple rhyme-schemes and also a kind of rhyme that introduces into modern poetry the surprises of leonine verse, but with greater precision and purpose.

It is clear that the worth of all these means can be verified only when they are set to work; and the dream of translating poems made as deliberately and with as much concentration as Poe's may be flattering, but must remain a dream. Poe wrote few poems; he sometimes expressed his regret at not being able to devote himself, not just more often but exclusively, to poetry, which he considered the noblest of all forms of writing. But his poetry has always a powerful effect. It is not the ardent effusion of Byron, or the soft, harmonious, distinguished melancholy of Tennyson, although, let us note in passing, Poe admired the latter almost like a brother. It is something deep and shining like a dream, something mysterious and perfect like crystal. I assume there is no need for me to add that American critics have often belittled Poe's poetry; very recently I found in a dictionary of American biographies an article in which it was accused of strangeness, in which the writer expressed fear that this muse in such sophisticated dress might form a literary school in the glorious fatherland of utilitarian morality, and where, finally, regret was expressed that Poe had not applied his talents to stating moral truths instead of wasting them in search of a perverse ideal and of pouring out in his verses a mysterious, but sensual voluptuousness.

We are familiar with this kind of literary fencing. The reproaches made by bad critics to good poets are everywhere the same. As I was reading this article I seemed to be reading a translation of one of those numerous indictments drawn up by Parisian critics against those of our poets who are most in love with perfection. It is easy to guess which writers are preferred among us, and every mind that is attracted to pure poetry will understand me when I say that, amidst our antipoetic race, Victor Hugo would be less admired if he were a perfect poet, and that he has been able to win forgiveness for all his lyric genius only through introducing into his poetry, by force and brutality, what Edgar Poe considered the chief modern heresy—*the heresy of the didactic.*

Notes

1. Quoted from Poe's "Fifty Suggestions." (Ed.)
2. From "Fifty Suggestions." (Ed.)
3. In *The Poetic Principle.* (Ed.)
4. From "Fifty Suggestions." (Ed.)
5. Here and below the reference is to Poe's *Philosophy of Composition* (Ed.)

# Three Tales of Edgar Poe     Fyodor M. Dostoevski*

Two or three stories by Edgar Poe have already been translated and published in Russian magazines. Here we present to our readers three more. What a strange, though enormously talented writer, that Edgar Poe! His work can hardly be labeled as purely fantastic, and in so far as it falls into this category, its fantasticalness is a merely external one, if one may say so. He admits, for instance, that an Egyptian mummy that had lain five thousand years in a pyramid, was recalled into life with the help of galvanism. Or he presumes that a dead man, again by means of galvanism, tells the state of his mind, and so on, and so on. Yet such an assumption alone does not make a story really fantastic. Poe merely supposes the outward possibility of an unnatural event, though he always demonstrates logically that possibility and does it sometimes even with astounding skill; and this premise once granted, he in all the rest proceeds quite realistically. In this he differs essentially from the fantastic as used for example by Hoffmann. The latter personifies the forces of Nature in images, introduces in his tales sorceresses and specters, and

*Reprinted from Vladimir Astrov, "Dostoevsky on Edgar Allan Poe," *American Literature* 14 (March 1942):70–74. Original appeared in *Wremia* 1 (1861):230.

seeks his ideals in a far-off utterly unearthly world, and not only assumes this mysterious magical world as superior but seems to believe in its real existence. . . . Not so Edgar Poe. Not fantastic should he be called but capricious. And how odd are the vagaries of his fancy and at the same time how audacious! He chooses as a rule the most extravagant reality, places his hero in a most extraordinary outward or psychological situation, and, then, describes the inner state of that person with marvellous acumen and amazing realism. Moreover, there exists one characteristic that is singularly peculiar to Poe and which distinguishes him from every other writer, and that is the vigor of his imagination. Not that his fancy exceeds that of all other poets, but his imagination is endowed with a quality which in such magnitude we have not met anywhere else, namely the power of details. Try, for instance, yourselves to realize in your mind anything that is very unusual or has never before occurred, and is only conceived as possible, and you will experience how vague and shadowy an image will appear before your inner eye. You will either grasp more or less general traits of the inward image or you will concentrate upon the one or the other particular, fragmentary feature. Yet Edgar Poe presents the whole fancied picture or events in all its details with such stupendous plasticity that you cannot but believe in the reality or possibility of a fact which actually never has occurred and even never could happen. Thus he describes in one of his stories a voyage to the moon, and his narrative is so full and particular, hour by hour following the imagined travel, that you involuntarily succumb to the illusion of its reality. In the same way he once told in an American newspaper the story of a balloon that crossed the ocean from Europe to the New World, and his tale was so circumstantial, so accurate, so filled with unexpected, accidental happenings, in short was so realistic and truthful that at least for a couple of hours everybody was convinced of the reported fact and only later investigation proved it to be entirely invented. The same power of imagination, or rather combining power, characterizes his stories of the Purloined Letter, of the murder committed by an orangutan, of the discovered treasure, and so on.

Poe has often been compared with Hoffmann. As we have said before, we believe such a comparison to be false. Hoffmann is a much greater poet. For he possesses an ideal, however wrong sometimes, yet an ideal full of purity and of inherent human beauty. You find this ideal embodied even oftener in Hoffmann's nonfantastic creations, such as "Meister Martin" or the charming and delightful "Salvator Rosa," to say nothing of his masterpiece, "Kater Murr." In Hoffmann, true and ripe humor, powerful realism as well as malice, are welded with a strong craving for beauty and with the shining light of the ideal. Poe's fantasticalness, as compared with that, seems strangely "material," if such expression may be allowed. Even his most unbounded imagination betrays the true American. To acquaint our readers with this capricious talent we present meanwhile three of his tales.

# Letter to Sara
# Sigourney Rice

**Algernon Charles Swinburne***

November 9 [1875]

Dear Madam

I have heard with much pleasure of the memorial at length raised to your illustrious fellow-citizen. The genius of Edgar Poe has won on this side of the Atlantic such wide and warm recognition that the sympathy which I cannot hope fitly or fully to express in adequate words is undoubtedly shared at this moment by hundreds as far as the news may have spread throughout not England only but France as well; where as I need not remind you the most beautiful and durable of monuments has been reared to the genius of Poe by the laborious devotion of a genius equal and akin to his own; and where the admirable translation of his prose works by a fellow-poet, whom also we have now to lament before his time, is even now being perfected by a careful and exquisite version of his poems, with illustrations full of the subtle and tragic force of fancy which impelled and moulded the original song; a double homage due to the loyal and loving cooperation of one of the most remarkable younger poets and one of the most powerful leading painters in France—M. Mallarmé and M. Manet.

It is not for me to offer any tribute here to the fame of your great countryman, or to dilate with superfluous and intrusive admiration on the special quality of his strong and delicate genius, so sure of aim and faultless of touch in all the better and finer part of work he has left us. I would only, in conveying to the members of the Poe Memorial Committee my sincere acknowledgment of the honour they have done me in recalling my name on such an occasion, take leave to express my firm conviction that widely as the fame of Poe has already spread, and deeply as it is already rooted in Europe, it is even now growing wider and striking deeper as time advances; the surest presage that time, the eternal

---

*Reprinted from facsimile in *Edgar Allan Poe, A Memorial Volume*, ed. Sara S. Rice (Baltimore, Md.: Turnbull Bros., 1877), 69–72.

enemy of small and shallow reputations, will prove in this case also the constant and trusty friend and keeper of a true poet's full-grown fame.

I remain Dear Madam
Yours very truly,
A. C. Swinburne

# Under-Lines:
# On a Poet's Tomb

William J. Linton
[Able Reid, pseud.]*

Tomb'd in dishonor! Not like thine own Ghoul
Have I thus dug thee out, Unhappy One!
For critical devouring; but some words
Writ heedlessly above thee call for words
Of answering rebuke. If Israfel
In heaven needs his own heart-strings for his lyre—
The only organ of harmonious worth—
Shall not earth's poet? And if he be weak,
Rent by ill memories, harsh with sour desire,
Untunable, rejoicing not in good,
Can aught but discord issue? Speech absurd
Of "art for art's sake!" when art is not art
Out of the circles of the universe,
Out of the song of eternities,
Or unfit to attend the ear of God.
My mocking words aim at, not thee, but those
Who would strain praise for thee, disgracing Truth.

*Reprinted from *Pot-pourri* (New York: S. W. Green, 1875). I am indebted to Professor John E. Reilly for calling attention to this poem.

# Le Tombeau d'Edgar Poe

Stéphane Mallarmé*

Tel qu'en Lui-même enfin l'éternité le change,
Le Poète suscite avec un glaive nu
Son siècle épouvanté de n'avoir pas connu
Que la mort triomphait dans cette voix étrange!

*From S. S. Rice, ed., *Edgar Allan Poe: A Memorial Volume* (Baltimore: Turnbull, 1877).

Eux, comme un vil sursaut d'hydre oyant jadis l'ange
Donner un sens plus pur aux mots de la tribu
Proclamèrent très haut le sortilège bu
Dans le flot sans honneur de quelque noir mélange.

Du sol et de la nue hostiles, ô grief!
Si notre idée avec ne sculpte un bas-relief
Dont la tombe de Poe éblouissante s'orne,

Calme bloc ici-bas chu d'un désastre obscur,
Que ce granit du moins montre à jamais sa borne
Aux noirs vols du Blasphème épars dans le futur.

In a letter to Sara S. Rice, Mallarmé translated the earlier version of his sonnet into English, with a few notes on the meaning of key words. But as his translation is neither idiomatic nor reliable, it is not reproduced here.

By Eternity changed at last into what he essentially Is, the Poet with naked sword rouses up the epoch of his contemporaries, overwhelmed with horror to realize that they had never understood that death was triumphant in that strange voice.

Hearing, of old, that angel bestow a purer meaning upon the words of the tribe, they started up like the detestable Hydra, bawling out that his words were but a wizard's spell imbibed dishonorably from the draught of some dark brew.

If, out of the conflict of earth and heaven,—O grief!—our thoughts carve no bas-relief with which to adorn Poe's shining tomb—

Then, calm block of stone, here fallen from obscure disaster, may at least this granite forever thrust its barrier against dark flights of Blasphemy scattered throughout the years to come. (Translated by Doris G. Carlson.)

# Comments                                        Henry James*

For American readers, furthermore, Baudelaire is compromised by his having made himself the apostle of our own Edgar Poe. He translated, very carefully and exactly, all of Poe's prose writings, and, we believe, some of his very valueless verses. With all due respect to the very original genius of the author of the "Tales of Mystery," it seems to us

*The first comment, on Les Fleurs du Mal, The Nation, 27 April 1876, was reprinted in French Poets and Novelists (1878), 76. The second excerpt is from Hawthorne (New York: Harper, 1879), as reprinted in Edmund Wilson, ed., The Shock of Recognition, vol. 1 (New York: Grosset & Dunlap, 1955), 474–76.

that to take him with more than a certain degree of seriousness is to lack seriousness one's self. An enthusiasm for Poe is the mark of a decidedly primitive stage of reflection. Baudelaire thought him a profound philosopher, the neglect of whose golden utterances stamped his native land with infamy. Nevertheless, Poe was much the greater charlatan of the two, as well as the greater genius. [1876]

There was but little literary criticism in the United States at the time Hawthorne's earlier works were published; but among the reviewers Edgar Poe perhaps held the scales the highest. He, at any rate, rattled them loudest, and pretended, more than any one else, to conduct the weighing-process on scientific principles. Very remarkable was this process of Edgar Poe's, and very extraordinary were his principles; but he had the advantage of being a man of genius, and his intelligence was frequently great. His collection of critical sketches of the American writers flourishing in what M. Taine would call his *milieu* and *moment*, is very curious and interesting reading, and it has one quality which ought to keep it from ever being completely forgotten. It is probably the most complete and exquisite specimen of *provincialism* ever prepared for the edification of men. Poe's judgments are pretentious, spiteful, vulgar; but they contain a great deal of sense and discrimination as well, and here and there, sometimes at frequent intervals, we find a phrase of happy insight imbedded in a patch of the most fatuous pedantry. He wrote a chapter upon Hawthorne, and spoke of him, on the whole, very kindly; and his estimate is of sufficient value to make it noticeable that he should express lively disapproval of the large part allotted to allegory in his tales—in defence of which, he says, "however, or for whatever object employed, there is scarcely one respectable word to be said . . . The deepest emotion," he goes on, "aroused within us by the happiest allegory *as* allegory, is a very, *very* imperfectly satisfied sense of the writer's ingenuity in overcoming a difficulty we should have preferred his not having attempted to overcome. . . . One thing is clear, that if allegory ever establishes a fact, it is by dint of overturning a fiction"; and Poe has furthermore the courage to remark that the *Pilgrim's Progress* is a "ludicrously overrated book." Certainly, as a general thing, we are struck with the ingenuity and felicity of Hawthorne's analogies and correspondences; the idea appears to have made itself at home in them easily. Nothing could be better in this respect than *The Snow Image* (a little masterpiece), or *The Great Carbuncle*, or *Doctor Heidegger's Experiment*, or *Rappaccini's Daughter*. But in such things as *The Birth-Mark* and *The Bosom-Serpent* we are struck with something stiff and mechanical, slightly incongruous, as if the kernel had not assimilated its envelope. [1879]

# Edgar Poe's Significance          Walt Whitman*

Jan. 1, 1880.—In diagnosing this disease called humanity—to assume for the nonce what seems a chief mood of the personality and writings of my subject—I have thought that poets, somewhere or other on the list, present the most mark'd indications. Comprehending artists in a mass, musicians, painters, actors, and so on, and considering each and all of them as radiations or flanges of that furious whirling wheel, poetry, the centre and axis of the whole, where else indeed may we so well investigate the causes, growths, tally-marks of the time—the age's matter and malady?

By common consent there is nothing better for man or woman than a perfect and noble life, morally without flaw, happily balanced in activity, physically sound and pure, giving its due proportion, and no more, to the sympathetic, the human emotional element—a life, in all these, unhasting, unresting, untiring to the end. And yet there is another shape of personality dearer far to the artist-sense (which likes the play of strongest lights and shades), where the perfect character, the good, the heroic, although never attain'd, is never lost sight of, but through failures, sorrows, temporary downfalls, is return'd to again and again, and while often violated, is passionately adhered to as long as mind, muscles, voice, obey the power we call volition. This sort of personality we see more or less in Burns, Byron, Schiller, and George Sand. But we do not see it in Edgar Poe. (All this is the result of reading at intervals the last three days a new volume of his poems—I took it on my rambles down by the pond, and by degrees read it all through there.) While to the character first outlined the service Poe renders is certainly that entire contrast and contradiction which is next best to fully exemplifying it.

Almost without the first sign of moral principle, or of the concrete or its heroisms, or the simpler affections of the heart, Poe's verses illustrate an intense faculty for technical and abstract beauty, with the rhyming art to excess, an incorrigible propensity toward nocturnal themes, a demoniac undertone behind every page—and, by final judgment, probably belong among the electric lights of imaginative literature, brilliant and dazzling, but with no heat. There is an indescribable magnetism about the poet's life and reminiscences, as well as the poems. To one who could work out their subtle retracing and retrospect the latter would make a close tally no doubt between the author's birth and antecedents, his childhood and youth, his physique, his so-call'd education, his studies and associates, the literary and social Baltimore, Richmond, Philadelphia, and New York, of those times—not only the places and circumstances in

*Reprinted from Richard Bucke, et al., eds., *The Complete Writings of Walt Whitman*, 10 vols. (New York: G. T. Putnam's Sons, 1902), 1:284–87.

themselves, but often, very often, in a strange spurning of, and reaction from them all.

The following from a report in the Washington "Star" of November 16, 1875, may afford those who care for it something further of my point of view toward this interesting figure and influence of our era. There occurr'd about that date in Baltimore a public reburial of Poe's remains, and dedication of a monument over the grave.

> Being in Washington on a visit at the time, "the old gray" went over to Baltimore, and though ill from paralysis, consented to hobble up and silently take a seat on the platform, but refused to make any speech, saying, "I have felt a strong impulse to come over and be here to-day myself in memory of Poe, which I have obey'd, but not the slightest impulse to make a speech, which, my dear friends, must also be obeyed." In an informal circle, however, in conversation after the ceremonies, Whitman said: "For a long while, and until lately, I had a distaste for Poe's writings. I wanted, and still want for poetry, the clear sun shining, and fresh air blowing—the strength and power of health, not of delirium, even amid the stormiest passions—with always the background of the eternal moralities. Non-complying with these requirements, Poe's genius has yet conquer'd a special recognition for itself, and I too have come to fully admit it, and appreciate it and him.
>
> "In a dream I once had, I saw a vessel on the sea, at midnight, in a storm. It was no great full-rigg'd ship, nor majestic steamer, steering firmly through the gale, but seem'd one of those superb little schooner yachts I had often seen lying anchor'd, rocking so jauntily, in the waters around New York, or up Long Island sound—now flying uncontroll'd with torn sails and broken spars through the wild sleet and winds and waves of the night. On the deck was a slender, slight, beautiful figure, a dim man, apparently enjoying all the terror, the murk, and the dislocation of which he was the centre and the victim. That figure of my lurid dream might stand for Edgar Poe, his spirit, his fortunes, and his poems—themselves all lurid dreams."

Much more may be said, but I most desired to exploit the idea put at the beginning. By its popular poets the calibres of an age, the weak spots of its embankments, its sub-currents, (often more significant than the biggest surface ones), are unerringly indicated. The lush and the weird that have taken such extraordinary possession of Nineteenth century verse-lovers—what mean they? The inevitable tendency of poetic culture to morbidity, abnormal beauty—the sickliness of all technical thought or refinement in itself—the abnegation of the perennial and democratic concretes at first hand, the body, the earth and sea, sex and the like—and the substitution of something for them at second or third hand—what bearings have they on current pathological study?

# [Marginalia on "The Philosophy of Composition"]

**Remy de Gourmont***

Of all his mystifications, the "Genesis of a Poem" is the one that has been accepted most willingly and believed the longest. Baudelaire, who miraculously entered Poe's mind and even shared his manias, did not want to seem to question such positive statements. As for the ordinary reader, he was flattered to learn, from the poet himself, that poetry is only a deliberate combination of sounds carefully selected beforehand like the little squares of glass used by artists in mosaic. It is obvious that Poe amused himself enormously in writing his paradox: that is enough to make it legitimate. This paradox is in no way the revelation of Poe's method of work. His method, like all others, will remain forever unknown to us. We scarcely understand how we ourselves work, how our ideas came to us, how we carry them out; if we understood too well, we would no longer be able to work at all. Those are questions that a writer ought to avoid exploring. Besides, it is extremely dangerous to think too much about one's acts or life: the *"Know Thyself"* is perhaps the most harmful nonsense ever uttered.

Poe's system, in "The Raven," presupposes that a poet can imagine successively and in a short period of time all possible combinations of all the words that could be gathered around an idea. That is to say that it presupposes the absurd, since the principle of all verbal composition is the principle of association of ideas, images, sounds—association and linking. Now, one moves here in an infinite which is relative, to say the least; the direction of the will can be exercised only on the immediate, the known—on the senses, the ideas and images that evolve in the order of consciousness. The will cannot evoke, and the consciousness cannot know, what moves outside the present activities of the intelligence. In composition, then, an immense part is played by the unexpected. If a poet imagined that he constructed a poem rationally and deliberately, he would be the dupe of a psychological illusion. In short, one can choose an image in his mind only if the image rises, like a star, over the horizon of consciousness. We know nothing of how it rose and how it has become visible; that takes place in the impenetrable night of the subconscious.

*Reprinted from Jean Alexander, ed., *Affidavits of Genius*, by permission of Associated Faculty Press, Inc. © 1971 by Kennikat Press. From "Marginalia," 1904.

# Edgar Allan Poe                    George Bernard Shaw*

There was a time when America, the Land of the Free, and the birth-place of Washington, seemed a natural fatherland for Edgar Allan Poe. Nowadays the thing has become inconceivable: no young man can read Poe's works without asking incredulously what the devil he is doing in *that* galley. America has been found out; and Poe has not; that is the situation. How did he live there, this finest of fine artists, this born aristocrat of letters? Alas! he did not live there: he died there, and was duly explained away as a drunkard and a failure, though it remains an open question whether he really drank as much in his whole lifetime as a modern successful American drinks, without comment, in six months.

If the Judgment Day were fixed for the centenary of Poe's birth, there are among the dead only two men born since the Declaration of Independence whose plea for mercy could avert a prompt sentence of damnation on the entire nation; and it is extremely doubtful whether those two could be persuaded to pervert eternal justice by uttering it. The two are, of course, Poe and Whitman; and there is between them the remarkable difference that Whitman is still credibly an American, whereas even the Americans themselves, though rather short of men of genius, omit Poe's name from their Pantheon, either from a sense that it is hopeless for them to claim so foreign a figure, or from simple Monroeism. One asks, has the America of Poe's day passed away, or did it ever exist?

Probably it never existed. It was an illusion, like the respectable Whig Victorian England of Macaulay. Karl Marx stripped the whitewash from that sepulchre; and we have ever since been struggling with a conviction of social sin which makes every country in which industrial capitalism is rampant a hell to us. For let no American fear that America, on that hypothetic Judgment Day, would perish alone. America would be damned in very good European company, and would feel proud and happy, and contemptuous of the saved. She would not even plead the influence of the mother from whom she has inherited all her worst vices. If the American stands today in scandalous preeminence as an anarchist and a ruffian, a liar and a braggart, an idolater and a sensualist, that is only because he has thrown off the disguises of Catholicism and feudalism which still give Europe an air of decency, and sins openly, impudently, and consciously, instead of furtively, hypocritically, and muddle-headedly, as we do. Not until he acquires European manners does the

*Reprinted from *Pen Portraits and Reviews*, by Bernard Shaw (London: Constable & Co., 1932), 231–38, with the permission of The Society of Authors on behalf of the Bernard Shaw Estate. Originally published in the *Nation* (London), 16 January 1909.

American anarchist become the gentleman who assures you that people cannot be made moral by Act of Parliament (the truth being that it is only by Acts of Parliament that men in large communities can be made moral, even when they want to); or the American ruffian hand over his revolver and bowie knife to be used for him by a policeman or soldier; or the American liar and braggart adopt the tone of the newspaper, the pulpit, and the platform; or the American idolater write authorized biographies of millionaires; or the American sensualist secure the patronage of all the Muses for his pornography.

Howbeit, Poe remains homeless. There is nothing at all like him in America: nothing, at all events, visible across the Atlantic. At that distance we can see Whistler plainly enough, and Mark Twain. But Whistler was very American in some ways: so American that nobody but another American could possibly have written his adventures and gloried in them without reserve. Mark Twain, resembling Dickens in his combination of public spirit and irresistible literary power with a congenital incapacity for lying and bragging, and a congenital hatred of waste and cruelty, remains American by the local color of his stories. There is a further difference. Both Mark Twain and Whistler are as Philistine as Dickens and Thackeray. The appalling thing about Dickens, the greatest of the Victorians, is that in his novels there is nothing personal to live for except eating, drinking, and pretending to be happily married. For him the great synthetic ideals do not exist, any more than the great preludes and toccatas of Bach, the symphonies of Beethoven, the paintings of Giotto and Mantegna, Velasquez and Rembrandt. Instead of being heir to all the ages, he came into a comparatively small and smutty literary property bequeathed by Smollett and Fielding. His criticism of Fechter's Hamlet, and his use of a speech of Macbeth's to illustrate the character of Mrs. Macstinger, shew how little Shakespear meant to him. Thackeray is even worse: the notions of painting he picked up at Heatherley's school were further from the mark than Dickens' ignorance; he is equally in the dark as to music; and though he did not, when he wished to be enormously pleasant and jolly, begin, like Dickens, to describe the gorgings and guzzlings which make Christmas our annual national disgrace, that is rather because he never does want to be enormously pleasant and jolly than because he has any higher notions of personal enjoyment. The truth is that neither Dickens nor Thackeray would be tolerable were it not that life is an end in itself and a means to nothing but its own perfection; consequently any man who describes life vividly will entertain us, however uncultivated the life he describes may be. Mark Twain has lived long enough to become a much better philosopher than either Dickens or Thackeray: for instance, when he immortalized General Funston by scalping him, he did it scientifically, knowing exactly what he meant right down to the foundation in the natural history of human character. Also, he got from the Mississippi something that Dickens could not get from Chatham and Pentonville. But he wrote *A Yankee at the Court of King Arthur* just as Dickens wrote *A Child's History of England.* For the ideal of Catholic chivalry he had nothing but derision; and he exhibited it, not in conflict with reality, as Cervantes did, but in conflict with the prejudices of a Philistine compared to whom Sancho Panza is an Admirable Crichton, an Abelard, even a Plato. Also, he described *Lohengrin* as "a shivaree," though he liked the wedding chorus; and this shews that Mark, like Dickens, was not properly educated; for Wagner would have been just the man for him if he had been trained to understand and use music as Mr. Rockefeller was trained to understand and use money. America did not teach him the language of the great ideals, just as England did not teach it to Dickens and Thackeray. Consequently, though nobody can suspect Dickens or Mark Twain of lacking the qualities and impulses that are the soul of such grotesque makeshift bodies as Church and State, Chivalry, Classicism, Art, Gentility, and the Holy Roman Empire; and nobody blames them for seeing that these bodies were mostly so decomposed as to have become intolerable nuisances, you have only to compare them with Carlyle and Ruskin, or with Euripides and Aristophanes, to see how, for want of a language of art and a body of philosophy, they were so much more interested in the fun and pathos of personal adventure than in the comedy and tragedy of human destiny.

Whistler was a Philistine, too. Outside the corner of art in which he was a virtuoso and a propagandist, he was a Man of Derision. Important as his propaganda was, and admired as his work was, no society could assimilate him. He could not even induce a British jury to award him substantial damages against a rich critic who had "done him out of his job"; and this is certainly the climax of social failure in England.

Edgar Allan Poe was not in the least a Philistine. He wrote always as if his native Boston was Athens, his Charlottesville University Plato's Academy, and his cottage the crown of the heights of Fiesole. He was the greatest journalistic critic of his time, placing good European work at sight when the European critics were waiting for somebody to tell them what to say. His poetry is so exquisitely refined that posterity will refuse to believe that it belongs to the same civilization as the glory of Mrs. Julia Ward Howe's lilies or the honest doggerel of Whittier. Tennyson, who was nothing if not a virtuoso, never produced a success that will bear reading after Poe's failures. Poe constantly and inevitably produced magic where his greatest contemporaries produced only beauty. Tennyson's popular pieces, "The May Queen" and "The Charge of the Six Hundred," cannot stand hackneying: they become positively nauseous after a time. "The Raven," "The Bells," and "Annabel Lee" are as fascinating at the thousandth repetition as at the first.

Poe's supremacy in this respect has cost him his reputation. This is a phenomenon which occurs when an artist achieves such perfection as to place himself *hors concours*. The greatest painter England ever produced is Hogarth, a miraculous draughtsman and an exquisite and poetic colorist. But he is never mentioned by critics. They talk copiously about Romney, the Gibson of his day; freely about Reynolds; nervously about the great Gainsborough; and not at all about Rowlandson and Hogarth, missing the inextinguishable grace of Rowlandson because they assume that all caricatures of this period are ugly, and avoiding Hogarth instinctively as critically unmanageable. In the same way, we have given up mentioning Poe: that is why the Americans forgot him when they posted up the names of their great in their Pantheon. Yet his is the first—almost the only name that the real connoisseur looks for.

But Poe, for all his virtuosity, is always a poet, and never a mere virtuoso. Poe put forward his *Eureka*, the formulation of his philosophy, as the most important thing he had done. His poems always have the universe as their background. So have the figures in his stories. Even in his tales of humor, which we shake our heads at as mistakes, they have this elemental quality. Toby Dammit himself, though his very name turns up the nose of the cultured critic, is more impressive and his end more tragic than the serious inventions of most story-tellers. The short-sighted gentleman who married his grandmother is no common butt of a common purveyor of the facetious: the grandmother has the elegance and free mind of Ninon de l'Enclos, the grandson the *tenue* of a marquis. This story was sent by Poe to Horne, whose Orion he had reviewed as poetry ought to be reviewed, with a request that it might be sold to an English magazine. The English magazine regretted that the deplorable immorality of the story made it for ever impossible in England!

In his stories of mystery and imagination Poe created a world-record for the English language: perhaps for all the languages. The story of the Lady Ligeia is not merely one of the wonders of literature: it is unparalleled and unapproached. There is really nothing to be said about it: we others simply take off our hats and let Mr. Poe go first. It is interesting to compare Poe's stories with William Morris'. Both are not merely stories: they are complete works of art, like prayer carpets; and they are, in Poe's phrase, stories of imagination. They are masterpieces of style: what people call Macaulay's style is by comparison a mere method. But they are more different than it seems possible for two art works in the same kind to be. Morris will have nothing to do with mystery. "Ghost stories," he used to say, "have all the same explanation: the people are telling lies." His Sigurd has the beauty of mystery as it has every other sort of beauty, being, as it is, incomparably the greatest English epic; but his stories are in the open from end to end, whilst in Poe's stories the sun never shines.

Poe's limitation was his aloofness from the common people. Grotesques, negroes, madmen with delirium tremens, even gorillas, take the place of ordinary peasants and courtiers, citizens and soldiers, in his theatre. His houses are haunted houses, his woods enchanted woods; and he makes them so real that reality itself cannot sustain the comparison. His kingdom is not of this world.

Above all, Poe is great because he is independent of cheap attractions, independent of sex, of patriotism, of fighting, of sentimentality, snobbery, gluttony, and all the rest of the vulgar stock-in-trade of his profession. This is what gives him his superb distinction. One vulgarized thing, the pathos of dying children, he touched in "Annabel Lee," and devulgarized it at once. He could not even amuse himself with detective stories without purifying the atmosphere of them until they became more edifying than most of "Hymns, Ancient and Modern." His verse sometimes alarms and puzzles the reader by fainting with its own beauty; but the beauty is never the beauty of the flesh. You never say to him as you have to say uneasily to so many modern artists: "Yes, my friend, but these are things that men and women should *live* and not write about. Literature is not a keyhole for people with starved affections to peep through at the banquets of the body." It never became one in Poe's hands. Life cannot give you what he gives you except through fine art; and it was his instinctive observance of this distinction, and the fact that it did not beggar him, as it would beggar most writers, that makes him the most legitimate, the most classical, of modern writers.

It also explains why America does not care much for him, and why he has hardly been mentioned in England these many years. America and England are wallowing in the sensuality which their immense increase of riches has placed within their reach. I do not blame them: sensuality is a very necessary and healthy and educative element in life. Unfortunately, it is ill distributed; and our reading masses are looking on at it and thinking about it and longing for it, and having precarious little holiday treats of it, instead of sharing it temperately and continuously, and ceasing to be preoccupied with it. When the distribution is better adjusted and the preoccupation ceases, there will be a noble reaction in favor of the great writers like Poe, who begin just where the world, the flesh, and the devil leave off.

# Edgar Allan Poe                                    D. H. Lawrence*

It seems a long way from Fenimore Cooper to Poe. But in fact it is only a step. Leatherstocking is the last instance of the integral, progressive, soul of the white man in America. In the last conjunction between Leatherstocking and Chingachgook we see the passing out into the darkness of the interim, as a seed falls into the dark interval of winter. What remains is the old tree withering and seething down to the crisis of winterdeath, the great white race in America keenly disintegrating, seething back in electric decomposition, back to that crisis where the old soul, the old era, perishes in the denuded frame of man, and the first throb of a new year sets in.

The process of the decomposition of the body after death is slow and mysterious, a life process of post-mortem activity. In the same way, the great psyche, which we have evolved through two thousand years of effort, must die, and not only die, must be reduced back to its elements by a long, slow process of disintegration, living disintegration.

This is the clue to Edgar Allan Poe, and to the art that succeeds him, in America. When a tree withers, at the end of a year, then the whole life of the year is gradually driven out until the tissue remains elemental and almost null. Yet it is only reduced to that crisis of perfect quiescence which *must* intervene between life-cycle and life-cycle. Poe shows us the first vivid, seething reduction of the psyche, the first convulsive spasm that sets-in in the human soul, when the last impulse of creative love, creative conjunction, is finished. It is like a tree whose fruits are perfected, writhing now in the grip of the first frost.

For men who are born at the end of a great era or epoch nothing remains but the seething reduction back to the elements; just as for a tree in autumn nothing remains but the strangling-off of the leaves and the strange decomposition and arrest of the sap. It is useless to ask for perpetual spring and summer. Poe had to lead on to that winter-crisis when the soul is, as it were, denuded of itself, reduced back to the elemental state of a naked, arrested tree in midwinter. Man must be stripped of himself. And the process is slow and bitter and beautiful, too. But the beauty has its spark in anguish; it is the strange, expiring cry, the phosphorescence of decay.

Poe is a man writhing in the mystery of his own undoing. He is a great dead soul, progressing terribly down the long process of post-mor-

*This original version, which appeared in the *English Review* in April 1919, is reprinted with permission from *The Symbolic Meaning: The Uncollected Versions of Studies in Classic American Literature*, ed. *Armin Arnold* (Fontwell, Arundel, Sussex: Centaur Press, Ltd. 1962), 116–30. © 1961 by the Estate of the late Frieda Lawrence.

tem activity in disintegration. This is how the dead bury their dead. This is how man must bury his own dead self: in pang after pang of vital, explosive self-reduction, back to the elements. This is how the seed must fall into the ground and perish before it can bring forth new life. For Poe the process was one of perishing in the old body, the old psyche, the old self. He leads us back, through pang after pang of disintegrative sensation, back towards the end of all things, where the beginning is: just as the year begins where the year is utterly dead. It is only perfect courage which can carry us through the extremity of death, through the crisis of our own nullification, the midwinter which is the end of the end and the beginning of the beginning.

Yet Poe is hardly an artist. He is rather a supreme scientist. Art displays the movements of the pristine self, the living conjunction or communion between the self and its context. Even in tragedy self meets self in supreme conjunction, a communion of passionate or creative death. But in Poe the self is finished, already stark. It would be true to say that Poe had no soul. He lives in the post-mortem reality, a living dead. He reveals the after-effects of life, the processes of organic disintegration. Arrested in himself, he cannot realise self or soul in any other human being. For him, the vital world is the sensational world. He is not sensual, he is sensational. The difference between these two is a difference between growth and decay. In Poe, sensationalism is a process of explosive disintegration, phosphorescent, electric, refracted. In him, sensation is that momentaneous state of consciousness which concurs with the sudden combustion and reduction of vital tissue. The combustion of his own most vital plasm liberates the white gleam of his sensational consciousness. Hence his addiction to alcohol and drugs, which are the common agents of reductive combustion.

It is for this reason that we would class the "tales" as science rather than art: because they reveal the workings of the great inorganic forces, disruptive within the organic psyche. The central soul or self is in arrest. And for this reason we cannot speak of the tales as stories or novels. A tale is a concatenation of scientific cause and effect. But in a story the movement depends on the sudden appearance of spontaneous emotion or gesture, causeless, arising out of the living self.

Yet the chief of Poe's tales depend upon the passion of love. The central stories, "Ligeia" and "The Fall of the House of Usher," *are* almost stories; there is in these almost a relation of soul to soul. These are the two stories where love is still recognisable as the driving force.

Love is the mysterious force which brings beings together in creative conjunction or communion. But it is also the force which brings them together in frictional disruption. Love is the great force which causes distintegration as well as new life, and corruption as well as procreation.

It brings life together with life, either for production or for destruction, down to the last extremes of existence.

And in Poe, love is purely a frictional, destructive force. In him, the mystic, spontaneous self is replaced by the self-determined ego. He is a unit of will rather than a unit of being. And the force of love acts in him almost as an electric attraction rather than as a communion between self and self. He is a lodestone, the woman is the soft metal. Each draws the other mechanically. Such attraction, increasing and intensifying in conjunction, does not set up a cycle of rest and creation. The one life draws the other life with a terrible pressure. Each presses on the other intolerably till one is bound to disappear: one or both.

The story of this process of magnetic, self-less pressure of love is told in the story of "Ligeia", and this story we may take to be the clue to Poe's own love-tragedy. The motto to the tale is a quotation from Joseph Glanville: "And the will therein lieth which dieth not. Who knoweth the mysteries of the will, with its vigour? For God is but a great will pervading all things by nature of its intentness. Man doth not yield himself to the angels, nor unto death utterly, save only through the weakness of his feeble will."

If God is a great will, then the universe is a great machine, for the will is a fixed principle. But God is not a will. God is a mystery, from which creation mysteriously proceeds. So is the self a unit of creative mystery. But the will is the greatest of all control-principles, the greatest machine-principle.

So Poe establishes himself in the will, self-less and determined. Then he enters the great process of destructive love, which in the end works out to be a battle of wills as to which can hold out longest.

The story is told in a slow method of musing abstraction, most subtle yet most accurate. Ligeia is never a free person. She is just a phenomenon with which Poe strives in ill-omened love. She is not a woman. She is just a re-agent, a re-acting force, chimerical almost. "In stature she was tall, somewhat slender, and, in her later days, even emaciated. I would in vain attempt to portray the majesty, the quiet ease, of her demeanour, or the incomprehensible lightness and elasticity of her footfall. I was never made aware of her entrance into my closed study save by the dear music of her low, sweet voice as she placed her marble hand upon my shoulder."

Perhaps it is hardly fair to quote fragments of Poe's prose, for the careful style shows up a little meretricious. It is for their scientific progress in sensation that the tales should be studied, not as art.

When Poe comes to the clue of Ligeia he leaves a blank. He paints her portrait till he comes to the very look in her eyes. This he never meets, never knows. His soul never goes out to her in that strange conjunction where self greets self, beautiful and unspeakable. He only analyses her till he comes to the unanalysable, the very quick of her.

Speaking of her eyes, he goes on: "They were, I must believe, far larger than the ordinary eyes of our own race. They were even fuller than the fullest of the gazelle eyes of the tribe of Nourjahad. . . . The hue of the orbs was the most brilliant of black, and, far over them, hung pretty lashes of great length. The brows, slightly irregular in outline, had the same tint. The *strangeness*, however, which I found in the eyes was of a nature distinct from the formation, or the colour, or the brilliancy of the features, and must, after all, be referred to the *expression*. Ah, word of no meaning! behind whose vast latitude of sound we intrench our ignorance of so much of the spiritual. The expression of the eyes of Ligeia! How for long hours have I pondered upon it! How have I, through the whole of a midsummer night, struggled to fathom it! What was it—that something more profound than the well of Democritus—which lay far within the pupils of my beloved? What *was* it? I was possessed with a passion to discover. . . ."

This is the same old effort, to analyse and possess and know the secret of the soul, the living self. It is the supreme lust of possession. But the soul can never be analysed any more than living protoplasm can be analysed. The moment we start we have dead protoplasm. We may, with our own soul, behold and know the soul of the other. Look can meet look in pure recognition and communion. And this communion can be conveyed again in speech. But ever didactically. It is a motion of the whole soul in its entirety, whereas scientific knowledge is never more than a post-mortem residuum.

Of a piece with this craving to analyse the being of the beloved, to be scientifically master of the mystery of the other being, is the whole passion for knowledge which fills these two. The learning of Ligeia was immense, we are told, such as has never before been known in woman. It shows the unspeakable craving of those whose souls are arrested, to gain mastery over the world through knowledge. This is one of the temptations of Christ, when Satan offers him the world. To possess the world in deliberate, scientific knowledge, this is one of the cravings of the unrebuked human heart. It cannot be done. We can only know in full when we *are* in full. In the fulness of our own being we are at one with the mystery; in the deepest and most beautiful sense we know it. But as creatures of exact knowledge and deliberate will we exist in the world of post-mortem reality. Life is beyond us for ever, even as the strangeness of the eyes of Ligeia was beyond the man's probing and fathoming. He seemed so often *on the verge*, thrillingly, awfully. But that was all.

He decided that the clue to the strangeness was in the mystery of will. "And the will therein lieth, which dieth not. . . ." Ligeia had a "gigantic volition." . . . "An *intensity* in thought, action, or speech was possibly, in her, a result, or at least an index, of that gigantic volition which, during our long intercourse, failed to give other and more immediate evidence of its existence. Of all the women whom I have ever known, she, the outwardly calm, the ever-placid Ligeia, was the most violently a prey to the tumultuous vultures of stern passion. And of such passion I could form no estimate, save by the miraculous expansion of those eyes which at once so delighted and appalled me—by the almost magical melody, modulation, distinctness, and placidity of her very low voice—and by the fierce energy (rendered doubly effective by contrast with her manner of utterance) of the wild words which she habitually uttered."

Having recognised the clue to Ligeia in her gigantic volition, there must inevitably ensue the struggle of wills. But Ligeia, true to the great traditions, remains passive or submissive, womanly, to the man; he is the active agent, she the recipient. To this her gigantic volition fixes her also. Hence, moreover, her conquest of the stern vultures of passion.

The stress of inordinate love goes on, the consuming into a oneness. And it is Ligeia who is consumed. The process of such love is inevitable consumption. In creative love there is a recognition of each soul by the other, a mutual kiss, and then the balance in equilibrium which is the peace and beauty of love. But in Poe and Ligeia such balance is impossible. Each is possessed with the craving to search out and *know* the other, entirely; to know, to have, to possess, to be identified with the other. They are two units madly urging together towards a fusion which must break down the very being of one or both of them. Ligeia craves to be identified with her husband, he with her. And not until too late does she realise that such identification is death.

"That she loved me I should not have doubted; and I might have been easily aware that, in a bosom such as hers, love would have reigned no ordinary passion. But in death only was I fully impressed with the strength of her affection. For long hours, detaining my hand, would she pour out before me the overflowing of a heart whose more than passionate devotion amounted to idolatry. How had I deserved to be blessed by such confessions? How had I deserved to be cursed with the removal of my beloved in the hour of her making them? But upon this subject I cannot bear to dilate. Let me say only that in Ligeia's more than womanly abandonment to a love, alas! all unmerited, all unworthily bestowed, I at length reocgnised the principle of her longing with so wildly earnest a desire for the life which was now fleeing so rapidly

away. It is this wild longing—it is this vehement desire for life—*but
for life*—that I have no power to portray—no utterance capable of ex-
pressing."

Thus Ligeia is defeated in her terrible desire to be identified with
her husband, and live, just as he is defeated in his desire, living, to grasp
the clue of her in his own hand.

On the last day of her existence Ligeia dictates to her husband the
memorable poem, which concludes:—

> "Out—out are all the lights—out all!
>   And over each quivering form
> The curtain, a funeral pall,
>   Comes down with the rush of a storm,
> And the angels, all pallid and wan,
>   Uprising, unveiling, affirm
> That the play is the tragedy 'Man,'
>   And its hero the Conqueror Worm."

"'O God!' half shrieked Ligeia, leaping to her feet and extending
her arms aloft with a spasmodic movement, as I made an end of these
lines, 'O God! O Divine Father!—shall these things be undeviatingly so?
Shall this conqueror be not once conquered? Are we not part and parcel
in Thee? Who—who knoweth the mysteries of the will with its vigour?
Man doth not yield him to the angels, *nor unto death utterly*, save only
through the weakness of his feeble will.'"

So Ligeia dies. Herself a creature of will and finished consciousness,
she sees everything collapse before the devouring worm. But shall her
will collapse?

The husband comes to ancient England, takes a gloomy, grand old
abbey, puts it into some sort of repair, and, converting it into a dwelling,
furnishes it with exotic, mysterious splendour. As an artist Poe is un-
failingly in bad taste—always in bad taste. He seeks a sensation from
every phrase or object, and the effect is vulgar.

In the story the man marries the fair-haired, blue-eyed Lady Rowena Trevanion, of Tremaine.

"In halls such as these—in a bridal chamber such as this—I passed,
with the Lady of Tremaine, the unhallowed hours of the first month of
our marriage—passed them with but little disquietude. That my wife
dreaded the fierce moodiness of my temper—that she shunned me and
loved me but little—I could not help perceiving; but it gave me rather
pleasure than otherwise. I loathed her with a hatred belonging rather
to a demon than to a man. My memory flew back (Oh, with what intensity of regret!) to Ligeia, the beloved, the august, the entombed. I
revelled in recollections of her purity," etc.

The love which had been a wild craving for identification with
Ligeia, a love inevitably deadly and consuming, now in the man has

become definitely destructive, devouring, subtly murderous. He will slowly and subtly consume the life of the fated Rowena. It is his vampire lust.

In the second month of the marriage the Lady Rowena fell ill. It is Ligeia whose presence hangs destructive over her; it is the ghostly Ligeia who pours poison into Rowena's cup. It is Ligeia, active and unsatisfied within the soul of her husband, who destroys the other woman. The will of Ligeia is not yet broken. She wants to live. And she wants to live to finish her process, to satisfy her unbearable craving to be identified with the man. All the time, in his marriage with Rowena, the husband is only using the new bride as a substitute for Ligeia. As a substitute for Ligeia he possesses her. And at last from the corpse of Rowena Ligeia rises fulfilled. When the corpse opens its eyes, at last the two are identified, Ligeia with the man she so loved. Henceforth the two are one, and neither exists. They are consumed into an inscrutable oneness.

"Eleonora," the next story, is a fantasy revealing the sensational delights of the man in his early marriage with the young and tender bride. They dwelt, he, his cousin and her mother, in the sequestered Valley of Many-coloured Grass, the valley of prismatic sensation, where everything seems spectrum-coloured. They looked down at their own images in the River of Silence, and drew the God Eros from that wave. This is a description of the life of introspection and of the love which is begotten by the self in the self, the self-made love. The trees are like serpents worshipping the sun. That is, they represent the phallic passion in its poisonous or destructive activity. The symbolism of Poe's parables is easy, too easy, almost mechanical.

In "Berenice" the man must go down to the sepulchre of his beloved and take her thirty-two small white teeth, which he carries in a box with him. It is repulsive and gloating. The teeth are the instruments of biting, of resistance, of antagonism. They often become symbols of opposition, little instruments or entities of crushing and destroying. Hence the dragon's teeth in the myth. Hence the man in "Berenice" must take possession of the irreducible part of his mistress. "Toutes ses dents étaient des idées," he says. Then they are little fixed ideas of mordant hate, of which he possesses himself.

The other great story somewhat connected with this group is "The Fall of the House of Usher." Here the love is between brother and sister. When the self is broken, and the mystery of the recognition of *otherness* fails, then the longing for identification with the beloved becomes a lust. And it is this longing for identification, utter merging, which is at the base of the incest problem. In psychoanalysis almost every trouble in the psyche is traced to an incest-desire. But this will not do. The incest-desire is only one of the manifestations of the self-less desire for merging. It is obvious that this desire for merging, or unification, or identification of the man with the woman, or the woman with the man, finds its gratification most readily in the merging of those things which are already near—mother with son, brother with sister, father with daughter. But it is not enough to say, as Jung does, that all life is a matter of lapsing towards, or struggling away from, mother-incest. It is necessary to see what lies at the back of this helpless craving for utter merging or identification with a beloved.

The motto to "The Fall of the House of Usher" is a couple of lines from De Béranger.

"Son coeur est un luth suspendu;
Sitôt qu'on le touche il résonne."

We have all the trappings of Poe's rather overdone vulgar fantasy. "I reined my horse to the precipitous brink of a black and lurid tarn that lay in unruffled lustre by the dwelling, and gazed down—but with a shudder even more thrilling than before—upon the remodelled and inverted images of the grey sedge, and the ghastly tree-stems, and the vacant and eye-like windows." The House of Usher, both dwelling and family, was very old. Minute fungi overspread the exterior of the house, hanging in festoons from the eaves. Gothic archways, a valet of stealthy step, sombre tapestries, ebon black floors, a profusion of tattered and antique furniture, feeble gleams of encrimsoned light through latticed panes, and over all "an air of stern, deep, irredeemable gloom"—this makes up the interior.

The inmates of the house, Roderick and Madeline Usher, are the last remnants of their incomparably ancient and decayed race. Roderick has the same large, luminous eye, the same slightly arched nose of delicate Hebrew model, as characterised Ligeia. He is ill with the nervous malady of his family. It is he whose nerves are so strung that they vibrate to the unknown quiverings of the ether. He, too, has lost his self, his living soul, and become a sensitised instrument of the external influences; his nerves are verily like an aeolian harp which must vibrate. He lives in "some struggle with the grim phantasm, Fear," for he is only the physical, post-mortem reality of a living being.

It is a question how much, once the rich centrality of the self is broken, the instrumental consciousness of man can register. When man becomes self-less, wafting instrumental like a harp in an open window, how much can his elemental consciousness express? It is probable that even the blood as it runs has its own sympathies and responses to the material world, quite apart from seeing. And the nerves we know vibrate all the while to unseen presences, unseen forces. So Roderick Usher quivers on the edge of dissolution.

It is this mechanical consciousness which gives "the fervid facility of his impromptus." It is the same thing that gives Poe his extraordinary facility in versification. The absence of real central or impulsive being in himself leaves him inordinately mechanically sensitive to sounds and effects, associations of sounds, association of rhyme, for example—mechanical, facile, having no root in any passion. It is all a secondary, meretricious process. So we get Roderick Usher's poem, "The Haunted Palace," with its swift yet mechanical subtleties of rhyme and rhythm, its vulgarity of epithet. It is all a sort of dream-process, where the association between parts is mechanical, accidental as far as passional meaning goes.

Usher thought that all vegetable things had sentience. Surely all material things have a form of sentience, even the inorganic: surely they all exist in some subtle and complicated tension of vibration which makes them sensitive to external influence and causes them to have an influence on other external objects, irrespective of contact. It is of this vibrational or inorganic consciousness that Poe is master: the sleep-consciousness. Thus Roderick Usher was convinced that his whole surroundings, the stones of the house, the fungi, the water in the tarn, the very reflected image of the whole, was woven into a physical oneness with the family, condensed, as it were, into one atmosphere—the special atmosphere in which alone the Ushers could live. And it was this atmosphere which had moulded the destinies of his family.

In the human realm, Roderick had one connection: his sister Madeline. She, too, was dying of a mysterious disorder, nervous, cataleptic. The brother and sister loved each other passionately and exclusively. They were twins, almost identical in looks. It was the same absorbing love between them, where human creatures are absorbed away from themselves, into a unification in death. So Madeline was gradually absorbed into her brother; the one life absorbed the other in a long anguish of love.

Madeline died and was carried down by her brother into the deep vaults of the house. But she was not dead. Her brother roamed about in incipient madness—a madness of unspeakable terror and guilt. After eight days they were suddenly startled by a clash of metal, then a distinct, hollow, metallic, and clangorous, yet apparently muffled, reverberation. Then Roderick Usher, gibbering, began to express himself: "*We have put her living into the tomb!* Said I not that my senses were acute? *I now* tell you that I heard her first feeble movements in the hollow coffin. I heard them—many, many days ago—yet I dared not— *I dared not speak.*"

It is again the old theme of "each man kills the thing he loves." He knew his love had killed her. He knew she died at last, like Ligeia, unwilling and unappeased. So, she rose again upon him. "But then without those doors there *did* stand the lofty and enshrouded figure of the Lady Madeline of Usher. There was blood upon her white robes, and the evidence of some bitter struggle upon every portion of her emaciated frame. For a moment she remained trembling and reeling to and fro upon the threshold, then, with a low moaning cry, fell heavily inward upon the person of her brother, and in her violent and now final death-agonies bore him to the floor a corpse, and a victim to the terrors he had anticipated."

It is lurid and melodramatic, but it really is a symbolic truth of what happens in the last stages of this inordinate love, which can recognise none of the sacred mystery of *otherness*, but must unite into unspeakable identification, oneness in death. Brother and sister go down together, made one in the unspeakable mystery of death. It is the world-long incest problem, arising inevitably when man, through insistence of his will in one passion or aspiration, breaks the polarity of himself.

The best tales all have the same burden. Hate is as inordinate as love, and as slowly consuming, as secret, as underground, as subtle. All this underground vault business in Poe only symbolises that which takes place *beneath* the consciousness. On top, all is fair-spoken. Beneath, there is the awful murderous extremity of burying alive. Fortunato, in "The Cask of Amontillado," is buried alive out of perfect hatred, as the Lady Madeline of Usher is buried alive out of love. The lust of hate is the inordinate desire to consume and unspeakably possess the soul of the hated one, just as the lust of love is the desire to possess, or to be possessed by, the beloved, utterly. But in either case the result is the dissolution of both souls, each losing itself in transgressing its own bounds.

The lust of Montresor is to devour utterly the soul of Fortunato. It would be no use killing him outright. If a man is killed outright his soul remains integral, free to return into the bosom of some beloved, where it can enact itself. In walling-up his enemy in the vault, Montresor seeks to bring about the indescribable capitulation of the man's soul, so that he, the victor, can possess himself of the very being of the vanquished. Perhaps this can actually be done. Perhaps, in the attempt, the victor breaks the bounds of his own identity, and collapses into nothingness, or into the infinite.

What holds good for inordinate hate holds good for inordinate love. The motto, *Nemo me impune lacessit*, might just as well be *Nemo me impunne amat*.

In "William Wilson" we are given a rather unsubtle account of the attempt of a man to kill his own soul. William Wilson, the mechanical, lustful ego succeeds in killing William Wilson, the living self. The lustful ego lives on, gradually reducing itself towards the dust of the infinite.

In the "Murders in the Rue Morgue" and "The Gold Bug" we have those mechanical tales where the interest lies in following out a subtle chain of cause and effect. The interest is scientific rather than artistic, a study in psychologic reactions.

The fascination of murder itself is curious. Murder is not just killing.

Murder is a lust utterly to possess the soul of the murdered—hence the stealth and the frequent morbid dismemberment of the corpse, the attempt to get at the very quick of the murdered being, to find the quick and to possess it. It is curious that the two men fascinated by the art of murder, though in different ways, should have been De Quincey and Poe, men so different in ways of life, yet perhaps not so widely different in nature. In each of them is traceable that strange lust for extreme love and extreme hate, possession by mystic violence of the other soul, or violent deathly surrender of the soul in the self.

Inquisition and torture are akin to murder: the same lust. It is a combat between conqueror and victim for the possession of the soul after death. A soul can be conquered only when it is forced to abdicate from its own being. A heretic may be burned at the stake, his ashes scattered on the winds as a symbol that his soul is now broken by torture and dissolved. And yet, as often as not, the brave heretic dies integral in being; his soul re-enters into the bosom of the living, indestructible.

So the mystery goes on. La Bruyère says that all our human unhappiness *vient de ne pouvoir être seuls.* As long as man lives he will be subject to the incalculable influence of love or of hate, which is only inverted love. The necessity to love is probably the source of all our unhappiness; but since it is the source of everything it is foolish to particularise. Probably even gravitation is only one of the lowest manifestations of the mystic force of love. But the triumph of love, which is the triumph of life and creation, does not lie in merging, mingling, in absolute identification of the lover with the beloved. It lies in the communion of beings, who, in the very perfection of communion, recognise and allow the mutual otherness. There is no desire to transgress the bounds of being. Each self remains utterly itself—becomes, indeed, most burningly and transcendently itself in the uttermost embrace or communion with the other. One self may yield honourable precedence to the other, may pledge itself to undying service, and in so doing become fulfilled in its own nature. For the highest achievement of some souls lies in perfect service. But the giving and the taking of service does not obliterate the mystery of otherness, the being-in-singleness, either in master or servant. On the other hand, slavery is an avowed obliteration of the singleness of being.

# On Poe's *Eureka* Paul Valéry*

*To Lucien Fabre*

I was twenty and believed in the might of human thought. I found it a strange torment to be, and not to be. At times I felt I had infinite forces within me. They collapsed when faced with problems, and the weakness of my effective powers filled me with despair. I was moody, quick, tolerant in appearance, fundamentally hard, extreme in contempt, absolute in admiration, easy to impress, impossible to convince. I had faith in a few ideas that had come to me; I took their conformity with my nature, which had given them birth, to be a sure sign of their universal value. What seemed so definite to my mind seemed to be incontrovertible; convictions born of desire are always the clearest.

I guarded those ghosts of ideas as my state secrets. I was ashamed of their strangeness; I feared they might be absurd; I knew they were absurd, and yet not so. They were futile in themselves, but powerful by virtue of the remarkable force which I drew from keeping them hidden. My jealous watch over this mystery of weakness filled me with a sort of vigor.

I had ceased writing verse and almost given up reading. Novels and poems, in my opinion, were only impure and half-unconscious applications of a few properties inherent in the great secrets I hoped some day to discover, basing this hope on the unremitting assurance that they must necessarily exist. As for the philosophers, I had read little of their work and was irritated by that little because they never answered any of the questions that tormented me. They filled me only with boredom, never with the feeling that they were communicating some verifiable power. Then too, it seemed to me useless to speculate about abstractions without first defining them. Yet what else can we do? The only hope for a philosophy is to render itself impersonal. We must still wait for this great step to be taken, shortly before the end of the world.

I had dipped into a few mystics. One can hardly speak ill of them, for what one finds in their work is only what one brings to it.

This was the point I had reached when *Eureka* fell into my hands.

My studies under drab and dismal instructors had led me to believe that science was not love; that its fruits might be useful but its bark was terribly rough and its leafage full of thorns. I consigned mathematics to a species of tiresomely exact minds, incommensurable with my own.

Literature, on the other hand, had often shocked me by its lack of discipline, coherence, and necessity in handling ideas. Frequently its

*Reprinted from Paul Valéry, *The Collected Works in English*, Bollingen Series 45, vol. 8, *Leonardo, Poe, Mallarmé*, trans. Malcolm Cowley and James R. Lawler. © 1972 by Princeton University Press. Excerpt, 161–70, reprinted by permission of Princeton University Press.

object is trifling. French poetry ignores, or even fears, all the tragedies and epics of the intellect. When it sometimes ventures into that territory, it becomes bleak and boring. Neither Lucretius nor Dante was French. We simply have no poets of knowledge. Perhaps our feeling for the separation of literary genres—in other words, for the independence of the different activities of the mind—is such that we cannot tolerate the works in which they are mingled. If something can do without song, we are unable to make it sing. But our poetry, for the last hundred years, has revealed such a wealth of resources, such a rare power of renewal, that perhaps the future will not be slow to grant it some of those works, grand in style, noble in their severity, that dominate both senses and intellect.

In a few moments, *Eureka* introduced me to Newton's law, the name of Laplace, the hypothesis he proposed, and the very existence of speculations and researches that were never mentioned to adolescents—for fear, I suppose, that we might be interested, instead of measuring out the amazing length of an hour with yawning and dreaming. In those days, whatever was likely to stimulate the intellectual appetite was placed among the arcana. It was a time when thick textbooks of physics had not a word to whisper about the law of gravity, or Carnot's principle, or the conservation of energy; instead they were addicted to Magdeburg hemispheres, three-branched faucets, and the tenuous theories to which they were laboriously inspired by the problem of the siphon.

And yet, would it be a waste of academic time to give young minds at least a hint of the origins, the high goal, and the living virtue of the dry calculations and barren theorems that are now inflicted on them in no logical order and even with a remarkable degree of incoherence?

These sciences, so coldly taught, were founded and developed by men with a passionate interest in them. *Eureka* made me feel some of that passion.

I confess that I was astonished and only half persuaded by the vast pretensions and ambitions of the author, the solemn tone of his preamble, and the extraordinary discussion of method with which the volume opens. Those first pages, however, brought forward a ruling idea, while presenting it in a mysterious fashion that suggested partly a feeling of helpless awe and partly a deliberate reserve, the reluctance of an enthusiastic soul to reveal its most precious secret. All this was not calculated to leave me cold.

To attain what he calls the *truth*, Poe invokes what he calls *consistency*. It is not easy to give a definition of that consistency. The author does not do so, although he must have had a clear conception of its meaning.

According to him, the *truth* he seeks can be grasped only by immediate adherence to an intuition of such nature that it renders present, and in some sort perceptible to the mind, the reciprocal dependence of the parts and properties of the system under consideration. This reciprocal dependence extends to the successive phases of the system; causality becomes symmetrical. To a point of view that embraced the totality of the universe, a cause and its effect might be taken one for the other, might be said to exchange their roles.

Two remarks at this point. The first I shall merely indicate, for it would lead us far, both the reader and myself. The doctrine of final causes plays a capital part in Poe's system. The doctrine is no longer fashionable, and I am neither able nor eager to defend it. But we must admit that our notions of cause and adaptation lead almost inevitably in that direction (not to speak of the immense difficulties, and hence of the temptations, that are offered by certain facts, such as the existence of instincts, etc.). The simplest course is to dismiss the problem. Our only resources for solving it are those of pure imagination, which might better be applied to other tasks.

Let us pass to the second remark. In Poe's system, *consistency* is both the means of discovery and the discovery itself. Here is an admirable conception: an example and application of reciprocal adaptation. Poe's universe is formed on a plan the profound symmetry of which is present, to some degree, in the inner structure of our minds. Hence the poetic instinct should lead us blindly to the truth.

Fairly often one meets with analogous ideas among the mathematicians. They come to regard their discoveries not as "creations" of their mathematical faculties, but rather as booty seized by their attention from a treasure house of preexistent and natural forms, one that becomes accessible only through a rare conjunction of disciplined effort, sensibility, and desire.

All the consequences developed in *Eureka* are not deduced with the precision, or explained with the degree of clarity, that one might desire. There are dark places and lacunae. There are interventions inadequately explained. There is a God.

For a spectator of the drama and comedy of the intellect, nothing is more interesting than to observe the ingenuity, the insistency, the trickery and anxiety of an inventor at grips with his invention. He is admirably aware of all its defects. Necessarily he would like to display all its beauties, exploit its advantages, conceal its poverty, and at any cost make it the image of what he desires. A merchant dresses up his merchandise. A woman improves herself in front of the mirror. Preachers, philosophers, politicians, and, in general, all those who undertake to propound uncertainties, are always a mixture of sincerity and reticence (on the most favorable assumption). What they do not like to consider, they do not wish us to see. . . .

The fundamental idea of *Eureka* is nonetheless a profound and sovereign idea.

It would not be exaggerating its scope to recognize, in Poe's theory of consistency, a fairly shrewd attempt to define the universe in terms of its *intrinsic properties*. There is a proposition to be found in Chapter Eight of *Eureka: Each law of nature depends at all points on all the other laws.* Is this not a formula for generalized relativity, at least the expression of a will toward it?

That this tendency approaches recent conceptions becomes evident when, in the *poem* under discussion, we find an affirmation of the symmetrical and reciprocal relationship of matter, time, space, gravity, and light. I emphasize the word symmetrical, for the *essential characteristic of Einstein's universe is, in effect, its formal symmetry.* Therein lies its beauty.

But Poe does not confine himself to the physical constituents of phenomena. He introduces life and consciousness into his plan. How many things this brings to mind! The time is past when one could easily distinguish between the material and the spiritual. Formerly all discussion was based on the complete knowledge of "matter" that we claimed to possess; in a word, it was based on *appearance*.

The appearance of matter is that of a dead substance, a *potentiality* that becomes *activity* only through the intervention of something exterior and entirely foreign to its nature. From that definition, inevitable consequences used to be drawn. But the look of matter has changed. Our former picture of it was derived from pure observation; experiments have led to a wholly different conception. By creating, as it were, *relays* for our senses, modern physics has persuaded us that our ancient definition had no absolute or speculative value. We find that matter is strangely diverse and endlessly surprising; that it is an assemblage of transformations which continue on a smaller scale until they are lost in smallness, in the very abysses of smallness; we learn that perpetual motion is perhaps realized. There is an eternal fever in substances.

At present we no longer know what a fragment of any given substance may or may not contain or produce, now or in the future. The very idea of matter is distinguished as little as you will from that of energy. Everything at a deeper level consists of agitations, rotations, exchanges, radiations. Our own eyes, our hands, our nerves, are made of such things; and the appearances of death or sleep at first presented by matter, by its passivity and surrender to external forces, are conceptions built up in our senses, like the shadows obtained by a certain superposition of lights.

All this can be summarized in the statement that the properties of matter seem to depend only on the order of size in which we place the observer. But it follows that the classical attributes of matter—its lack of spontaneity, its essential difference from movement, and the continuity or homogeneity of its texture—are merely superficial and can no longer be absolutely contrasted with such concepts as life, sensibility, or thought. Within the category of size in which rough observations are made, all former definitions prove incorrect. We are certain that unknown properties and forces are exerted in the *infra-world,* since we have discovered a few that our senses were not designed to perceive. But we can neither enumerate those properties and forces nor assign a definite number to the increasing plurality of chapters in the science of physics. We cannot even be sure that most of our concepts are not illusory, when transported into the realms that limit and support our own. To speak of iron or hydrogen is to presuppose entities the existence and permanence of which can only be inferred from experiments of very limited extent and duration. Moreover, there is no reason to believe that our space, our time, and our causality preserve any meaning whatever in those realms where the existence of our bodies is *impossible.* Naturally the man who attempts to picture the inner reality of objects can only apply to it the ordinary categories of his thinking. But the more he pursues his researches and, in some measure, the more he increases his ability to record phenomena, the farther he travels from what might be called the *optimum* of his perceptions. Determinism is lost among inextricable systems, with billions of variables, where the mind's eye can no longer trace the operation of laws and come to rest on some durable fact. When discontinuity becomes the rule, the imagination, which was once employed in giving final form to a truth guessed at by one's perceptions and woven into a single piece by one's reasoning, must confess to being helpless. When *averages* become the objects of our judgments, we are ceasing to consider events in themselves. Our knowledge is tending toward power and has turned aside from a coordinated contemplation of things; prodigies of mathematical subtlety are required to restore some degree of unity to it. We have stopped talking about first principles, and physical laws have become mere instruments, always capable of being improved. They no longer govern the world, but are matched with the weakness of our minds; we can no longer rely on their simplicity; always, like a persistent point, there is some unresolved decimal that brings us back to a feeling of uneasiness, a sense of the inexhaustible.

One can see from these remarks that Poe's intuitions regarding the general nature of the physical, moral, and metaphysical universe are neither proved nor disproved by the extremely numerous and important discoveries made since 1847. Some of his views might even be incorporated, without too much effort, into fairly recent conceptions. When he measures the duration of his Cosmos by the time necessary to realize all possible combinations of the elements, one thinks of Boltzmann's theories and his estimates of probability as applied to the kinetic theory of gas. Carnot's principle—the second law of thermodynamics—is also foreshadowed in *Eureka,* and is the representation of that principle by the mechanics of diffusion. The author seems to have been a precursor of those bold spirits who would rescue the universe from certain death by means of an infinitely brief passage through an infinitely improbable state.

Since it is not my present intention to make a complete analysis of *Eureka*, I shall have very little to say about the author's use of the nebular hypothesis. When Laplace advanced the theory, his object was limited. He proposed only to reconstitute the development of the solar system. He assumed the existence of a gaseous mass in the process of cooling. The core of the mass had already reached a high degree of concentration, and the whole rotated on an axis passing through its center of gravity. He assumed the existence of gravity, as well as the invariability of mechanical laws, and made it his sole task to explain the direction of rotation of the planets and their satellites, the slight eccentricity of their orbits, and the relatively slight degree of inclination. In these conditions, being subjected to centrifugal force and the process of cooling, matter would flow from the poles toward the equator of the mass and, at the points where gravity and centrifugal acceleration balanced each other, would be disposed in a zone. Thus a nebulous ring was formed; it would soon be broken, and the fragments of the ring would finally coalesce to form a planet. . . .

Readers of *Eureka* will see how Poe has extended the application of both the nebular hypothesis and the law of gravity. On these mathematical foundations he has built an abstract poem, one of the rare modern examples of a total explanation of the material and spiritual universe, a *cosmogony*.

It belongs to a department of literature remarkable for its persistence and astonishing in its variety; cosmogony is one of the most ancient literary forms. . . .

# Modern Criticism: 1950–1985

## Poe as a Literary Critic

Edmund Wilson*

Poe, at the time of his death in 1849, had had the intention of publishing a book on *The Authors of America in Prose and Verse*. He had already worked over to a considerable extent the material of his articles and reviews; and the collection of critical writing printed by Griswold after his death is something between a journalistic chronicle like Bernard Shaw's dramatic notices and a selected and concentrated volume like Eliot's *The Sacred Wood*.

Poe as a critic has points of resemblance both to Eliot and to Shaw. He deals vigorously and boldly with books as they come into his hands day by day, as Shaw did with the plays of the season, and manages to be brilliant and arresting even about works of no interest; and he constantly insists, as Eliot does, on attempting, in the practice of this journalism, to formulate general principles. His literary articles and lectures, in fact, surely constitute the most remarkable body of criticism ever produced in the United States. Henry James, as will be seen in his study of Hawthorne, called it "probably the most complete and exquisite specimen of *provincialism* ever prepared for the edification of men." But, though Poe had his share of provincialism as all American writers did in that period, the thing that most strikes us today is his success in keeping himself above it. Intellectually he stands on higher ground than any other American writer of his time. He is trying to curb the tendency of the Americans to overrate or overpraise their own books, and at the same time he is fighting a rearguard action against the overinflation of British reputations and the British injustice to American writers; and he has also a third battle: to break down the monopolistic instincts of the New

*The text here is that of the introduction to the section on Poe in *The Shock of Recognition*, by Edmund Wilson, vol. 1 (New York: Grosset & Dunlap, 1955), 79–84, a revision of the original version in the *Nation* 155 (1942):452–53. Reprinted by permission of Farrar, Straus and Giroux, Inc., © 1955, renewed © 1969 by Edmund Wilson.

109

Englanders, who tended to act as a clique and to keep out New Yorkers and Southerners.

On one plane, Poe grapples realistically with the practical problems of writers in the United States of that time: the copyright situation and the growth of the American magazine, with its influence on literary technique; and on another plane, he is able to take in the large developments of Western literature. With his general interest in method, he has definite ideas about the procedures in a variety of departments of literature: fiction, poetry, satire, travel, criticism. And he can be elevated, ironic, analytical, as the subject in hand requires. His prose is as taut as in his stories, but it has cast off the imagery of his fiction to become simply sharp and precise: our only first-rate classical prose of this period. His mind is like a bright vivid shaft that picks out the successive objects in the American literary landscape just as the searchlight on the Albany night-boat picks out houses along the Hudson; so that, just as we are drawn to gaze at even undistinguished mansions in their new relief of spectral intensity, so with Poe we read even the articles on insignificant figures whose dead faces the critic irradiates in the process of speeding them to oblivion. When we have put the whole picture together, we seem to behold it as clearly as the geography of the surface of the moon under an unattainably powerful telescope. There is no other such critical survey in our literature.

But Poe had tweaked the beard of Longfellow, and he had made people laugh at a Channing, and the lurking rancor of New England seems to have worked against the acceptance of his criticism. There is an anecdote in W. D. Howells' book, *Literary Friends and Acquaintance,* which shows both the attitude of New England and the influence of this attitude on others. Howells had visited Boston for the first time when he was twenty-three, and he had gone to see Emerson in Concord. Poe had been dead ten years. "After dinner," says Howells, "we walked about in [Emerson's] 'pleached garden' a little, and then we came again into his library, where I meant to linger only till I could fitly get away. He questioned me about what I had seen of Concord, and whom besides Hawthorne I had met, and when I told him only Thoreau, he asked me if I knew the poems of Mr. William Ellery Channing. I have known them since, and felt their quality, which I have gladly owned a genuine and original poetry; but I answered then truly that I knew only from Poe's criticisms: cruel and spiteful things which I should be ashamed of enjoying as I once did. 'Whose criticisms?' asked Emerson. 'Poe's,' I said again. 'Oh,' he cried out, after a moment, as if he had returned from a far search for my meaning, *'you mean the jingle-man.'*

"I do not know why this should have put me to such confusion, but if I had written the criticism myself I do not think I could have been more abashed. Perhaps I felt an edge of reproof, of admonition, in a characterization of Poe which the world will hardly agree with; though I do not agree with the world about him, myself, in its admiration. At any rate, it made an end of me for the time, and I remained as if already absent, while Emerson questioned me as to what I had written in the *Atlantic Monthly*."

It is true that Poe had not much admired Emerson and had written rather insultingly about him in *A Chapter of Autography*; and that Channing had been a sort of disciple and protégé of Emerson's. But an entry in Emerson's journal for 1855 shows that his private opinion of Channing was not so very different from Poe's: "Ellery Channing's poetry has the merit of being genuine, and not the metrical commonplaces of the magazines, but it is painfully incomplete. He has not kept faith with the reader; 'tis shamefully insolent and slovenly. He should have lain awake all night to find the true rhyme for a verse, and he has availed himself of the first one that came; so that it is all a babyish incompleteness."

The prejudice of New England against Poe was supported by the bad reputation that had been given him by Griswold's mendacious memoirs. It is not so long ago that it was possible for President Hadley of Yale to explain the refusal of the Hall of Fame to admit Poe among its immortals on the ground that he "wrote like a drunkard and a man who is not accustomed to pay his debts"; and it was only in 1941 that Professor A. H. Quinn showed the lengths to which Griswold had gone, by producing the originals of Poe's letters and printing them side by side with Griswold's falsifications.

We have often been told of Poe's criticism that it is spiteful; that it is pretentious; that it is vitiated by Poe's acceptance of the sentimental bad taste of his time. In regard to the first two of these charges, it must be admitted that the essays do give us unpleasant moments: they do have their queer knots and wrinkles; they are neurotic as all Poe's work is neurotic, and the distortions do here sometimes throw us off as they do not do in the stories, because it is here a question of judgment, whereas in his fiction the distortions itself is the subject of the story. It is true, as Mr. Joseph Wood Krutch has said, that there is constantly felt in Poe's criticism the same element of obsessive cruelty that inspires his tales of horror. Yet certainly Poe in his criticism makes an effort to hold his tendency in check—with an occasional effect of inconsistency of opinion as well as of tone, as when he will begin by telling us that certain passages in some book he is reviewing are among the best things of their kind to be found in contemporary poetry, and then go on to pick the poet to pieces slowly, coldly, and at a length of many pages. It is also true that Poe pretends sometimes, or at least sometimes lets us infer, that he has read things he has not read. The psychology of the pretender is always a factor to be reckoned with in Poe.

The child of a fascinating actress, who died when he was two years old, he had been adopted by a Scotch merchant in Richmond, brought up as a Southern gentleman, and then cast off with no job and no income at the end of his first year of college. His foster father had even failed to provide money for his necessary expenses, so that Poe, as he said, had been unable to associate with any students "except those who were in a similar situation with myself." He had always been in the false situation of not being Allan's son and of knowing that in the society he was bred to his parents had been *déclassés*; and now he was suddenly deprived of his role of a well-heeled young Southern gentleman with prospects of inheriting a fortune, and found himself a poor man with no backing who had to survive in the American Grub Street. He had the confidence of faith in superior abilities, and the reports of his work at his English school and at the University of Virginia show that he excelled as a student. But his studies had been aborted at the same time as his social career, and a shade of the uncertainty of the "gentleman" was communicated also to the "scholar." Perhaps, also, though Poe's mind was a first rate one, there was in him a dash of the actor who delights in elaborating a part. Out of his consciousness of being a pretender, at any rate, with its infliction of an habitual secretiveness, came certainly Poe's love of cryptograms, his interest in inventing and solving crimes, and his indulgence in concocting and exposing hoaxes. If Poe sometimes plays unavowed tricks by cheating the reader a little as to what he has written or read, the imposture is still almost as gratuitous, as innocent, and as unimportant as Stendahal's disguises and aliases and his weakness for taking ladies from the provinces through Paris and misinforming them about the public monuments. And with this we must also write off Poe's rather annoying mania of accusing his contemporaries of plagiarism—a harsh name he is in the habit of brandishing to indicate borrowings and echoes of a kind which, whether more or less abject, are usually perfectly harmless. Poe himself was certainly guilty—in his imitations of Chivers, for example—of borrowings of precisely the same kind. But the consciousness of borrowing at all was enough to touch off the pretender.

As for the charge of Poe's acquiescence in the mawkish bad taste of his period, it is deserved to only a slight degree. He more often ran counter to this taste, as when he came down on Fitz-Greene Halleck; and, for the rest, his excessive enthusiasm for poets like Mrs. Osgood is attributable to the same sort of causes as, say, the praises of Bernard Shaw for the plays of Henry Arthur Jones: the writer who is potentially a master sees in the inferior writer a suggestion of the kind of thing that he wants to do himself—a kind of thing of which the possibility will hardly be plain to anyone else till the master himself has made it actual.

We must recognize these warpings of Poe's line; but we must not allow them as serious impugnments of the validity of his critical work.

His reading *was* wide and great; and his culture was derived from a plane of the world of thought and art which had hardly been visited by Longfellow, with his patient, persistent transposition of the poetry of many lands and ages into terms of his own insipidity or by Lowell with his awful cozy titles for the collections of his literary essays: *My Study Windows* and *Among My Books*. The truth was that literary America has always resented in Poe the very superiority which made him so quickly an international figure. He must have been a difficult person, with his accesses of hatefulness and depression, though certain people seem to have got on very well with him; but it seems hard to explain the virulence with which Griswold pursued him after his death and the general hostility toward him which has haunted us ever since, except on the ground that he puts us out by making so much of our culture seem second-rate. In our childhood we read *The Gold Bug* and *The Murders in the Rue Morgue,* and everybody knows *Annabel Lee* and *Ulalume* and *The Raven* and *The Bells*; but Poe is not, as he is with the French and as he ought to be with us, a vital part of our intellectual equipment. It is rare that an American writer points out, as Waldo Frank once did, that Poe does not belong at all with the clever contrivers of fiction like O. Henry and S. S. Van Dine, but, in terms of his more constricted personality, with the great inquiring and versatile minds like Goethe. So that in any presentation of American writing it is still necessary to insist on his value. In the darkness of his solitary confinement, Poe is still a prince.

# Style and Meaning in "Ligeia" and "William Wilson"    Donald Barlow Stauffer*

From his own lifetime to the present, controversy has flourished between those holding the widely accepted but inadequately demonstrated view that Poe was a master stylist and those who condemn his style for its awkwardness and lack of taste. Judgments upon his style, in fact, differ as widely as those making them. Hawthorne praising his "force and originality," Mark Twain finding his prose unreadable. Baudelaire's practically unrestrained praise of Poe's "admirable style, pure and bizarre" is balanced by the twentieth-century condemnation of Yvor Winters, who holds that Poe was always a bad writer, accidentally and temporarily popular.[1]

Many readers whose opinions lie somewhere between these extremes

*Reprinted from *Studies in Short Fiction* 2 (Summer 1965):316–30, by permission of the author and of *Studies in Short Fiction*.

still often too hastily condemn Poe's style because they are using standards of "taste" or propriety which are seldom related to consideration
of the style in the individual tales themselves. No judgment of the
quality of a style can legitimately be made separately from a critical
consideration of the work in which it is found. It is often disturbing
to find remarks about the style of an author which seem to be based on
the reader's own personal tastes, rather than upon his awareness that
the style is inseparable from the work itself and must therefore, like
its symbols, its metaphors, and its paradoxes, be organically related to
it. Such an assumption must be insisted upon in the instance of Poe,
who was not a careless, haphazard writer, but a conscious and skilled
craftsman—technician even—who carefully calculated the means by which
to bring about his celebrated "unity of effect."

Allen Tate, who is more generous to Poe than many other modern
critics, still has reservations about his style in some of his tales. Setting
two passages together, one from "William Wilson" and one from "Ligeia,"
Tate concludes that he finds it difficult to admire what he calls the
"ungrammatical rubbish" of the "Ligeia" passage. But, he says,

> . . . if Poe is worth understanding at all (I assume that he is), we
> might begin by asking why the writer of the lucid if not very dis-
> tinguished passage from "William Wilson" repeatedly fell into the
> bathos of "Ligeia." I confess that Poe's serious style at its typical
> worst makes the reading of more than one story at a sitting an almost
> insuperable task.

Poe's subjects, he writes, are done up in a "glutinous prose" that "so
fatigues one's attention that with the best will in the world one gives
up, unless one gets a clue to the power underlying the flummery."[2]

There is the strong suggestion in these and other remarks by Tate
that, stylistically, "William Wilson" and "Ligeia" are poles apart, and
that the former, which is "perspicuous in diction and on the whole
credible in realistic detail," is therefore to be preferred to the latter.
But is the matter this simple? Closer inspection shows us that some of
what looks very much like the "ungrammatical rubbish" of "Ligeia"
can be found in "William Wilson." And much of "Ligeia," on the other
hand, is written in a style not so different from that in many passages
of "William Wilson." Actually, as I shall attempt to show, the same
stylistic elements appear in both stories. The difference in the total
effect produced by stylistic means derives from the difference in order
and proportion of various stylistic ingredients rather than from the kind
of polarity which Tate's remarks suggest.

In the following study, an analysis of the style of each of these
stories, I shall try to do two things: first, to describe the elements
of style found in each story; and, second, to analyze the function of

these elements in each story in order to see what relationship exists between the style of the tale and its meaning.

The choice of these two stories for analysis is based partly on Tate's provocative remarks and partly on the assumption that Poe himself regarded neither of them as hackwork, or as satire or burlesque. It is evident that Poe, in spite of his insistence that he considered none of his stories better than others, was especially partial to "Ligeia," on one occasion calling it his best because it is "of the highest imagination." He resented Duyckinck's exclusion of both "Ligeia" and "William Wilson" from his 1845 *Tales,* since the selection as it stood did not, he said, represent his mind in its various phases.[3] In a letter to Lowell a year earlier, Poe had listed both "William Wilson" and "Ligeia" among his favorite tales.[4] We may therefore reasonably assume that since he had a high regard for both these tales, he had taken an equal amount of pains with each. This assumption is further strengthened by his introduction to *Tales of the Grotesque and Arabesque* (1840), in which both appeared:

> There are one or two of the articles here, (conceived and executed in the purest spirit of extravaganza,) to which I expect no serious attention, and of which I shall speak no farther. But for the rest I cannot conscientiously claim indulgence on the score of hasty effort. I think it best becomes me to say, therefore, that if I have sinned, I have deliberately sinned. These brief compositions are, in chief part, the results of matured purpose and very careful consideration.

## I

Looking first at "Ligeia,"[5] we notice that the style is in many ways extravagant, lying somewhere between the youthful exuberance and heterogeneity of "The Assignation," and the ratiocinative and expository prose of "The Murders in the Rue Morgue." One of the first things we notice about the style of "Ligeia" is its incantatory quality, which makes us feel that the narrator is intoning his story. Rhythm and sound effects, especially in the opening paragraphs, are extremely important in establishing the tone of the tale. The rhythmical quality of the opening sentence is maintained through the entire first paragraph and is echoed at various points throughout the story:

-  /  -  -  -  /  -  /  -  /  /  -  /  -  -  /  -

I cannot, for my soul, remember how, when, or even precisely

/  -  /  -  -  -  /  -  -  -  /  -  -  /  -

where, I first became acquainted with the lady Ligeia.

The phrase "how, when, or even precisely where" is particularly emphatic rhythmically and makes it obvious that Poe is directing his prose to the ear as well as to the mind. The techniques of analysis of prose rhythm are still in too primitive and even chaotic a state to insist on any kind of metrical or rhythmic pattern without some understandable and necessary reservations. Nevertheless, we would be closing our ears to an essential feature of the prose of "Ligeia" if we ignored the part that rhythm plays in creating its haunting, incantatory, emotional style. We seldom find in Poe the kind of metrical regularity that appears in passages of Melville, many of which may be turned into blank verse lines, but an analysis of the rhythm of sentences in "Ligeia" will reveal a loose sort of regularity. The two prevailing feet are, in the technical language of prosodists, the *amphibrach* (-/-), and the *third paeon* (--/-). The word *Ligeia* is itself an amphibrach, which Poe exploits for its rhythmical quality. The other of these two dominant metrical forms, the third paeon, appears in such lines as:

```
 -    -    / -|  - -  / -|/ - - | - -  /  / |--
"and the thrilling and enthralling eloquence of her low musical
 /   -
language"; and, at the end of the paragraph and therefore in a
```

particularly emphatic position:

```
- / - -|/ -  | - / - |- -  / |- -  / - |- - / - |
idolatrous Egypt, presided, as they tell, over marriages ill-omened,
  -   -    / -| -  - / - | - -   /
then most surely she presided over mine.
```

The predominance of this metrical pattern sets the tone of the paragraph as a whole.

Even without concluding that Poe deliberately set out to write in specific rhythms, we may still assert that his ear governed the choice and arrangements of words in this tale. His strongly rhythmic poetry is clear enough evidence of his reliance on and taste for a marked beat. Let us look at the last sentence of the opening paragraph again:

```
 -  -   /  -|-  - /  -  |  -   -   / -|  -  - / -|- -   /
over marriages ill-omened, then most surely she presided over mine.
```

We notice two things here: first, the accent on the last syllable firmly ends a series of feet each ending with a weak beat, and also ends the paragraph on an emphatic beat. Second, the inversion of "marriages ill-omened" not only creates the kind of emphasis always created by a deviation from normal word order, but here it also preserves a rhythm pattern in a sentence which sounds halting indeed if one were to restore the adjective and noun to their normal order.

Before leaving the subject of rhythm in "Ligeia," let us put Poe's sense of rhythm to two more tests. First, let us look at a sentence from another tale, which is very similar in meaning, but totally different in tone and manner of treatment, and compare it rhythmically (other differences exist as well) with the opening sentence of "Ligeia."

```
 -  /  -  /   /  - /  -   /  -  /  -  /   /    -
I cannot just now remember when or where I first made the
 /  /    -    -    -  /  - /   /  -   /  -   /  -  /  -  -
acquaintance of that truly fine-looking fellow, Brevet Brigadier-
 /  -    -  /  /  /    /
General John A. B. C. Smith. ["The Man That Was Used Up"]
 -  /  - |  -  -   /  | - /   -  |  /    /   | - /  - | -  / | -
I cannot, for my soul, remember how, when, or even precisely
 /   |- /  -  | -   -    /   -|  -   -   / -| - / -
where, I first became acquainted with the lady Ligeia.
```

My divisions into feet may be quarrelled with, but a reading aloud will reveal the absence of any sort of rhythmic pattern in the first passage and the presence of such a pattern in the second. The first is closer to the rhythm of good prose than to that of "rhythmic prose."

A glance at Poe's revisions gives further evidence of his awareness of rhythm. The phrase "giving a hideous and uneasy animation to the whole," for example, has an unmistakable rhythmic pattern that is closer to verse than to prose. The 1838 *American Museum* version prints "vitality" rather than "animation," which first appears in the *Tales of the Grotesque and Arabesque* of 1840. "Animation," of course, gives the phrase its rhythmical regularity. And when he changed from a single to a double *Ligeia* in the opening paragraph of the *Broadway Journal* version, Poe was probably again counting on its rhythmical quality.

Parallelism may also be considered a form of rhythm, and Poe's parallelisms, although they appear infrequently in "Ligeia," are sometimes both logically and rhythmically parallel. This phrase, for example, is closer to the eighteenth century in construction and tone than to the nineteenth; it has the quality of balance associated with the style of Johnson:

```
  -    -  /  -  -   /  - /  -  -  -   /   -
which belong to the superstitions of the Normans
  -  - /  -  -   /  -  /  -  -  -    /
or arise in the guilty slumbers of the monk
```

But in another example of Poe's use of parallel construction, the emphasis is upon emotion rather than reason; the parallelism is not so much an aid to logical clarity as it is an emphatic statement of paradox: "How had I deserved to be so blessed by such confessions?—how had I deserved to be so cursed with the removal of my beloved in the hour of her making them?"

Other stylistic traits which occur to a noticeable extent in the rest of Poe's fiction as well as in "Ligeia" are repetition, inversions, and parenthetical expressions. Repetition, like the use of certain rhythmic patterns, gives his style an incantatory quality: "her wild desire for life—for life—*but* for life. Ligeia's voice "grew more gentle—grew more low." And emphasis is achieved by such expressions as "far more, very far more" and "a too-too glorious effulgence." The irrational quality of this kind of writing becomes even more evident when we pull from context the phrases of which it is composed. Such is the case also with inversions of normal word order, a device which gives the style a distant, archaic, otherworldly tone: "In the classical tongues was she deeply proficient." (Note the choice of *tongues* instead of *languages*, and note also how different in tone is a more nearly normally ordered phrase: "In the classical languages she was deeply proficient," or "She was deeply proficient in the classical languages."). Other inversions occur throughout the story: "... not until the last instance ... was shaken the eternal placidity of her demeanor"; "... in death only was I fully impressed"; "For long hours ... would she pour out ... the overflowing of a heart."

Poe consistently uses parenthetical expressions in "Ligeia" to emphasize or heighten the mood. Frequently they are in the form of interjections or exclamations: "a love, alas! all unmerited, all unworthily bestowed"; "And (strange, oh, strangest mystery of all!)"; "I could restore her to the pathways she had abandoned—ah, *could* it be forever?—upon the earth." All of these heighten the emotional tone, or in some way emphasize the disturbed psychological state of the narrator. Another smacks of Poe's particular brand of hokum, but it, too, is consistent with the mood of the passage, "And there are one or two stars in heaven (one especially, a star of the sixth magnitude, double and changeable, to be found near the large star in Lyra) in a telescopic scrutiny of which I have been made aware of the feeling."

The use of what W. M. Forrest, in a discussion of the biblical qualities of Poe style,[6] has described as the "genitive of possession" is another syntactical feature giving an archaic or exotic texture to the style. "The learning of Ligeia"; "the eyes of Ligeia"; "the person of Ligeia"; "the fetters of Death"; "the acquistion of Ligeia" are more frequent than "Ligeia's eyes" or "Ligeia's beauty." The effect of this construction, and others in which *of* appears, such as "The hue of the orbs was the most brilliant of black, and, far over them, hung jetty lashes of great length," is, like the effect of inversion, repetition, and the use of exclamatory parentheses, a heightening, an emotionality, a sense of the mysterious, the irrational and the unreal.

Much, but by no means all, of "Ligeia" is written in this half-hysterical, highly emotional style, since Poe varies the style in this tale as he does in almost all his serious tales. Later in the tale we discover a much more measured, rational tone, as the narrator describes the fantastic interiors of the English abbey to which he retires after the death of Ligeia. The center portion is marked by complex, compound, and compound-complex sentences quite different from the simpler syntax of sentences in the early part of the tale. In his recollections of Ligeia he has been rhapsodic, conveying to the reader the frame of mind into which the memory of her puts him; now, in the second half of the tale, as he recalls the sequence of events leading up to the reappearance of Ligeia, he attempts to get a grip on himself and his emotions as he recounts the early history of Rowena dispassionately and with apparent detachment. He tries to view his actions and his taste for arabesque interiors with some objectivity—and even asks how the bride's family permitted her to "pass the threshold of an apartment *so* bedecked." But as he again recalls the evidence of his own senses, the narrator dwells on details of the appearance of the dying woman in a "naturalistic" description as he endeavors by this means to explain the inexplicable. He reports the "facts" as nearly as he can remember them. But as he draws nearer in memory to the appearance of Ligeia, he becomes more and irrationally affected by that memory, and the last paragraph differs markedly in style from those preceding it. Inversions, repetitions, questions, exclamations, dashes, italics, capitals are all there, ending with the wild speech of the narrator himself with Poe's calculated use of repetition and parallelism for a maximum of emotional effect: "can I never—can I never be mistaken—these are the full, and the black, and the wild eyes—of my lost love—of the lady—of the LADY LIGEIA."[7]

This is not to suggest that the style of "Ligeia" is faultless, or that the reader may ignore Poe's frequent lapses into awkwardness or banality. He writes of the "shadow of a shade"; he says, ". . . we had been precipitate in our preparations"; and he relies heavily on the sound values of such words as *utter, utterly,* and *uttermost.* These jiggling phrases, in addition to his excessive use of some of the rhetorical patterns already discussed, remind us that Poe is not a flawless writer, and that his style, despite the evidence of his efforts to improve and revise it, remains to a certain degree simply turgid and ineffective.

Analysis of its style shows us quite clearly what we would suspect: Poe wrote "Ligeia" mainly in the language of emotional and dramatic involvement, with a strong marked rhythm underlying much of the narrator's obsessive delivery. Parallel constructions, when used, and repetitions emphasize this rhythmic quality, often at the expense of logic. Inversions, parentheses used as intensifiers, the genitive of possession, and archaic diction are combined to produce a tale written in a predominantly emotional, "arabesque" style.

But many passages in the second half indicate quite clearly that Poe was in control of his material and knew what he was about in his treatment of it. Balanced sentence structure and a painstaking building-up of circumstantial detail surrounding the reappearance of Ligeia demonstrate that he was carefully and patiently combining—denying as usual the office of inspiration in the act of creation. The emotion of the narrator of "Ligeia" should not, of course, be confused with the emotion of the author, and such obvious devices as the narrator's parenthetical "(what marvel that I shudder while I write?)" should be read as part of Poe's deliberate effort to give the narrator's emotions an air of verisimilitude. In dismissing the style of "Ligeia" as ungrammatical rubbish, then, Tate most certainly exaggerates, for most of it *is* grammatical and indeed much of it is highly ordered, highly formal prose. The predominantly emotional quality of its style may be defended by its appropriateness to both the agitated mental state of the narrator and to the supernatural events he relates. From the beginning of this tale the reader is in the realm of the supernatural; he is not gradually drawn into it by various devices to suggest verisimilitude, as he is in "MS. Found in a Bottle." The very vagueness of the origins and conditions surrounding the narrator's first meeting with Ligeia plunges the reader immediately into an irrational world. Like Poe's poetry, "Ligeia," the most poetic of his tales, is in the realm not of "Truth" but of "Beauty"—Poe's mythical region of absolute unity of matter and spirit. Ligeia herself becomes the narrator's contact with this realm—a realm which words themselves are inadequate to describe. Like the words in Poe's poetry, the words in "Ligeia" are symbolic, suggesting merely the ideas of things rather than the things themselves. From the expression in Ligeia's eyes, the narrator derives a sentiment which he says he can neither define nor analyze, and for the expression itself he can find only "a circle of analogies." Likewise, Poe himself in his use of language throughout much of "Ligeia" is forced to use a "circle of analogies" rather than direct statement. Hence the exotic, sometimes archaic, style, which conveys emotion rather than reason. The tale is successful finally not because of the lucidity of its prose, but because the reader's rational faculties are momentarily suspended and lulled by its haunting, irrational melodies.

## II

Analysis of the style of "William Wilson" shows it to be a carefully written story. Although it is interspersed with passages reminiscent of the style of "Ligeia," it is dominated by the eighteenth-century *ordonnance* mentioned by Tate. The style, for the most part, is highly ordered, marked by connectives and transitional elements, balanced and periodic sentences, a relatively high level of abstraction, little concrete imagery (outside of the descriptions of the school of Wilson's boyhood), few vivid adjectives, and a precision of diction. Certain key passages deviate from this pattern, notably the first and last paragraphs.

In this tale Poe seems to be concentrating not on creating a poetic effect but rather on telling a tale rationally and logically. Mood is therefore secondary to the orderly development of a series of causally related events. Certain qualities which were latent in the style of his early tales, and which are more evident in his critical writing, are highly developed and fully exploited here: parallelism; a measured rhythm (the rhythm of good prose, not "rhythmic prose," as in "Ligeia"); and abstract diction, which is sometimes latinate, sometimes cumbersome and even ludicrous. This diction combines with the orderliness of his sentence structure to give his prose a particularly eighteenth-century quality. The pace of the story, which is dictated by the formal style resulting from longer sentences, is leisurely but not halting, measured rather than uneven.

But the tale opens in a quite different style. At the beginning we are reminded of "Ligeia" and the mental state of the narrator which the style of that tale reflects. Rhetorical questions, apostrophes, inversions of word order, dashes, repetitions, and archaic diction together produce a heightened, oratorical style that is part of the self-characterization of a doomed Byronic hero:

> Let me call myself, for the present, William Wilson. The fair page now lying before me need not be sullied with my real appellation. This has been already too much an object for the scorn—for the horror—for the detestation of my race. To the uttermost regions of the globe have not the indignant winds bruited its unparalleled infamy? Oh, outcast of all outcasts most abandoned!—to the earth art thou not forever dead? to its honors, to its flowers, to its golden aspiration?—and a cloud, dense, dismal, and limitless, does it not hang eternally between thy hopes and heaven?

These extravagant opening sentences, in which the narrator meditates upon the causes of his ruin, precede others only slightly less emotionally charged. The dominant stylistic note of the tale is not struck until the third paragraph, in which the narrator begins to relate the sequence of events in a dispassionate, rational, analytical style. Analysis is the keynote of Wilson's remarks; in fact, we may say that Poe wrote "William Wilson" in the language of *analysis*, as contrasted to the language of emotion in which he wrote most of "Ligeia." The narrator of "William Wilson" constantly subjects himself and the motives for his actions to a careful scrutiny, evidently in an effort to answer the questions he has so passionately posed in the opening paragraph. The narrative intention of this scrutiny is clear enough. Wilson, at a loss to account satisfactorily for the state of spiritual death and moral depravity in which he finds himself at the opening of the tale, attempts to exercise his faculties of reason and analysis over the sequence of events which led to its disastrous conclusion. He therefore begins by carefully noting his inherited characteristics: he is descended from a race of "imaginative and easily excitable temperament"—and he develops into a child who is "self-willed, addicted to the wildest caprices, and a prey to the most ungovernable passions." Driven by his impulse to recall and analyze his extraordinary behavior, Wilson then turns to "minute recollections" of his first school days. Like Egæus in "Berenice," he seeks relief in "the weakness of a few rambling details." But he also attributes meaning to these details: "... the first ambiguous monitions of the destiny which afterward so fully overshadowed me." These school-day recollections take up fully a third of the story, recollections which he finds "stamped upon memory in lines as vivid, as deep, and as durable as the *exergues* of the Carthaginian medals." Most of them relate to the character of the school-mate with the remarkable resemblance to himself. Only a great many quotations would demonstrate the analytic quality of the style of this section of the tale: the number of times which Wilson speculates on the possible causes for having understood or misunderstood the conduct of his double, and the descriptions of his relationship with him. I shall quote two:

> I could only conceive this singular behavior to arise from a con-summate self-conceit assuming the vulgar airs of patronage and pro-tection. Perhaps it was this latter trait in Wilson's conduct, conjoined with our identity of name, and the mere accident of our having entered the school upon the same day, which set afloat the notion that we were brothers, among the senior classes in the academy.

> Wilson's retaliations in kind were many; and there was one form of his practical wit that disturbed me beyond measure. How his sagacity first discovered at all that so petty a thing would vex me, is a question I never could solve; but having discovered, he habit-ually practised the annoyance. I had always felt aversion to my uncourtly patronymic, and its very common, if not plebian praenomen.

Both of these passages are typical of the dominant style of the tale: highly abstract, rather stilted—even mannered. Because it is not heavily latinate, the latinate expressions themselves seem actually to be affecta-tions: *sagacity, consummate*; and sometimes even absurd: *patronymic, plebian praenomen*. These words give a weightiness to certain sentences which the subject hardly demands. But more to the immediate point is the language of speculation and conjecture: *perhaps, conceive, solve*. These words suggest that the narrator is constantly attempting to analyze and explain rationally the motives for his actions; something which the narrator of "Ligeia" does not do.

Formality and order, then, are the chief characteristics of the dom-inant style of "William Wilson," and parallelism is one of the syntacti-cal devices through which Poe achieves these. Note, for example, the eighteenth--century quality of this passage: "... a profligacy which set at defiance the laws, while it eluded the vigilance of the institution." Or this: "He appeared to be destitute alike of the ambition which urged, and of the passionate energy of mind which enabled me to excel." These parallelisms are different in their logical clarity from the predominantly emotional quality of similar constructions in "Ligeia."

Formality of sentence structure is achieved in other ways as well. In this sentence are three successive phrases, each composed of three elements, and in the final coupling of two phrases modifying *affectionateness*, each phrase contains three modifiers:

> In his rivalry he might have been supposed actuated solely by a whimsical desire to thwart, astonish, or mortify myself; although there were times when I could not help observing, with a feeling made of wonder, abasement, and pique, that he mingled with his injuries, his insults, or his contradictions, a certain most inappropriate, and assuredly most unwelcome *affectionateness* of manner.

Such formal groupings of three elements are often found in Poe's periodic sentences (periods also occur more frequently in "William Wilson" than they do in "Ligeia"): "That the school, indeed, did not feel his design, perceive its accomplishment, and participate in his sneer. . . ." Less formal groupings of threes occur not only in the formal rational style, but also in Poe's emotional style, as in the first paragraph of "William Wilson," suggesting, therefore, that such groupings are a characteristic trait of all of Poe's styles.

But the stylistic trait which at the same time links these two tales and indicates their essential differences is the parenthetical expression. "Ligeia," we have observed, is full of parentheses. "William Wilson" has many, if not more. But while in the former they are used to heighten or emphasize the mood or atmosphere by their exclamatory or interjectional character, in this tale they slow down the pace by qualifying and amplifying ideas. The parentheses in "William Wilson" are halting, hesitant, fussy, over-precise, reflecting the deliberations of a mind committed to discovering the truth. They contain additional, sometimes gratuitous, information that seems to satisfy the narrator's overwhelming need for facts and details. They also reflect the complexity of his mind, a complexity already more than once suggested by the references to the "many little nooks and recesses" of which the school mansion is composed. If the tale is symbolically a mental journey, this "wilderness of narrow passages" suggests the labyrinthine quality of the mind itself. Thus the style, which is itself full of similar nooks and recesses, becomes organically related to Wilson's own psychological state. The following passage illustrates the kinds of parentheses (indicated by brackets)—and parentheses within parentheses—typical of the style of "William Wilson":

> . . . but, [in the latter months of my residence at the academy,] [although the intrusion of his ordinary manner had, [beyond doubt,] [in some measure,] abated,] my sentiments, [in nearly similar proportion,] partook very much of positive hatred. Upon one occasion he

saw this, [I think;] and afterward avoided, [or made a show of avoiding] me.

It was about the same period, [if I remember aright,] that, [in an altercation of violence with him,] [in which he was more than usually thrown off his guard, and spoke and acted with an openness of demeanor rather foreign to his nature,] I discovered, [or fancied I discovered,] in his accent, in his air, and general appearance, a something which first startled, and then deeply interested me, by bringing to mind dim visions of my earliest infancy—wild, confused and thronging memories of a time when memory herself was yet unborn.

The general character and function of these parentheses in "William Wilson," then, differ radically from those of the intensifying parentheses of "Ligeia." Here they are authorial comments written not in an emotional frenzy but in the coolness of recollection. They often have not only an analytic but a strong moralistic tone as well. For example: "It was no doubt the anomalous state of affairs existing between us, which turned all my attacks upon him (and there were many, either open or covert) into the channel of banter or practical joke (giving pain while assuming the aspect of mere fun)...." Or even more overtly moral in tone: "I was anxiously seeking (let me not say with what unworthy motive) the young, the gay, the beautiful wife of the aged and doting Di Broglio." Syntax in this tale, then, is actually a means of characterization, since the narrator's use of parentheses gives the impression of a man extremely interested in being both accurate and honest.

Although "William Wilson"[8] is written predominantly in an analytical, intellectual style, there are nevertheless passages in the tale which recall the emotional style of "Ligeia." Emotional heightening occurs at some key points in the tale, as when Wilson recognizes the close resemblance of his double after the card game at Oxford, and at intervals from that point to the end. In these closing paragraphs the narrator alternates between emotion and reason as the details of the events he recalls bring him closer to the overwhelming conclusion. He tries to maintain his objectivity and balance, but his emotions get the better of him. One paragraph is almost incantatory in tone, both beginning and ending with the sentence, "I fled in vain." Alternating with this is the "rational" style of the following paragraph, which ends "Poor indemnity for natural rights of self-agency so pertinaciously, so insultingly denied!" The next ends almost hysterically, but the narrator forces himself to continue his tale:

Could he, for an instant, have supposed that, in my admonisher at Eton—in the destroyer of my honor at Oxford,—in him who thwarted my ambition at Rome, my revenge at Paris, my passionate love at Naples, or what he falsely termed my avarice in Egypt,—

that in this, my archenemy and evil genius, I could fail to recognize the William Wilson of my school-boy days,—the namesake, the companion, the rival,—the hated and dreaded rival at Dr. Bransby's? Impossible!—But let me hasten to the last eventful scene of the drama.

In the final paragraph, when Wilson II speaks his final lines to Wilson I, he speaks in Poe's most strongly moral manner—in a style similar to that of his parabolic tales, "Shadow," "Silence," and "The Masque of the Red Death":

> "You have conquered, and I yield. Yet henceforward art thou also dead—dead to the World, to Heaven, and to Hope! In me didst thou exist—and, in my death, see by this image, which is thine own, how utterly thou hast murdered thyself."

But in the course of his narration Wilson I has become increasingly irrational, as he recalls the growing disintegration of his personality. He is telling the tale from the other side, with a chastened but hopeless awareness of the place of the moral sense in the life of man. Like the narrator in "MS. Found in a Bottle," he has undertaken a voyage of exploration beyond the limits of normal human experience. But Wilson has gone beyond morality as well as reason, and in this uncharted region has found only that in this transcendence lies oblivion. This "mechanism of destructive transcendence," as Richard Wilbur has aptly described it,[9] underlies both "Ligeia" and "William Wilson," as well as many other Poe tales. The narrator of "Ligeia," too, has found a way to transcend the physical world, but for him that way lies madness—and madness with none of Wilson's self-awareness.

At first reading, "Ligeia" and "William Wilson" seem entirely dissimilar in style, yet the more closely we examine them, the more similarities we find. The reason for these similarities—as well as the differences—lies partly in the similarity of structure and theme. In "Ligeia" the narrator is attempting to reproduce the state of mind he was in when he was in contact with Ligeia. This state of mind is evoked in the beginning and vanishes with the death of Ligeia. With the narrator's move to England and the return of his rational faculties, the style resembles the rational style of "William Wilson." But as the symptoms of Rowena's disease become more and more evident, the narrator gradually discards the rational style, in which he has attempted clinically to recall every detail of the circumstances of Ligeia's return, and returns to the state of mind he was in on that memorable night. His final outburst recalls the style, and even echoes some of the words, of the opening passages of the tale, thereby relating the beginning of the tale to the end. The mood and attitude of the speaker are primarily nostalgic, or evocative, as he attempts to reproduce in his own mind, as well as in the mind of the reader, an idea of what he experienced. This attempt to relate the barely perceived world, of which only the poet may achieve momentary glimpses, to the things of this world which bear only an imperfect relation to them, is the attempt Poe makes in all his poetry. But language fails him, as he himself is aware, and only by calling up an atmosphere roughly analogous to what he has perceived can the narrator-hero-poet hope to put what is untranslatable into words.

We may similarly read "William Wilson" as a parable of the war between the external world and the world of the spirit. Whereas in "Ligeia" the hero has renounced the physical world and achieved a momentary union with the absolute, in this tale Wilson has succumbed to the corrupting material world and has thereby lost his soul. Both tales begin in recollection and end in hysteria, but "William Wilson" is not so much an attempt to reproduce the quality of his experience, which he finds almost unendurably painful, as an attempt to trace the *causes* leading up to it. The experience itself, therefore, although it comes at a climactic moment in both tales, is not as important in "William Wilson" as are the causally related events leading up to it. One indication of the difference in emphasis in the two tales is that in "Ligeia" we know from the outset that she is dead, but we do not learn of the death of Wilson's double until the end; we know only that Wilson has committed an "unpardonable crime." The direction of "William Wilson is towards rediscovery—not of the moment of confrontation, which nevertheless is inevitable, but of the sequence of events leading up to it. In short, the narrator of "William Wilson" finds himself in a fallen state and seeks a rational explanation for it; the narrator of "Ligeia" finds himself in a state of lost happiness and seeks to reproduce that happiness—hence the difference in stylistic organization and emphasis.

Notes

1. See Nathaniel Hawthorne, letter to Poe, June 17, 1846, in Edgar Allan Poe, *Complete Works*, James A. Harrison, ed. (New York, 1902), xvii, 232–233; Mark Twain, letter to William Dean Howells, Jan. 18, 1909, in *Mark Twain-Howells Letters*, Henry Nash Smith and William M. Gibson, eds. (Cambridge, Mass., 1960), ii, 841; Charles Baudelaire, "Edgar Poe: sa Vie et ses Oeuvres," introduction to *Histoires Extraordinaires par Edgar Poe* (Paris, 1856); and Yvor Winters, "Edgar Allan Poe: A Crisis in the History of American Obscurantism," *Maule's Curse* (Norfolk, Conn., 1938), p. 93.

2. Allen Tate, *The Forlorn Demon* (Chicago, 1933), p. 90.

3. Letter to Philip Pendleton Cooke, Aug. 9, 1846, in Edgar Allan Poe, *Letters*, John Ward Ostrom, ed. (Cambridge, Mass., 1948), ii, 328–329.

4. Letter to James Russell Lowell, July 2, 1844, in Ostrom, *Letters*, i, 258.

5. Edgar Allan Poe, *Complete Works*, James A. Harrison, ed. (New York, 1902), ii, 248–268. The "Virginia Edition." All textual citations are from this edition.

6. William M. Forrest, *Biblical Allusions in Poe* (New York, 1928), p. 86.

7. I am following the reading by James Schroeter in "A Misreading of Poe's 'Ligeia,'" *PMLA*, LXXVI (1961), 397–406, which examines and rejects many of the hypotheses made by Roy P. Basler in his well-known and influential essay "The Interpretation of 'Ligeia,'" *College English*, V (1944), 363–372.

8. Poe, *Complete Works*, III, 299–325.

9. "Introduction," Edgar Allan Poe, *Complete Poems*, Richard Wilbur, ed. (New York, 1959), pp. 16–18.

# Poe and the Gothic Clark Griffith*

Despite the emphasis in his criticism upon a need for novelty, Poe's tales of terror are clearly indebted to some literary forebears. From Gothic fiction of the English eighteenth century, Poe took the *imagery* of terror: the blighted, oppressive countryside; the machinery of the Inquisition; in particular, the haunted castle, swaddled in its own atmosphere of morbidity and decay. From the nineteenth-century Gothicized tales in *Blackwood's Magazine*, which he both ridiculed and admired, he took the *form* of terror: a first-person narrator, lingering typically over a single, frightening episode, and bringing matters to a climax in which he has grown deaf to every sound except the noise of his unique sensations. So close are the resemblances that one passes from Anne Radcliffe's architecture to the effusions of a *Blackwood's* speaker, convinced that Poe's effects often result from his combining the murky details of the one with the inveterate, uninterrupted talkativeness of the other. Yet I wish to argue that even as Poe borrowed, he also made a significant contribution. Imperfectly at first, but then with greater assurance, he was concerned with shifting what I shall call the locus of the terrifying. This change in stance is one measure of his originality as a practitioner in the Gothic mode. And to watch him make it is to find special meaning in his famous declaration that the terror of which he wrote came not from Germany but from the soul.

As the basis for contrast, let us glance briefly at Emily St. Aubert, before the Castle of Udolpho. Confronting it for the first time, she can only see the castle as a real and utterly objective fact. For Emily is a true child of the *Essay Concerning the Human Understanding*. It would please her to suppose that she has somehow been transported into "one of those frightful fictions in which the wild genius of the poet delights."

*Reprinted from *Papers on Poe: Essays in Honor of John Ward Ostrom*, ed. Richard P. Veler (Springfield, Ohio: Chantry Music Press at Wittenberg University, 1972), 21–27.

But aware that there is nothing in the mind not first in the senses, she recognizes that she has no grounds for distrusting her perceptions; hence she must scorn as "delusion" and "superstition" the notion that the source of her agitation is anywhere except in the world around her. In Emily's case, therefore (as throughout Mrs. Radcliffe and the eighteenth-century Gothic generally), the direction of the horrifying is from without to within: from setting to self. Terror comes in consequence of what no less an authority than Horace Walpole had called the "extraordinary position," is it impinges upon "mere men and women" to alarm and dismay them.[1]

The situation seems identical in the early portions of "MS. Found in a Bottle" (1833). The storm at sea, which overtakes Poe's narrator, or the engulfing waves that "surpass . . . anything [he] had imagined possible": both appear to be examples of the received, physical ordeal, such as Walpole and Mrs. Radcliffe had devised. Halfway through "MS.," however, a change in emphasis occurs. Now, for the first time, the narrator speaks of strange "conceptions" which are arising from inside his mind. They consist of "feelings" and "sensations" to which no name can be given; nevertheless, they cause him to spell out the word "Discovery" as he beholds—in any case, apparently beholds—an entire new order of experience. At this point, I suggest, Poe has commenced to modify the traditional Gothic relationship. If terror is to be the effect of inner conceptions, it is no longer necessary to regard his narrator as a "mere man," beset and beleaguered by appalling circumstances. Instead, one can as readily think of him as Creative Man, and of the circumstances themselves as the products of his terrible creativity. At least potentially, the locus of the terrifying has passed from the spectacle into the spectator.

Admittedly, though, the change remains no more than implied and potential in "MS. Found in a Bottle." It breaks down ultimately, because the scenery in the tale still seems too much founded upon the eighteenth-century convention of the "outer wonder." What Poe needed, if he intended to psychologize the Gothic, was nothing so spacious or openly exotic as the South Indian Ocean. He required the smaller, less public *mise-en-scène*, one which could more plausibly be transfigured by his narrators, and, above all, one which would dramatize the processes of transfiguration in action. He is best off, in short, when he returns to the dark, secluded interiors of eighteenth-century fiction, but portrays them in such a way that the interiors are made suggestive of the human mind itself. And this of course is the technique he has perfected two years later, with the publication in 1835 of "Berenice," his first example of a genuinely new Gothic.

Sitting within his ancestral mansion, Poe's Egaeus turns out to be both projector and voice, the source of a strange predicament as well as its spokesman. He has spent a lifetime gazing for "long unwearied

hours" at objects which he half-suspects are trivial and without purpose—and watching while, gradually and inexplicably, they acquire
some momentous significance. The story makes it clear, however, that
the details present this heightened aspect only to Egaeus's "mind's
eye"; whatever the meaning they come to possess, it is due solely to his
fierce concentration upon them. Obviously, then, there has ceased to
be any distance, or difference, between the terror and the terrified.
Egaeus's realities are the realities of his own making; his world resembles a mirror in a madhouse, wherein distortions and phantasms appear, but only as the reflections of a particular sort of observer. And
nowhere is this fact more evident than in his obsession with the teeth
of Berenice:

> The teeth!—the teeth! they were here, and there, and everywhere,
> and visibly and palpably before me; long, narrow, and excessively
> white, with the pale lips writhing about them. . . .

At first glance, we are likely to be struck by the sheer, intense
*physicalness* of these dreadful molars. Superficially, in fact, they may
well seem of a kind with the highly tangible horrors which *The Monk*
presents. Yet they function in quite another way. M. G. Lewis's ghoul-
ish occurrences were rooted in a thoroughly Lockean landscape. The
putrefying head, in the convent vaults at St. Clare, had to exist inde-
pendently of Agnes de Medina, first to accost Agnes's senses and then
to register on her appalled sensibility. By contrast, the teeth in Poe have
no meaningful existence outside a sensibility; as Egaeus acknowledges,
*"tous ses dents étaient des idées."* What the teeth might be like apart
from Egaeus, or, whether, for that matter, they even have an identity
except in his vision of them: these are issues of no real moment. So
successfully has Poe internalized the Gothic that the old "outer wonders"
of the eighteenth century now disappear into the stream of consciousness. They have become the conditions and consequences (if one likes,
the "objective correlatives") of a psychic state.

The strategy of "Berenice" is one that with the slightest variations
Poe would continue to utilize for the rest of his life. Barring the allegorical "Masque of the Red Death" and the fact-bound *Pym* (with its
return to a glamorous out-of-doors), I know of none of the horror tales
in which the perceiving mind does not seem much more nearly the
originator of the terrifying than it is a mere passive witness. Moreover,
I am convinced that to read them as though they were notes composed
from within is often to clarify and enrich the stories. For example, the
real key to the somewhat baffling "Fall of the House of Usher" (1839)
appears to me to lie in the way it opens by re-enacting an episode out
of Mrs. Radcliffe, but repeats the event for a totally different purpose.

Like Emily St. Aubert, Poe's speaker also rides up, at the end of a long day's journey, before an apparently haunted castle. He too feels it to be a massive and brooding presence in the foreground. And then, in an effort to dispell the alarm with which it quickly envelopes him, he decides to examine the place from a different perspective. But when he reins in his horse and proceeds to the new location, nothing happens. Where Emily could always look forward to being physically delivered from peril, the physical change in Poe only means that his narrator seems menaced anew. The "ghastly tree stems" and "vacant eyelike windows" continue to glare back at him with the same old ominousness.

Of course nothing happens. The truth about the speaker in "Usher" is that he has all along been engaged in a kind of symbolic homecoming. When at length he crosses the causeway and goes indoors, he finds himself among rooms and furnishings that are oddly familiar, because he has arrived at nothing less than the depths of his own being. Thereafter, it is not his talkativeness—his descriptive abilities, in the usual sense—that summon up Roderick and Madeline. The Ushers are products of the narrator's psyche; for they and their behavior become the embodiments of his trance, or they appear at the *personae* in his dream vision, or perhaps their incestuous relationship is a working out of his own, dark, tabooed, and otherwise inexpressible desires. Thus every subsequent event in "Usher" is prepared for by an opening tableau in which the power to terrorize could not be blotted from the landscape, because it had actually been brought into the landscape by the mind of the narrator. The organic unity, of which Poe makes so much, is a unity between the single creating self at the center of the story, and those shapes and forms which radiate outward as the marks of his continuous creative act. To me at least, no other interpretation of the tale can justify the amount of attention paid its narrator, or is so true to the form and manner of his narration.[2]

Poe's tinkerings with tradition are probably less eccentric and ultra-personal than, at first look, they appear to be. Behind them, after all, one discerns nothing more remarkable than a particular manifestation of the Romantic Movement. If the terrors of the eighteenth century were accountable in terms of Locke's *Essay*, then what is terror for Poe except an adjunct to the thirteenth chapter of the *Biographia Literaria?* That is, the horrifying now looms up out of a world in which the imagination "dissolves, diffuses, dissipates, in order to recreate" and wherein imaginative tendencies are "essentially *vital*, even as all objects (*as* objects) are essentially fixed and dead."

Granted that they represent extreme cases. Poe's narrators have to be understood as figures who are deeply involved in just the activity that Coleridge describes. Until their inner lives impinge upon the outer, the outer, if it is consequential at all, remains a dull and prosaic affair. It gains its extraordinary qualities, as we have seen, through the trans-

forming and the transfiguring capacities of an imaginative self. To cite
a last example, we are told by the speaker in "Ligeia" (1838) of how
the *décor* in Lady Rowena's bedchamber "partook of the true character of the Arabesque only when regarded from a single point of view."
As we read, however, it is to find that the single point of view has
nothing to do with physical positioning. Rather, it seems expressive
of the narrator's personality, an extension of his inward state. One
concludes therefore that it is akin to Coleridge's "secondary imagination." In Poe's hands this faculty has become more nearly an instrument of the appalling than it is a strictly aesthetic principle. Nevertheless,
it still operates as the means of discovering relevance, pattern, even
a certain sort of beauty and ideality in objects which, left to themselves,
would be "essentially fixed and dead."

Small wonder, consequently, that Poe's fiction is better unified
but, at the same time, darker and much gloomier than the eighteenth-
century Gothic had been. With their stress upon horror as an objective phenomenon, the earlier Gothic writers could introduce a whole
range of tones and effects. As they evoked terror from the outside,
so they were likewise free to suspend and withdraw it from without.
Having opened what amounted to a trapdoor onto the world of men-
ace, they found it possible to snap the door shut again, and so to conduct their characters back into a world of happy endings: of order,
security and (typically) the celebration of marriage vows. The waking
nightmare succeeded by the nuptials! It is the regular drift of events
from *The Castle of Otranto* to *The Monk* and on into *Blackwood's*.[3]

Put Poe possessed no such latitude. Since the stimulus for terror
comes from within, there can, in the tale he tells, be no real survivors,
no remissions of the terrible, no protagonists who, by pluck or by
luck, either earn or are at least vouchsafed the right to turn backward
through the trapdoor. Self-afflicted and self-victimized (so to speak,
their own executioners), Poe's characters must perform a persistently
downward journey, sinking further and further into voluble wonder-
ment at themselves, until they arrive at one of those shattering silences
with which their narratives customarily end. And yet, even as they
descend, they are granted a kind of glory which no hero of the earlier
Gothic could ever have matched. We may feel that the next step for
Poe's narrators will be the tomb or the lunatic asylum. During a single,
transcendent moment, however, they have had the privilege of calling
up out of their very beings a totally new order of reality. They are
Romantic heroes without peer, for they have been the masters, because
the creators, of all that they survey.

And small wonder, finally, that *their* creator was fascinated by
what he called "the power of words." Once he had got hold of his
true theme, it was never enough for Poe simply to set a scene, describe
an action, use words to provoke a shudder or two; that was the

business of those attuned to the terrors of Germany. The test of language in his work lay in its ability to delve deeply within and bring to light the most hidden crannies of a suffering, yet oddly prolific self. Thus the descriptive devices of his Gothic predecessors re-emerge as Poe's metaphors of mind; their rhetorical flourishes are turned by him into a rhetoric of revelation. Out of the magic of words, Poe brings forth the symbolic countryside, self-contained and self-sustaining, utterly devoid of connections with the world as it is, yet recognizable still in the terms of its own special topography. And behind the countryside, he shows us the figure of the owner. This is the soul of man, cloaked in the works which it has made, and rendered thereby into a visible and articulate entity.

### Notes

1. Walpole's formula appears in his preface to the second edition of *The Castle of Otranto*. It was still being echoed, forty years later, by an anonymous contributor to *Blackwood's*, who asserted that the occasions for horror come "from the cases . . . or circumstances of life." Before Poe, the real issue among Gothic writers was not whether fear was externally motivated (that was taken for granted), but whether "outer wonders" had to be natural and plausible (as in Mrs. Radcliffe) or could legitimately be supernatural visitations (as in Walpole and, sometimes, M. G. Lewis).

2. Though the opening of "Usher" seems closest to *The Mysteries of Udolpho*, it will also bear comparison with the preface to *The Castle of Otranto*. In a striking reversal of Walpole's formula, Poe's speaker transfers the quality of *mereness* away from himself and attaches it to the landscape. The prospect "out there," he feels, is a "mere" house, a domain with "simple features"; it ought not to alarm as it does. My position is, of course, that he is quite right: seen apart from the narrator's purview, the landscape might very well be "mere" and "simple"; without at all knowing it, he is an exceedingly complex fellow. And more and more of late, he is being restored to what seems to me his proper place in the story. See Richard Wilbur's "Introduction" to *Poe: Complete Poems* (New York, 1959) and James M. Cox, "Edgar Poe: Style as Pose," *VQR*, XLIV (Winter 1968), 67–89.

3. If the lurid high point of *The Monk* is Ambrosio's transformation from saint to devil, we should not miss another major movement in the book. In our last glimpse of Agnes and Raymond, they are a wedded couple, to whom all future vicissitudes will "seem as zephyrs which breathe over summer seas." Presumably, Raymond has earned this bliss by securing a decent Christian burial for the Bleeding Nun, while Agnes's entitlement to happiness derives from her simply having endured the outrages of the past.

# The Tales                                    David Halliburton*

In prose fiction Poe found that he could have it both ways. He could continue to deal with the problems that interested him: power and powerlessness, arbtitrary victimization, the reciprocity of body and soul, the need for unity and affirmation, and so on. At the same time he could expand into novel areas or explore old areas in ways that were not admissible under the tenets of his severe poetic theory. Thus one continues to find, as in the poems, victimizations that are subtle, problematic, or complex ("Ligeia," "The Fall of the House of Usher") but also out-and-out crimes against the person ("The Tell-Tale Heart," "The Mystery of Marie Rogêt"), performed in a social setting wider and more varied in texture than any to be found in the verse. Similarly, in the detective tales Poe reaches out to examine patterns of human events in all their interrelatedness, and even tries to convey a sense of urban life. Yet few would suggest that these works are less serious than the poems, or that they presented less of a challenge to Poe's creative consciousness. The same applies to *Pym*, in which Poe depicts the vicissitudes of maritime travel and exploration without prejudice to the story's metaphysical claims. "Landor's Cottage," with its New York setting and its comfortable domesticity, confirms that Poe no longer feels the antipathy between the "ideal" and the "every-day" that is implicit in his verse and explicit in his aesthetic theory. Even a work centered in a hermetic consciousness, such as "Berenice," pays its dues to the real world. Indeed, it is because Poe allows the world to enter, in the person of the servant, that we have a norm by which to judge the aberrations of Egaeus.

In the tales Poe grapples more openly with space and time, filling his pages with chambers, houses, apartments, vaults, boats, clocks, writing instruments, torture devices, and sundry other mechanisms, and describing the sensations of mind and body when they are subject to duration, expectation, and the thought of death. It is not that Poe ceases to portray the anxieties a man feels when threatened by the "other"; interest in this type of fear is a constant of his fiction as of his verse. What happens, rather, is that he widens the field. He is now able to show that man victimizes himself equally through the manmade environment, which represents an alienated human power still human enough to resent its alienation and powerful enough to seek its revenge. He is able also to suggest that the agonies he portrays, as in "The Pit and the Pendulum," say something fundamental about the human condition. He tried of course to say something fundamental in the poems as well.

*Reprinted from *Edgar Allan Poe: A Phenomenological View*. 366–74. Reprinted with permission of Princeton University Press. © 1973 by Princeton University Press.

The difference between the poems and the tales is that the latter, while showing the same interest in radical existential states, show a much greater interest in the world, and take on thereby a quality of fullness that Poe did not achieve in his verse because he did not seek it.

This expanding process is accompanied by an increase in consciousness, or at least in the overtly conscious treatment of earlier patterns. In the verse, terror and guilt, for example, are intensely felt but rarely described in detail and rarely analyzed. By contrast, tales like "The Fall of the House of Usher" and "The Black Cat" give such feeling an ample embodiment; if everything about them is not "explained," we have at least a fuller content from which to draw hermeneutic inferences, hints, and clues. Thus the close attention to peculiarities of physical constitution, such as Usher's hypersensitivity; thus the attempt, in "The Black Cat," to trace uncanny phenomena back to chemical causes, and to analyze the psychological origins of delusion. The problem of "interpretation" itself undergoes a similar evolution. In "The Raven" or "Ulalume" a man stakes his centeredness on his ability to interpret some strange thing that seems to hold great meaning for him. So, of course, do Pym and Peters, who must decide whether certain earthworks embody a signifying intention, or the male lovers, who must solve the mystery of a woman's identity. But interpretation also assumes in the tales a conscious and pragmatic form. The hero of "The Gold-Bug" offers what amounts to an essay on cryptography, and applies his interpretative powers to a search for buried treasure. Dupin offers fully developed guidelines for interpreting the intentions, motives, and behavior of other human beings. The first-person of "The Black Cat" interprets his own behavior in the light of an elaborate philosophy of perverseness.

"The intellect of man is forced to choose, as Yeats said, and Poe chose to perfect the work as well as he could."[1] Although Stephen Mooney is speaking here of the individual work, the same applies to groups or series of works and to the canon as a whole. Once Poe has done a thing it is likely that he will do it again, wholly or in part. As a result we find recurring types of stories and recurring patterns within them. It is also likely that he will try to do the thing better, in which case the result is not necessarily improvement so much as a kind of purification or heightening, testifying to Poe's persistent quest for the ideal. Let us examine this pattern now in a broad selection of tales, beginning with "Berenice." This tale sets a pattern for the love relations in other tales and offers a portrait of a human being unnaturally preoccupied with himself. The trouble with the story was not merely that it was too gruesome, as Poe said, but that it tended to affirm the reality of death: Berenice expires and does not come back. In the subsequent tales about women, Poe makes up for this by having the women return from death, thus confirming the indestructibility of life. This is not to say that the later works are mere correctives to the first. It is to say that Poe wanted to make a more affirmative and fuller statement than he had managed to do in the earlier tale; it is also to say that he discovered, after his first effort at this class of narrative, that much remained to be done if he was to develop the type to its full potential.

In the detective tales we find more people and more plot; we also find, if not more conscious experience, at least more conscious use of reason and imagination. The desire for greater fullness and for greater ideality is seen in "The Mystery of Marie Rogêt," which, as an explicit sequel to "The Murders in the Rue Morgue," is longer than the earlier work, and is to be thought of as implying a parallel between its earthly events and some "ideal series of events" in a realm above the human. If Dupin is drawn forward by the unfolding of the design of human events, Poe's metaphysical voyagers are drawn forward as by some preternatural undertow to whose force they half-consciously surrender. Here the goal is not conscious knowledge but something more instinctual and primal, a kind of divine but material vision that can be quite indeterminate, as in "MS. Found in a Bottle," or literally embodied, as in *Pym*.

The metaphysical voyager faces an open-ended time, a future he cannot know because it has never been. The Ushers, by contrast, face a future that is also, strangely, the past, for they can only become, in a manner of speaking, what they already were. Prisoners of time, they are equally prisoners of space; in this work the hermetic space of the chamber is expanded into an entire house and its environs. More fully embodied than other living-spaces in Poe, the House is also more human (it shares its being with its occupants) and more self-sufficient (it is a complete microcosmic world with its own laws). William Wilson, too, is determined by the past, although in his case fate takes longer to fulfill itself: thus the story assumes, uniquely, the form of a complete biography or "life." Wilson's problem is too much self. What is unusual about him is his tendency to think, if belatedly, in moral terms. In "The Black Cat" Poe portrays a miscreant who matches Wilson for cruelty but surpasses him, through his philosophy of perverseness, in the theory of evil, while in "The Tell-Tale Heart" he portrays an egoist whose experience carries further the aural dimension contained in the typical confessional narrative. Meanwhile, another egotist, Prince Prospero, tries in vain to create an entire, self-contained world, only to see it claimed by a power higher than his own.

Whereas these protagonists are victimized by their own desires, the hero of "The Pit and the Pendulum" is victimized—and rescued—by something outside himself, the fact that he escapes testifying to Poe's yearning for an affirmative outcome, even at the expense of a hurried ending for which there is no preparation. The hero of "The Premature Burial" suffers a different and in a way a greater bondage, being the victim of his own excessive fears. His physical constitution, moreover, makes him eminently eligible for the worst of all terrors. Yet his will to affirmation is such that he escapes by effecting his own permanent cure. By conquering the terror within, he is able truthfully to say that "out of Evil proceeded Good" (v, 273).

In the landscape tales the good has even greater scope. It spreads before our eyes and stretches beneath our feet; it is the extended embodiment of the ideal. Woman is an embodiment, too; the advantage of the landscape is that here man, the  artist, is in control of the design. In landscape, therefore, there is no antagonism or threat, but harmony, plenitude, repose. Landscape, as the embodiment of harmonious creative design, is greater than woman, with the result that such female presence as we see in these tales is reduced and literally contained. Where other protagonists build walls between themselves and their women, the lord of the landscape merely keeps his indoors.

It may be that Poe's desire for fullness and ideality is not always realized. Such is the case, perhaps, with "The Mystery of Marie Rogêt," or *The Journal of Julius Rodman,* neither of which, for all its breadth, breaks much new ground. A standard remark would be that Poe was feeling the pressures of a market that he could accommodate only by exploiting what had already proved to be a good thing. To be sure, one should never underestimate the influence on an author's work of financial need and contemporary taste. But is could also be argued that the works in a group represent different stages of an effort to fulfill all the possibilities of a given aesthetic type—an effort that would well produce an impression of redundancy or mere elaboration.

To refer to the master of design as a lord, as I have done, is to suggest that there is something godlike about conceiving and carrying out, in earth, one's original designs. Poe implies as much himself. It is evident, furthermore, that he was fascinated by power relations that tended toward the hierarchical (master and slave, sovereign and subject, victimizer and victim). When we consider that these relations in Poe are arbitrary and absolute, we recognize that there *is* an important sense in which Poe tries to get God, or a god-figure, or a godly power, into his stories. In a recent article Robert Daniel sees such a figure in the person of Dupin, whose ratiocinative feats amount to "miracles."[2] But the detective corresponds, it seems to me, to a fourth type, the seer or enlightened one who is elevated to a sacred place by those who lack his vision. His function is certainly different from that of the master of design. The latter increases the order in the material world, creating beauty where none exists, adding to it where it does. The master of design is forward-tending. He looks ahead to new horizons, both literally and figuratively, and projects his vision across the land toward them. The detective, on the other hand, is an interpreter who reveals a design that already exists. He neither makes nor alters. Least of all does he devote himself to the improvement of the countryside. The detective accepts the existing order, and, when it is threatened, as by the actions of a lawbreaker, he does what he can to set it right again. His method is to work backwards, retracing in time and space the design of human movements and motives. The designer, in summary, is a creator whose medium is the material world, while the detective is an interpreter whose medium is the social world.

"Supreme irony," says Karl Solger, "reigns in the conduct of God as he creates man and the life of men. In earthly art Irony has this meaning—conduct similar to God's."[3] The Poe characters who undertake a conduct similar to God's are the egotists like Prospero or the murderer in "The Tell-Tale Heart," who seek to become (to borrow from a discussion above) the absolutes of their own fiction. In his own eyes the pseudo-God is masterly, rational, omnipotent, a superior being who rises above the ordinary world and its denizens. But the reader, standing apart from him, sees him ironically. To us he is simply brutal, bizarre, or mad. We perceive furthermore, that such a being, for all his show, is in the grip of some force greater than himself.

The victimizer-god is revealed to be an extreme form of the being who cannot love enough. The innocence of his victim merely heightens the guilt for which, through the power of words, he punishes himself. Poe's "detective god" is not so culpable. He is guilty, at worst, of the more conventional degree of failure that according to Poe's moral theology characterizes man by virtue of his being man. Even this failure (which takes the form of disdain) may be the necessary complement of his superiority to other men. The limitation of such an interpreter is that he must necessarily perform after the fact: he has no gift of prophecy, save in the restricted sense that he can see now what other men will see slightly later. What is therefore still lacking in Poe's system up to this point (and what he eventually provides) is an interpreter who speaks to others, as it were, *while there is still time.* How Poe meets this need will be seen in the chapter that follows.

A second form of transcendental being in the tales is embodied in the female presence at the end of "Ligeia," "Morella," and "Eleonora," or the numinous figure at the end of *Pym.* In this relation the god-figure is presented through the eyes of the lowly. It is contemplated, in other words, much as God or an image of God is contemplated by a believer in real life. In the landscape tales the godliness is more diffused, embodied now in the female presence (Annie, the Fay, the portraits of ladies), now in the master of design and his theories, now in the earth itself. If these works represent an "advance" on the others, it is because they manage to bring man, world, and God closer together. They suggest that the creativity of God and the creativity of man are somehow parallel, and that man is most godlike when he is most fully himself.

The final and most obvious "conduct like God's" is of course that of the author himself. His is the power of the creator and the lawgiver, his the supreme authority and the supreme responsibility. In the end there is no absolute within a fiction that can compare to the power that shapes it from without. To exist within a fiction is to exist by grace of that creative consciousness which alone determines the design of the work and the forms of being it bodies forth.

The romantic philosophy to which Poe subscribed considered that "the artist is the man who goes out into the empty space between man and god and takes the enormous risk of attempting to create in that vacancy a new fabric of connections between man and the divine power. . . .The new type of man is the romantic artist, the man who in the absence of a given world must create his own. The central assumption of romanticism is the idea that the isolated individual, through poetry, can accomplish the 'unheard of work,' that is, create through his own efforts, a marvelous harmony of words which will integrate man, nature, and God."[4]

Ellison was one example of such artist; Edgar Allan Poe was another.

### Notes

1. "Poe's Gothic Wasteland," p. 282.

2. "Poe's Detective God" (see n. 21 above).

3. Quoted in G. G. Sedgewick, *Of Irony, Especially in Drama*, 2nd ed. (Toronto, 1948), p. 17.

4. Miller, *The Disappearance of God*, pp. 13–14.

## Eleonora                                    Richard Wilbur*

At the end of "Eleonora"'s second paragraph, Poe invites the reader to play Oedipus to the riddle of his tale's conclusion, and one pertinently recalls that the riddle of the Sphinx, which Oedipus guessed, had to do with the ages of man's life. "Eleonora" is a first-person account or depiction of four stages in the life of a particular sort of man, a man who was born with an inherited "vigor of fancy" and has developed into a visionary whose dreams explore the "light ineffable" and the *mare tenebrarum* or "sea of darkness." Given such

*Reprinted from the special edition of "Eleonora" for The Print Club of Cleveland, Ohio, © 1979 by Richard Wilbur. Reprinted with the permission of Richard Wilbur and The Print Club of the Cleveland Museum of Art.

a narrator, we should not look for any mundane realism in his narrative; it is clear from the beginning that we shall not be told what
the characters have for dinner, or whether they wear socks and shoes.
On the other hand, it would be a pity to mistake this story for the
airy fabrications and mis-rememberings of a madman. "Eleonora"'s
poet-hero tells his tale, and tells it truly, but as so often in Poe the narrative mode is allegory.

For the gnostic or neo-Platonist, the soul's adventure entails an
original unity with God, a descent into incarnate life and the corruption of this world, and a subsequent effort to extricate itself and return
to its first condition. Poe's fiction repeatedly employs this story-pattern,
in whole or in part; we have it in that focal story "Ligeia," for example,
but there the allegory is ambiguous and dark; the later "Eleonora,"
for all its luxury of detail, is perhaps the clearest and most charming
embodiment of Poe's essential plot. Like Ligeia, the seraphic Eleonora
stands for "the Idea of Beauty," that mediatory principle through which
the divine is known to men, and the hero's relation to her, during the
first stage of his life, represents the unfallen condition of his soul. That
condition is reflected in the original aspect of the Valley, which is
Edenically isolated from the "world," which partakes of the eternal (as
we feel through the prominence of such words as "always" and "forever,") and which through all of its beauties speaks to the hero "of
the love and of the glory of God." The second phase of the hero's life
begins when his love of Beauty is tarnished by the activation of his
hereditary "ardor of passion." The state of soul which ensues is mirrored
in the color, life, and melody of the transformed Valley, which for all
its splendor is a garish parody of blessedness and implies a spiritual
fall. A prisoner of Eros and of Venus (Hesper), Poe's poet-hero has
forsaken "the Beauty above" for a physical passion incompatible with
it, and must therefore suffer the loss of his mediatrix. With Eleonora's
death, there comes a third period in which the Valley withers and
grieves, and the hero's damaged soul is solaced only by his memories of
Eleonora, and by her occasional visitations. It will be noted that the
Eleonora with whom he now fitfully communes is not an object of passion but the angelic spirit whom first he knew; his grief is thus to be
seen as purgative, and a fortifying preparation for the trials of the
fourth phase of his life. Leaving the Valley for a city in which he en-
counters "the vanities and the turbulent triumphs of the world," the
hero finds himself subject to every base temptation, and in danger of
forgetting his original harmony with God. This is restored through the
seeming infidelity of his marriage to Ermengarde—seeming, I say, because it is quite plain that Ermengarde is somehow Eleonora *rediviva*.
Both names begin with an E; Ermengarde is not of the city or "world,"
but comes to it from a far, far distant and unknown land"—Helusion,

or the Valley; like Eleonora she is bright, seraphic, and conducive to worship; she is authenticated by a voice from Heaven; and her "memorial eyes" (like those of Ligeia) can signify only that the hero, through her, is once again able to ignore the world and "remember his Creator." It is fruitless to try to decide by what means—reincarnation, possession, angelic visitation—Eleonora has returned. On the plane of plot the final action is mysterious, but as allegory it is transparent: Eleonora and Ermengarde (on whose likeness the first version of the tale was still more insistent) together constitute the *forma specifica* which guarantees the hero's salvation, and the hero's marriage is allegorically an *anamnesis*, the regaining of a previous state of awareness in which the hero's intact soul participated in supernal harmony and beauty

Commentators sometimes speak of Poe's "style," as if he had but one way of writing. The fact is that he chose numerous styles for his several modes and purposes, distinguishing between the means appropriate to criticism, fiction, and verse, and attuning the language of his tales to their genres ("grotesque," "arabesque," or other) and the natures of his narrators. Poe's literary theory permitted the prose tale a degree of "truth" or verisimilitude, and a fullness and clarity of plot not appropriate in poetry; at the same time he required that the tale possess, if it hoped for any imaginative effect, a deep "undercurrent" of allegorical meaning. The poem, on the other hand, was to be vague, bewildering, incantatory, and full of "novel combinations" of the beautiful, to the end of inducing in its reader a dizzy foretaste of unimaginable unities belonging to a higher world of the spirit. In the light of these general prescriptions, "Eleonora" is obviously a hybrid performance. It is a prose tale with a simple plot, but it is wholly lacking in quotidian "truth," and its allegorical "undercurrent" is more readily sounded than any other in Poe's fiction, unless it be "William Wilson" 's. Furthermore, the style of the tale patently aims at certain of the effects which Poe deemed proper to poetry. "Mazy," "wandering," "dazzling," "besprinkled," and "interweaving" are words which appear in Poe's text, and which apply not merely to his subject matter but to the "arabesque" manner of its writing: that is to say, the tale imitates in language a decorative style which the *Britannica* describes as "a fantastic or complicated interweaving" of tendrilous, foliate or floral forms, often (as at Pompeii) heterogeneously incorporating "birds and animals, human figures and chimeras." Poe's intricate and profuse sentences mingle the natural with the preternatural—the buttercup and daisy, for instance, with the "writhing" violet and "fantastic" tree—in such a way as to produce those "novel combinations" by which poetry (à la Poe) seeks to estrange us from the known and impel us toward the beyond. Another aspect of Poe's arabesque style is his mingling of rhetorics: there is the plainness of "We will say, then, that I am mad;" there is also such a phrase as

"Suddenly these manifestations they ceased, and the world grew dark before mine eyes," in which we find both a French construction and an archaism; while in the paragraph concerning Eleonora's death there is a cascade of "Biblical" sentences beginning with "And." One is reminded, in experiencing Poe's shifts of style, of the dazzling eclecticism of such arabesque interiors as he describes in "The Assignation" or "Ligeia."

It need hardly be pointed out that there are further devices, in this prose tale, which are calculated to produce what Poe meant by the poetic effect. The phrase, "brighter than all save the eyes of Eleonora," is repeated with variations, and suggests a verse refrain. The technique of recapitulation, so prominent in late incantatory poems like "Ulalume" and "Annabel Lee," is liberally used, and especially so in the descriptive paragraph which follows Eleonora's death; one might say of this tale, as its narrator says of the poetry of Hafiz, that in it "the same images are found occurring, again and again, in every impressive variation of phrase." Finally, it will be noted that the penultimate paragraph threatens, in its first four words, to break into emphatic meter and rhyme.

Poe's arabesque prose in "Eleonora," with its strange fusions and its supporting poetic devices, is clearly intended, then, not merely to tell a tale but to excite in the reader "the Poetic Sentiment;" I take this as a further certification that the narrator's concluding visions are not to be discounted as "mad," but accepted and in a measure shared. When prose or poetry sets out to enchant and enthrall, and to any extent succeeds, it is possible for the reader to grow passively unaware of particular words and strategies, and I therefore wish to conclude by mentioning a few details of "Eleonora"'s deliberate texture. There is, for one thing, an admirably subtle use of light and dark and shadow throughout the story. The "forever" of the Valley's first state is tellingly altered in the second to "as if forever," and there are many such deft modulations to be found. The narrator's opening words about "the wisdom which is of good" and "the mere knowledge which is of evil" hint at Eden and the Fall, and prepare one to discern foreboding elements in the Valley as first described: the asphodel (which ambiguously symbolizes both death and Elysian immortality) is accordingly not white or yellow but an unnatural "ruby-red," and there are trees which resemble serpents. When the hero succumbs to Eros, it is appropriately "beneath the serpent-like trees," and thereafter the asphodel, unambiguously suggestive of passion and death, crowds out the purity of the white daisies.

More often than is generally appreciated, Poe reinforces his meaning by the artful employment of allusion or echo. It may well be that "Eleonora"'s use of the asphodel is intended, among other things, to evoke the carnal context of *Paradise Lost*, IX, 1040, and that the violets which weep for Eleonora's death recall Laertes' words at Ophelia's graveside (*Hamlet*, V, i, 261 ff.) We may be sure, however, that the phrase "We spoke no words during the rest of that sweet day" is reminiscent of the famous line in *Inferno*, V, where Francesca, having told of her (and Paolo's) fall into carnal sin through the reading of a poem about Lancelot, concludes by saying *quel giorno più non vi leggemmo avante*—"That day we read in it no further." Still more surely, the Valley's "many-colored grass" puts us in mind of Shelley's famous lines

> Life, like a dome of many-colored glass,
> Stains the white radiance of Eternity.

and sends us back also to the description of Nesace's palace in Poe's own early poem "Al Aaraaf," where a circular diamond window, set into the dome, diffracts the light of God's Truth into the many colors of Beauty. Finally, when Poe's hero bows down at Ermengarde's footstool "in the most abject worship of love," it seems to me that our memory of Psalm 99—"Exalt ye the Lord our God, and worship at his footstool"—confirms our sense of what sort of emissary she is.

# Explained Gothic ["The Fall of the House of Usher"]
### G. R. Thompson*

The structural configuration of ambiguously explained Gothic informing "Ligeia" and "Usher" may be clarified by reference to another nineteenth-century tale. In *Heart of Darkness* (first published in *Blackwood's*, 1898–99), Joseph Conrad's first narrator comments on the conception of the meaning of a narrative held by Marlow, who is himself the narrator of the basic tale of his pursuit of his psychological double, Kurtz, and to whom Conrad's first narrator listens as one sitting in darkness waiting for light. This first narrator comments that Marlow, unlike other tale-spinning sailors, saw the significance of a narrative not as a core-meaning of some kind but as a system of structures: "The yarns of seamen have a direct simplicity, the whole meaning of which lies within the shell of a cracked nut. [But to Marlow] the meaning of an episode was not inside like a kernel but outside, enveloping the tale which brought it out only as a glow brings out a haze, in the likeness of one of these misty halos that sometimes are made visible by the spectral illumination of moonshine." So it is with "The Fall of the House of Usher," which bears a number of surprising similarities in theme,

*Reprinted from *Poe's Fiction* (Madison: University of Wisconsin Press, 1973), 87–97, 225–27, by permission of the author and The University of Wisconsin Press.

imagery, and structure to *Heart of Darkness*.[1] Like "Ligeia," "Usher" is a structure of interpenetrating structures that shifts its aspect with a slight shift of perspective by the reader. Given the initial focus of a reader, the primary answer to any question presented by the story varies, though the relationships among the various structures of the story do not.

This can be partially iluustrated by reference to the recurrent concerns of critics of the tale; most of the critical commentary returns obsessively to a few central points, compulsively repeating with slightly altered angles of vision the same set of haunting questions. What is the significance of the close resemblance of Roderick Usher and his sister, and are the two the product of, and guilty of incest? Did Roderick intentionally try to murder Madeline, and did Madeline actually return from her tomb, vampirelike, to claim her brother's life? Is the physical house actually "alive" and by some preternatural force of will controlling the destinies of the Ushers? Or is the story not a tale of the supernatural at all, but rather a work of psychological realism? What then is the precise role of the narrator? And can the work be read in Freudian or Jungian terms? If the tale is a psychological or symbolic work, what is the meaning of the interpolated story of the "Mad Trist of Sir Launcelot Canning"? What significance have the titles of the books in Usher's library, and what significance are we to attach to Usher's strange, neurasthenic art works? The very fact that these questions persist year after year suggests that at the dark heart of the story lies an essential ambiguity, carefully insinuated and carefully wrought.

Thus, just as with "Ligeia," it is misleading to conceive of the meaning of the tale as devolving solely upon any single and fixed subject, such as the supernatural character of the house, or of Madeline Usher, *as opposed* to a Gothic homily on the neurasthenia of the ultimate in narcissistic artist heroes, or as opposed to the incestuous guilt and hereditary curse of the family. The tale is a concatenation of all these, and not an either / or question. Nevertheless, there is, as with "Ligeia," a basic structure that integrates all the others, a set or system of relationships that remains constant and primary, enveloping the rest with a further meaning without disturbing each as a coherent system within itself. This primary structure is the product of the objective synthesis generated by our perceiving as readers the double aspects of the tale as simultaneously supernaturalistic (symbolic of deep structures in the human mind or not) and yet also realistic in a conventional sense. This multiple perception of the simultaneous or parallel levels of the tale derives principally from our perception of the subjectivity of the narrator. As in "Ligeia," we experience a series of "supernatural" events (which have Freudian and Jungian resonances) through the mind of a narrator whom we recognize as disturbed—so that we simultaneously are subjectively involved in and detached from these experiences. The whole system of interpenetrating levels or structures of both tales leads ultimately to Poe's ironic mockery of the ability of the human mind ever to know anything with certainty, whether about the external reality of the world or about the internal reality of the mind.

Much of the discussion of "Usher" to follow dervies from Darrel Abel's brilliant analysis of the tale as a psychodrama of the mutual hysteria of the narrator and Roderick Usher.[2] What I offer as progressive to our understanding of the tale is principally addenda to such evidence in terms of a reconsideration of the principal symbols of the tale within the primary structural context proposed—that is, the structure wherein the subjectivity of the narrator provides the basic system of structures holding in tension all the others. I shall attempt to demonstrate the pervasiveness of this primary structure principally by reference to the pattern of the double and its redoubled manifestations (Roderick and Madeline, Roderick and the house, Roderick and the narrator, Madeline and the narrator, the narrator and the house). This pattern is again redoubled by the imagery of the face or skull, which ultimately inverts back on the self as a symbol of the "reality" seen from the inward perspective of characters caught in a labyrinth of mental surmise.

On its most obvious level, the tale is concerned with the traditional Gothic subjects of death and madness and fear. The matters of madness (especially Roderick's) and fear have been frequently commented on, but the other pervading subject of death (physical, familial, spiritual, and mental) has not been closely enough linked to the themes of fear and madness. It is curious, for example, that no one has ever seen fit to remark that when the narrator rides up to the house of Usher, he is immediately confronted with a death's-head looming up out of the dead landscape. Poe obviously intended the image of the skull-like face of the house to dominate as the central image of the tale, for he returns to it again and again, placing the most extended descriptions of it at symmetrically located places in the narrative. Eventually, the pervasive image of the psychically split face reflects the internal landscape of the narrator himself (rather than just Usher), so that the primary structure of the tale merges with its central image. Even when the house sinks into the pool at the end, the motifs of the skull and face (Usher's, the house's, that of the mind gone mad in "The Haunted Palace," and the narrator's) represent the internal spiralling of the complete subjectivity of consciousness. That is, the sinking of the house into the reflecting pool dramatizes the sinking of the rational part of the mind, which has unsuccessfully attempted to maintain some contact with a stable structure of reality outside the self, into the nothingness that is without and within.

Usher's weird painting of what might be a tomb for the burial of the body of Madeline, imaging nothing but rays of light rolling throughout a passage without outlet, is also reflective of the death and burial of consciousness and rationality themselves; thus, it is a painting of Usher's internal void, which is objectified by the final collapse of the house into the image of itself in the pool. The spiralling further and further inward leads us to the mocking irony of the ultimate theme of nothingness, which is all the mind can ever truly know, if it can know anything. The nothingness without (in the landscape) and the nothingness within (in the minds of Usher and the narrator) are mirror images or doubles reflecting the theme of nothingness in the tale. And the collapse of the universe of Roderick Usher includes the double collapse of his mind along with the narrator's—productive of an overall structure of collapse mirroring the pattern of the universe itself, as expressed in *Eureka*.

That Usher's mind disintegrates as the tale progresses is obvious. Both Usher and the narrator comment variously on the matter. The inciting event, in fact, is Usher's written appeal to the narrator to preserve him from the final collapse of his mind. Moreover, as mentioned, a major concern in the tale is the mechanism of fear itself, which has perversely operated on Roderick Usher before the narrator arrives, and which operates on the narrator through Usher afterwards, so that we apprehend the basic dramatic action of the tale as psychological—the presentation of the progressive hallucination of the two protagonists. In the supernaturally charged atmosphere of the first level of the story, the narrator seems to serve as a corroborating witness to the actual return of Madeline, and to the strange, simultaneous "deaths" of the Ushers and of their house. But Poe meticulously, from the opening paragraph through to the last, details the development of the narrator's initial uneasiness into a frenzy of terror, engendered by and parallel to Usher's terrors. The tale opens with the narrator's account of his lonely autumn journey through a "singularly dreary tract of country" in response to a "wildly importunate" summons from Usher (H 3:273–74). At nightfall, as the "melancholy" house of Usher comes into view, the narrator feels a sense of "insufferable gloom" pervading his spirit. He pauses to look at the "mere house," trying to account rationally for its total weird effect. But the scene still produces in him "an utter depression of soul which I can compare to no earthly sensation more properly than to the afterdream of the reveller upon opium . . . an iciness, a sinking, a sickening of the heart—an unredeemed dreariness of thought. . . . it was a mystery all insoluble; nor could I grapple with the shadowy fancies that crowded upon me as I pondered" (H 3:273–74). The primary effect of the opening paragraphs, of course, is to suggest something horrible and supernatural about the house of Usher. But, as in Poe's other tales, there is no overstepping of the real; the strange impression of the scene is relegated to the "fancies" of the narrator. Because the narrator tries to account for the effect rationally, however, we are led, for the time being, to attribute the weirdness of the scene not to his subjective impressions but to the scene itself.

Yet Poe uses this apparent rationality to heighten the irrational. The narrator reflects on the possibility that "there *are* combinations of very simple natural objects" that have the power to affect the mind, but "the analysis of this power lies among considerations" beyond our "depth"; and at this moment, he looks down into a "black and lurid tarn," to see the reflected, remodeled, and inverted images of the "gray sedge, and the ghostly tree-stems, and the vacant and eye-like windows" (H 3:274). This effect of this vision in the pool is to produce in him a "shudder even more thrilling than before" and to "deepen the first singular impression": "There can be no doubt that the consciousness of *the rapid increase of my superstition*—for why should I not so term it?—served mainly *to accelerate the increase itself*. Such, I have long known, is the paradoxical law of *all sentiments having terror as a basis*" (H 3:276; my italics). After this objective recognition of an inward self-division that results in yet further subjectivity, he again lifts his eyes "to the house itself, from its image in the pool" and he becomes aware of a "strange fancy" growing in his mind: "I had *so worked upon my imagination as really to believe* that about the whole mansion and domain there hung . . . a pestilent and mystic vapour, dull, sluggish, faintly discernible, and leaden-hued" (H 3:276; my italics). But Poe then reasserts the narrator's rationality: "Shaking off from my spirit what *must* have been a dream, I scanned more narrowly the real aspect of the building" (H 3:276). The paragraph is organized, however, so as to bring the "real" description back again to the "impression" the scene makes upon the narrator's "fancy." Although the narrator begins his "analysis" of the house at the (rational) roof, with its fine tangled web-work of fungi, his eye travels down along a zigzag fissure to become again "lost in the sullen waters of the tarn" (H 3:277), by now clearly emblematic of the subconscious mind.

The apprehensive, fanciful, superstitious, but "rational" narrator then goes into the house to meet Usher, where, during the course of the next several days, he comes increasingly under the influence of Usher's own wild superstitions. "In the manner of my friend," the narrator says, "I was at once struck with an incoherence—an inconsistency. . . ."

> To an anomalous species of terror I found him a bounden slave. "I shall perish," said he, ". . . in this deplorable folly. Thus, thus, and not otherwise shall I be lost. . . . I have, indeed, no abhorrence of danger, except in its absolute effect—in terror. In this unnerved—in this pitiable condition—I feel that the period will sooner or later

arrive when I must abandon life and reason together, in some struggle with the grim phantasm, FEAR." (H 3:280)

Usher's statement of his own condition applies also to the narrator, who struggles with the same phantasm, heightened by Usher's own phantasms. It is Usher, for example, who remarks to the suggestible narrator that the house is alive and has exerted a malignant influence on his mind. Later the narrator, looking for something to read, finds that the only books in Usher's library are accounts of strange journeys, eerie meetings, and deathwatches (some of which, like Tieck's *Blue Distance* are partially satiric). Then Usher reads his strange poem about the decay of reason (H 3:284–6), the single extended metaphor of which suggests the "face" of the house of Usher itself, and extends the pattern of descent from roof to basement, of rationality to irrationality, and the inverse ascent of irrationality welling up to overwhelm the rational. Soon after the reading, Madeline dies, and Usher and the narrator bury her in a crypt in the cellar. She has the "mockery of a faint blush of life" upon her skin and a terrible "lingering smile" upon her lips, phenomena that the "rational" narrator attributes to the peculiar ravages of her cataleptic disorder but which Usher intimates is something less natural (H 3:289). Then, as Usher's behavior becomes even more distracted (a continual "tremulous quaver, as if of extreme terror, habitually characterized his utterance"), the narrator confesses to himself his own increasing apprehensiveness. Slowly, although he tries to see in Usher's behavior the "mere inexplicable vagaries of madness," the narrator feels growing in himself a vague fear that Usher has some horrible "oppressive secret" to divulge (H 3:289). "Rationally," however, the narrator acknowledges that Usher's "condition terrified . . . it *infected* me. I felt creeping upon me, by slow yet certain degrees, the wild influences of his own fantastic yet impressive superstitions" (H 2:289–90; my italics).

Symmetrically, the psychological themes of the first part of the tale are exactly repeated in the second, but with the fears of both Usher and the narrator at a higher pitch. Shortly after Madeline's burial, the narrator is unable to sleep, especially since, as with the reflected image of the house in the tarn, he is aware of his increased terror: "an irrepressible tremour gradually pervaded my frame; and, at length, there sat upon my very heart an incubus" of "utterly causeless alarm" (H 3:290). "Overpowered by an intense sentiment of horror," the narrator begins pacing nervously; suddenly he is startled by a light footstep outside his door. But it is only Usher. Usher's intensely agitated condition, however, is the more unnerving, especially when he suggests that a supernatural and luminous vapor has surrounded the house in spite of the rising wind without.

What is perhaps the clearest of clues to the theme of doubled and redoubled fear comes next. The narrator, in an attempt to calm Usher, reads from a volume called the "Mad Trist." The title calls attention to the basic situation in which the narrator finds himself.[3] Usher is about to keep a mad tryst with Madeline, even as the narrator has kept his mad tryst with Usher. The tale, this "Mad Trist," is an absurd parody of a medieval romance about the delusive meeting of the knight Ethelred with a hermit who disappears and changes his form into that of a fearful dragon. The narrator's reading of the "Mad Trist" to Usher is interrupted by strange sounds of creaking wood, of shrieking, and of grating metal. These sounds, beginning at the bottom of the house and moving upward toward them, eerily (and ludicrously) correspond with the sounds evoked in the chivalric romance. The sounds, of course, are supposed to be the results of the cataleptic Madeline's efforts to free herself from her tomb. Usher, at least, tells the narrator that this is so and that she is, in fact, now standing outside the door. And, in the end, the narrator sees her too: bloody, frail, emaciated, trembling, and reeling to and fro, falling upon Usher in her "now final death agonies" and bearing Usher "to the floor a corpse, and a victim to *the terrors he had anticipated*" (H 3:296; my italics). As a last emphatic psychological detail, Poe has the narrator tell us that "from that chamber and from that mansion, I fled aghast." Thus we do not know for sure that the house splits apart and sinks into the tarn in a lurid blaze, for the narrator has by now been revealed to be completely untrustworthy.

Yet, even here, Poe provides one more turn of the screw, for, buried in the details about the house, is the information that the oxygenless dungeon has been a storage place for gunpowder or "some other highly combustible substance" (H 3:288). Thus if the house cracks open and crumbles, rather than a necessarily supernatural occurrence, as it seems to the hysterical narrator, it is explainable as the combustion generated when the lightning of the storm crackles near the previously airless crypt—the inrushing electricity being conducted along the copper floor and igniting the remnants of powder. Yet these mocking clues are not all. The miasma enshrouding the house provides yet another, for marsh gas was then thought to have hallucinatory effects, and Poe elsewhere mentions this very effect.[4]

If the stated terrors of the narrator are not convincing enough for a complete psychological interpretation of the supernaturally charged events, the recurrent dream imagery and the very order of the opening paragraphs regarding the images of the house in the pool should confirm such a reading. The dream images culminate in the return of Madeline and in the "Mad Trist." Madeline, supposedly the victim of a cataleptic fit, is presumably not a ghost or other supernatural manifestation, even though her appearance at Usher's door produces a ghostlike effect in the best tradition of supernatural Gothic. We do get our Gothic thrill, even though she is not a supernatural being. Yet, if she is not, then how, in her frail and emaciated condition, would she be capable of breaking open the coffin, the lid of which, the narrator specifically tells us, had been screwed down tight? Or of pushing open the door, "of massive iron" and of such "immense weight" that its movement "caused an unusually sharp grating sound, as it moved upon its hinges"? (See H 3:288). These details of Madeline's entombment, given us at the midpoint of the tale, underscore the dream motif and link her dreamlike manifestation directly to the psyche of the narrator; for Poe also makes a point of having the narrator tell us that Madeline's tomb is at great depth, immediately beneath that portion of the building in which was "my own sleeping apartment" (H 3:288). The images of sleep, mist, water, and descent, recurring throughout the tale, forcibly suggest Poe's focus on the subconscious mind. The night of Madeline's return, just before the reading of the "Mad Trist," the narrator cannot sleep, and a detailed description of his troubled drowsiness is given. Neither can Usher sleep, for he is troubled by the dreamy mist enshrouding the house. Finally, the events, the disappearances, the transformations, and the correspondences of sounds in the tale of the "Mad Trist" which follows, all have the order of a dream, and, moreover, move from the depths of the house upward toward Usher and the narrator.

Yet the "Mad Trist" is made purposefully ludicrous; it reads like a parody, and even the narrator comments on its absurdity. The correspondence of sounds, especially, heightens the ludicrous effect. But the intruded tale of the "Mad Trist" also has a clear ironic effect; it destroys the Gothic illusion. As in "Metzengerstein" and "Ligeia," Poe intrudes an ironic distance clearly and suddenly between the narrator and the reader, here calling attention to the real psychological situation of the two protagonists engaged in their own mad tryst.

Connected with the dream images and reinforcing the suggestion of subconscious action is the dreamlike reflection of the house of Usher in the pool and its parallel in Usher's arabesque face. In fact, Usher's famous face (supposedly a pen portrait of Poe's own according to biographically oriented critics), with its parallels in the appearance of "The Haunted Palace" of Usher's wild poem and in the appearance of the house itself, provides a major clue to the irony insinuated into, under, and around the apparent Gothic surface of the story. Usher's face in a sense is the image of the narrator's own, whose mind, if not disintegrating also, is capable of slipping in an instant into the same kind of madness or hysterical fear to which Usher is subject. The narrator, as he becomes absorbed in his "superstitious" reflections, says that he had to shake off from his fancy "what *must* have been a dream." The narrator's first impression of the house is that it is like a human face, especially with its two vacant eyelike windows. Then he looks down into the pool, but sees only the reflection of the "face" of the house. What is equally likely, of course, is that he should see imaged there his own reflected features, since Poe is careful to point out that the narrator wheels his horse up to "the precipitous brink" of the tarn and thus gazes straight down (H 3:274). Then he remembers Usher's hysterical letter and mentions, along with Usher's "mental disorder," that he had been Usher's close and only friend. Next he remembers that the peasants refer to both the building and the family as the House of Usher and immediately returns to the image of the "face" in the pool (H 3:275–76). When he looks up at the house again, he tries to "analyze" its weird effect, and describes once more its prominent details, especially the overspreading fungi "hanging in a fine tangled web-work from the eaves" (H 3:276). The nervous narrator, conscious of his own vague terror and therefore the more apprehensive, goes into the house to meet Usher, and his attention is focused on the odd appearance of Usher's face. Usher's face has a generally decayed aspect, like the house itself, but especially noticeable are his large and luminous eyes and his hair "of more than web-like softness and tenuity." This tangled, "web-like," "silken hair," of a "wild gossamer texture," thus imagistically merges the facelike structure of the house with Usher's face, the "arabesque expression" of which the narrator cannot "connect with any idea of simple humanity" (H 3:278–79). As we have seen, the narrator grows "terrified" and "infected" with Usher's hysteria. He becomes like Usher. In meeting Usher, he is symbolically staring into the face of his psychological double, and when he steps through the "Gothic" archway of Usher's house into the dark, black-floored hall with its carved, niched, fretted architectural features, lit by "feeble gleams" of "encrimsoned" light that barely makes its way through elaborately "trellised panes," it is clear that the narrator has stepped into the confused, subjective world of Gothic terror and horror. Once inside, in another absurdist touch, he is taken by a servant who "ushers" him into Usher's presence (H 3:277). Thus, Usher's "arabesque" face and the face of the house are the same, and when the narrator gazes into the pool, the reflected "arabesque" face is merged with his own—symbolically is his own. The image of the face is then reemphasized in Usher's poem about the attack of "madness" on the "haunted" castle.

The ghosts in the tale of Usher, then, are those of the mind. Such an analysis does not deny the supernaturalistic surface level of the tale, or other significant patterns such as the incest motif, the eerie hint of vampirism, the use of abstract art to suggest sexuality, entombment, or nothingness, or the carefully balanced themes of order and sentience that other critics have noted.[5] Rather, such a reading incorporates them into its overall pattern, while wrapping a layer of dramatic irony about the whole. As in other of Poe's Gothic tales, the delusiveness of the experience is rendered in and through the consciousness of the narrator so that we participate in his Gothic horror while we are at the same time detached observers of it. In the image of the house as skull or death's-head and the merging of the narrator's face with the face of the house which is also Usher's face in the pool, we see once again in Poe the subtly ironic paralleling of the narrative structure of the tale to its visual focal point. And by having the facelike house of Usher sink into its own image, the final collapse into that void which is both the self and the universe simultaneously is complete. This, then, is the larger pattern of meaning generated by the overall narrative system enveloping the other levels of narrative. And yet there is, by implication, a further enlargement. Since, just as in "Ligeia," it is clear that we do not know that anything the narrator has told us is "real," the whole tale and its structures may be the fabrication of the completely deranged mind of the narrator. Nothing at all may have happened in a conventional sense in the outside world—only in the inner world of a narrator's mind. Of this redoubled nothingness, then, also comes nothing. And as with "Ligeia," this further perception of the structures of nothingness becomes our ultimate perception of the tale as simultaneously involved and detached observers.

## Notes

1. The double, the skull motif, and theme of mental and moral collapse are the most obvious similarities, and I propose here the further similarity of the conception of the meaning of a narrative. See Joseph Conrad, *Heart of Darkness* (New York: New American Library, 1950), p. 68.

2. Several studies of "The Fall of the House of Usher" may be mentioned here. Darrel Abel in "A Key to the House of Usher," *University of Toronto Quarterly* 18 (1949):176–85, shows how the environment and Usher's fear terrorize the narrator to the point of hallucination. Abel's essay, a pioneering statement on the issue of the supernatural *vs.* the psychological reading of "Usher," has for twenty years almost never been given due acknowledgment. Leo Spitzer's often cited "A Reinterpretation of 'The Fall of the House of Usher,'" *Comparative Literature* 4 (1952):351–63, for example, essentially repeats and finally obfuscates what Abel pointed out four years later. J. O. Bailey, "What Happens in 'The Fall of the House of Usher'?" *American Literature* 35 (1964):445–66, argues for a supernatural interpretation based on vampire lore but clearly sets up the ironic dramatic tension between the two points of view of the tale. Also pertinent here is Maurice Lévy's "Poe et la tradition 'gothique,'" *Caliban: Annales de la Faculté des Lettres de Toulouse* 4 (1968):35–51; translated and revised in *ESQ* 18 (1972):19–29; Lévy rejects certain biographical Freudian interpretations of Poe's Gothic tales, and suggests instead that Poe was perfectly aware of a variety of Gothic techniques and that his imagery reflects a psychological archetype that the Gothic embodies. Thus

we have three kinds of "psychological" approaches which must be carefully differentiated: (1) a biographical, "psychoanalytic" approach in which Poe himself is the subject; (2) a "psychological" interpretation of the characters and their actions and perceptions in the dramatic world of the tale; (3) an "archetypal" approach, which sees certain universal human responses deeply embedded in the works.

3. See Jean Ricardou, "L'Histoire dans l'histoire; La Mise en abyme...," in *Problèmes du Nouveau Roman* (Paris: Le Seuil, 1968), pp. 171–76, for a slightly different discussion of the "Mad Trist" as a synecdoche of the story itself, and as representing a kind of preknowledge for the narrator of the inevitable outcome of the main narrative. See Claude Richard, "Poe Studies in Europe: France," *Poe Newsletter* 2 (1969): 22.

4. See H 14:167 for Poe's comment on miasmata; although he says that "injury" to the public from miasmata is questionable, his comment shows his awareness of the *supposed* properties of such gas (cf. H 14:168), thus making it a proper device for a fictional narrative. See I. M. Walker "The 'Legitimate Sources' of Terror in 'The Fall of the House of Usher,'" *Modern Language Review* 61 (1966): 585–92, for discussion of this and for a lucid "psychological" analysis of the dramatic action.

5. See in particular Maurice Beebe, "The Fall of the House of Pyncheon," *Nineteenth Century Fiction* 11 (1956):1–17, and "The Universe of Roderick Usher," *Personalist* 37 (1956): 146–60; Joseph Gold, "Reconstructing the 'House of Usher,'" *Emerson Society Quarterly*, no. 38 (1964), pp. 74–76; John S. Hill, "The Dual Hallucination in 'The Fall of the House of Usher,'" *Southwest Review* 48 (1963): 396–402; Lyle Kendall, "The Vampire Motif in 'The Fall of the House of Usher,'" *College English* 24 (1963): 450–53; D. H. Lawrence, Chapter VI of *Studies in Classic American Literature* (1923; reprint ed., New York: Viking, 1964); Bruce Olson, "Poe's Strategy in 'The Fall of the House of Usher,'" *Modern Language Notes* 75 (1960): 556–59; Patrick F. Quinn, "That Spectre in My Path," Chapter VII of *The French Face of Edgar Poe* (Carbondale: Southern Illinois University Press, 1957); Paul Ramsey, Jr., "Poe and Modern Art: An Essay on Correspondence," *College Art Journal* 18 (1959): 210–15; E. Arthur Robinson, "Order and Sentience in 'The Fall of the House of Usher,'" *PMLA* 76 1961): 68–81; William B. Stein, "The Twin Motif in 'The Fall of the House of Usher,'" *Modern Language Notes* 75 (1960): 109–11; Allen Tate, "Our Cousin Mr. Poe" in *Collected Essays* (Denver: Alan Swallow, 1959); Richard Wilbur, "The House of Poe," pp. 255–77. A symposium on "Usher," including six essays, a review-essay on three recent casebooks on "Usher," and a "Checklist of Criticism Since 1960," appeared in *Poe Studies* 5 (1972):1–23.

# A Misreading of Poe's "The Fall of the House of Usher"

Patrick F. Quinn*

D. H. Lawrence advised readers of fiction to trust the book and not the author, but he neglected to say what or who should be trusted when the book consists of a story told by a narrator who is unreliable. Presumably one then looks for guidance from that convenient abstraction, the critic, who, along with his other duties, attempts to clarify the author's intention and to unmask narrators with bogus claims to credibility. In *Poe's Fiction: Romantic Irony in the Gothic Tales* (Madison: University of Wisconsin Press, 1973), G. R. Thompson argues that it was part of Poe's intention as an ironical author to make the most of the unreliable narrator device, and that he did so in a good many of his most famous tales, including "MS. Found in a Bottle," "Ligeia," and "The Fall of the House of Usher."

Having long believed that Poe wanted his readers to give credence to, indeed to identify with, the visitor to Usher's house, and finding myself unpersuaded by the opposite proposals in Thompson's book, I should like to review the matter in some detail. Taking up four points that are worth more or less discussion: the appearance of the house, the narrator's experience, the ending of the story, and its theme, I shall try to show that in this case it may be the critic of the story rather than its narrator whose reliability is more open to question.

## THE APPEARANCE OF THE HOUSE

"It is curious," Thompson writes, "that no one has ever seen fit to remark that when the narrator rides up to the house of Usher he is immediately confronted with a death's head looming up out of the dead landscape. Poe obviously intended the image of the skull-like face of the house to dominate as the central image of the tale, for he returns to it again and again, placing the most extended descriptions of it at symmetrically located places in the narrative."

There can be no objection to describing as "dead" the landscape in which the house is sited, but two other assertions are made here which are not so self-evident. To take the house first: what does it look like? Very few architectural specifications are given, but it is obvious that the house is very old and very large. It dates back to feudal times

*Reprinted from *Ruined Eden of the Present: Hawthorne, Melville, and Poe*, ed. G. R. Thompson and Virgil L. Lokke (Purdue University Press, 1981), 303–12. Reprinted with permission of the author and the Purdue University Press, © 1981, by Purdue Research Foundation, West Lafayette, IN 47907. These pages are followed by a second exchange between Professors Thompson and Quinn on pp. 313–53.

and, though no doubt remodeled since then, remains what it originally was, a castle. Poe's misuse of the recherché words *donjon* and *donjon-keep* does not inspire one with confidence in his expertise about castles, but he conveys, nonetheless, a sufficiently graphic picture: the house of Usher is a castellated mansion of medieval origin. And of considerable size. "Vast" is the narrator's word for it, when, in the final paragraph, he records his last look at the front of the house. Approximately *how* vast may be inferred from the dimensions of Usher's "studio," the windows of which are at "so vast a distance from the black oaken floor as to be altogether inaccessible from within." If this is only the studio, imagine the scale of the great hall! But the question is whether a vast, castellated mansion, seen from in front, where the entrance is, can have a plausible resemblance to a death's head. I would say no. The proportions of the building, its generally rectilinear structure, its turrets, and above all its dimensions make this resemblance extremely difficult to visualize. And so I, for one, do not find it curious that the alleged house-skull resemblance has, prior to Thompson, gone unremarked.

Nor can I go along with Thompson's other contention, that the image of the skull-like facade of the house dominates the tale, with Poe returning to it again and again to give it more extensive treatment. The disagreement here may be reduced to a matter of statistics. "The Fall of the House of Usher" has 41 paragraphs. Counting "The Haunted Palace" as part of paragraph 18, and scrutinizing the text for evidence Thompson would use to support his view, I come up with only paragraphs 1, 4, 5, 18, possibly 19, and 41. In these paragraphs I do not find "extended descriptions," nor do I find them, as Thompson does, "at symmetrically located places in the narrative."

## THE EXPERIENCE OF THE NARRATOR

It is of importance to Thompson's case that a close link be discerned between the narrator and his host, since the essence of the case is that the two are psychological doubles and hence the initial uneasiness felt by the narrator develops into a "frenzy of terror, engendered by and parallel to Usher's terrors." As evidence of such a link, Thompson adduces the three-way relationship he sees between the face of the narrator, the facade of the house, and the face of Usher. He pairs the first two this way:"The narrator's first impression of the house is that it is like a human face, especially with its two vacant eyelike windows. Then he looks down into the pool, but sees only the reflection of the 'face' of the house. What is equally likely, of course, is that he should see imaged there his own reflected features, since Poe is careful to point out that the narrator wheels his horse up to 'the precipitous brink' of the tarn and thus gazes straight down."

So far there is no mention of a *three-way* connection, but two passages on a later page deal with this emphatically: "Usher's 'arabesque' face and the face of the house are the same, and when the narrator gazes into the pool the reflected 'arabesque' face is merged with his own—symbolically is his own ... [plus] the image of the house as skull or death's head and the merging of the narrator's face with the face of the house which is also Usher's face in the pool."

In my opinion, the evidence offered for a three-way tie-up is unconvincing, for these reasons:

1. The narrator's first impression of the house is that it is "melancholy," and to such a degree that he feels overcome by a "sense of insufferable gloom." Neither in the first scene nor elsewhere does he allude, even distantly, to a resemblance between the house and a human face, much less a skull. To be sure, there would be some basis for imputing to the narrator the impression of such a resemblance if the text read, per Thompson's paraphrase, "two vacant eyelike windows." In fact, the numeral *two* is not used by the narrator. (It is probable that Thompson borrowed it from the third stanza of "The Haunted Palace," but Usher's poem is hardly relevant evidence about the narrator's first impression of the house.)

2. When the narrator gazed at the tarn, could he have seen his face reflected, overlaid, as it were, on the reflected image of the house? It seems to me that, given his initial position, across the water from the house, he could have seen one or the other, but not both. Only after crossing over the causeway, standing with his back to the house, and *then* looking down could he have seen his reflection, within the frame of the reflected facade of the house. But since he does not cross the causeway until after his visual experiment is made, the laws of geometric optics would seem to rule out the possibility of the double-reflection phenomenon.

3. Another reason for questioning the face-facade theory may be worth mentioning. When the narrator enters the house and meets his host, his attention, Thompson says, "is focused on the odd appearance of Usher's face," which recalls to the reader "the facelike structure of the house." In a very general way this deduction is correct, for a basic *donnée* of the story is that some kind of occult connection, necessarily imprecise, exists between the house and its owner. But by giving such minute attention to Usher's face—its luminous eyes, its curved lips, its delicately shaped nose (distinguished, moreover, by an unusual "breadth of nostril")—the description negates Thompson's earlier suggestion that, *de rigueur*, an association is to be made between the house and a skull or death's head.

A more important contention in Thompson's argument is that the story is essentially about the mental collapse of the narrator, and that the stages of the collapse are given careful documentation: "Poe meticulously . . . details the development of the narrator's initial uneasiness into a frenzy of terror," etc. The word *uneasiness* is perhaps not sufficiently strong to do justice to the state of mind of the narrator when he has a *mauvais quart d'heure* in the opening scene. But once he is inside the house does this uneasiness augment by differentiated stages and eventually partake of the terrors that afflicted Usher? This is not shown.

Between paragraphs 6 and 24 the narrator's account does not reflect any progressive deterioration of mind or feeling. How could it? For his account is concerned almost entirely with Usher, his appearance, behavior, and obsessions with several varieties of fear. And rather than respond to and interiorize these obsessions, the narrator attempts to distract Usher from them. For several days after his arrival, he says, "I was busied in earnest endeavors to alleviate the melancholy of my friend." Following the interment of Madeline, "some days of bitter grief having elapsed," Usher's condition takes a serious turn for the worse. As he reads the symptoms, the narrator is unsure whether to diagnose their cause as "extreme terror" or "the more inexplicable vagaries of madness." Either way, Usher's condition has become terrifying, and it is *now*, after perhaps a week of residence in the house, that the narrator begins to feel real distress. Up to this point there has been no meticulous recording of a developing uneasiness. The development starts now, but it does not approach the intensity ("frenzy of madness") of Thompson's estimate.

Thompson's version of what takes place at this crucial juncture (paragraphs 24, 25, 26) adds some details to the text and, inexplicably, ignores others. The text reads: "There were times, indeed, when I thought his [Usher's] unceasingly agitated mind was laboring with some oppressive secret, to divulge which he struggled for the necessary courage." In Thompson's version of this statement the emotional ante is raised considerably: ". . . the narrator feels growing in himself a vague fear that Usher has some horrible 'oppressive secret' to divulge." Recognizing that Usher's terror is becoming contagious, the narrator says: "I felt creeping upon me, by slow yet certain degrees, the wild influence of his own fantastic yet impressive superstitions." Thompson renders this as "slow yet uncertain degrees"; but whether certain or uncertain, the degrees by which the infection spreads are not itemized.[1] Instead, Poe at once sets his final scene, which is enacted a week or so after Madeline's burial.

The scene begins with the narrator's account of experiencing "the full power of such feelings"—that is, those induced by Usher's condition. He is, to quote Thompson again, "unable to sleep, especially since, as with the reflected image of the house in the tarn, he is aware of his increased terror: 'an irrepressible tremor gradually pervaded my frame; and, at length, there sat upon my very heart an incubus [of] utterly

causeless alarm.'" What the resumé as quoted does not reflect are two
sentences in the text which describe the narrator's efforts to deal with,
to dispel, his feelings of terror. The resumé continues: "'Overpowered
by an intense sentiment of horror,' the narrator begins pacing nervously;
suddenly he is startled by a light footstep outside his door. But it is only
Usher. Usher's intensely agitated condition is the more unnerving, especially when he suggests that a supernatural and luminous vapor has
surrounded the house in spite of the rising wind without."

Here also is an omission of some consequence. The narrator does
not pace to and fro *because*, as Thompson seems to imply, he feels
"overpowered by an intense sentiment of horror." Rather, he resorts to
this action as a means of fighting back, "to arouse myself," as he puts it,
"from the pitiable condition into which I had fallen." He is not "startled"
(nor could he be) by Usher's light footstep; the sound merely "arrested
[his] attention." He does not find Usher's distraught appearance "the
more unnerving." What he says is quite simply and credibly this: "His
air appalled me—but anything was preferable to the solitude which I
had so long endured, and I even welcomed his presence as a relief."

Usher does not "suggest that a supernatural and luminous vapor"
has surrounded the house; all he does, without comment, is open a
casement window. The narrator sees for himself an "unnatural" light
glowing about the house. It seems, then, that one of Usher's specific
fears—that the house would become increasingly sentient, with increasingly ominous implications for himself—is in fact borne out. But instead
of succumbing to this fear the narrator tries to explain away both it
and the apparent basis for it. The phenomenon, he tells Usher, is only
hallucinatory. "You must not—you shall not behold this!" he exclaims,
and further to deflect Usher's attention he begins reading aloud from
the "Mad Trist." As things turn out, the reading proves less than therapeutic, but the intention behind it was certainly sane.

At this point the action of the story is within a few moments of
its close. Surely by now, if Thompson is right, the narrator, despite himself, would reveal how he is being victimized by a "frenzy of terror" on
a par with Usher's. He is not so victimized. Usher is the one who succumbs, "a victim to the terrors he had anticipated." The narrator, on the
other hand, "unnerved" and "aghast" as he understandably is, retains
sufficient *sang-froid* to get out of the house in time and witness what
happened to it.

## WHAT HAPPENED TO THE HOUSE?

The question is not as frivolous as it looks, for it involves one of the
major theses of Thompson's book. The thesis is that Poe, as an ironical
writer in the romantic mode of irony, characteristically provides in his
tales one kind of meaning for the average, untutored reader, and plants,

or "insinuates," another meaning, which, in Poe's words, "only minds congenial with that of the author will perceive." In the present instance, the thesis applies in this way: The reader of average gullibility will not think of questioning the veracity of Usher's visitor, and his account of what took place will be appreciated for the uncanny kind of excitement the tale gives rise to; whereas an inner circle of readers, aware that Poe's technique is one of "deceptive, ironic, psychological realism," will read the story for its clues (Thompson's word), just as a detective does in a mystery story. Therefore we either accept the narrator's word about what happened to the house, or, following Thompson's lead, we "clue in" to a different hypothesis.

According to the narrator, the house of Usher, almost immediately after his exit from it, split into two great sections and sank into the tarn. Since Thompson's opinion is that the man is revealed as "completely untrustworthy," he sees no reason why this professedly eyewitness report should be accepted as definitive. He offers an alternative explanation. The copper-floored vault in which Madeline was interred, he points out, was once a storage place for powder or some other highly combustible substance. This is textually exact. And so, Thompson continues, "if the house cracks open and crumbles, rather than a necessarily supernatural occurrence, as it seems to the hysterical narrator, it is explainable as the combustion generated when the lightning of the storm crackles near the previously airless crypt—the inrushing electricity being conducted along the copper floor and igniting the remnants of powder." This is an ingenious explanation, but it depends on too many improbabilities.

It seems improbable, for instance, that there was enough residual gunpowder in what is described as a small and damp vault to cause (when ignited) an explosion adequate to blow up the house; for the house, it can be assumed, is "vast." I have no idea what critical mass of gunpowder would be required to blow up a castle of even average size, but what Thompson refers to as "remnants of powder" would not seem to be nearly enough, for the phrase suggests only a few scattered, unswept grains. (The text, incidentally, makes no mention of such "remnants." It was apparently the copper sheathing that led the narrator to infer that the place had once been a powder magazine.)

If we assume that there was gunpowder in sufficient quantity to cause, when ignited, the blowing up of the house, a question arises as to the agency that might have caused the ignition. Thompson's theory is that a lightning bolt, finding access to and then conducted along the copper flooring, provided the spark. What is not explained is how such a bolt could have found access to the burial vault. Located "at great depth" underground, and therefore windowless, and of course damp, it would seem as lightning proof as any interior chamber could imaginably be.

There is the further (or rather preliminary) question as to whether the storm produced lightning. Rain is not mentioned, or thunder, and as for lightning, all that is said on this score is: "nor was there any flashing forth of the lightning." Thompson would certainly have a better case if the statement were less negative. I think it is possible that one reason why the tempestuous final night of the story is described as "wildly singular" is that all the makings of a thunderstorm were present— but, singularly, there was neither rain, nor thunder, nor lightning. Since, however, the text is not absolutely negative on this point, the possibility may be entertained that there was lightning that night. It was not seen as "flashing forth" because, presumably, it was concealed by the cloud cover, which was very dense and hung low enough to "press upon the turrets of the house." Such lightning as there may have been, therefore, was of the cloud-to-cloud variety, for flashes from cloud to ground, given the unnatural visibility of the occasion, would have been seen. So perhaps a bolt or two may have struck one of the turrets. But an explanation is still in order as to the route and the conducting material by which an electric charge traversed the anfractuous distance between turret level and the vault, sequestered well below ground level. The text offers no basis for such an explanation.

## THE THEME OF THE STORY

In "The Fall of the House of Usher," as Thompson interprets it, Poe, through the narrator's account of his experience, ironically mocks "the ability of the human mind ever to know anything with certainty, whether about the external reality of the world or the internal reality of the mind." I find it impossible to reconcile this definition of the story's theme with the contention, variously phrased, that the narrator of the story is mentally unstable, disturbed, prone to hysteria and hallucination—that he is, in fine, "completely untrustworthy." Surely it was as obvious to Poe as it is to us that a deranged mind, mired in its own subjectivity, is unable successfully to perceive objective reality, much less cope with it. There would be no point, ironical or otherwise, in mocking such inability. Therefore, only if the narrator's mental credentials are in good order, and the story he tells is accepted as reliable, can there be any possibility that the thematic drift of the story is as Thompson describes it.

Note

1. In his reply (*Ruined Eden of the Present*, p. 331) Professor Thompson acknowledged this error and claimed that the accurate text supports his argument. [Editor's note.]

# Poe and the Art of Suggestion    Richard Wilbur*

Poe well understood that people of strongly prosaic turn of mind are often drawn to mystic or imaginative literature, which they read with a fascinated resistance. The initially skeptical narrator of "MS. Found in a Bottle" has long enjoyed the German moralists, "not," he says, "from any ill-advised admiration of their eloquent madness, but from the ease with which my habits of rigid thought enabled me to detect their falsities." And the hero of "Berenice," once his visionary disposition has been destroyed by disease, is attracted to St. Augustine's *City of God* because of what he calls its "imaginative and inconsequential nature." Some scholars seem to approach Poe himself in a similar spirit of charmed mistrust, confining their often valuable studies to matters of fact, or apparent fact, while resisting Poe's repeated advice that imaginative writing be searched for undercurrents of meaning.

One recent resister of Poe is Julian Symons, whose book *The Tell-Tale Heart* asserts, among other things, that while "William Wilson" is "absolutely clear" as symbolic fiction, Poe's work in general is intrinsically vague and incapable of interpretation. Though I hesitate to agree with Mr. Symons about anything, I think him correct in saying that "Wilson" is one of the few fictions in Poe which have the suggestive clarity of a Hawthorne story. We must be grateful that we have, in "Wilson," a common ground on which all readers of Poe may meet— a story which plainly concerns the gradual division of a once harmonious soul into warring faculties; which embodies the conflict between the degraded will and the moral sense in the persons of Wilson and his double; which involves not only earth but Heaven and Hell; and which ends in spiritual death. Where I differ with Mr. Symons is in his inclination to dismiss as insoluble anything less perspicuous than "William Wilson." "Wilson" may be atypical in its clarity, but it is typical of Poe in its concerns, in its images and locutions, in its first-person narration, and in its symbolic or allegorical method. The thing to do, I think, is to push off from "Wilson" into the *mare tenebrarum* of the other works—seeing, for example, whether the high and low voices of the two Wilsons may help one to understand the variable registers of Roderick Usher, or of Dupin, or whether it is significant that the mummer who represents the Red Death moves with a step "solemn and measured," like Dr. Bransby in "William Wilson" or the figure of Conscience in *Politian*. Because Poe's machinery of suggestion can be

*A talk delivered to the Poe Studies Association at the *MLA* convention, December 1981. Reprinted from *UMSE* 3 (1982): 1–13, by permission of the author and of Benjamin Franklin Fisher IV, Editor, *UMSE*.

submerged and sly, such a quest must involve confusion and error, but at least it will have the virtue of responding to what is there.

We all know how slow a work of Poe's may be to release its meaning. I have been reading "Israfel," on and off, for most of my life, and I have always regarded it as a simple, flawed, and occasionally felicitous piece in which an earthly poet, while not apologizing for his own limited efforts, applauds the superior lyric powers of an angel. I still read the poem in the same general way, but not long ago I was made suddenly aware that the poem is subtler and more argumentative than I had thought, and that it may be taken, from beginning to end, as a treatise on the place of passion in poetry. Poe's poetic theory, which reached its full development in "The Poetic Principle," distinguishes as we know three primary divisions of the "world of mind": the intellect, which pursues truth; taste, which has for its object beauty; and the moral sense, which concerns itself with duty. Poetry being a wild effort to capture supernal beauty, it is the province of taste alone. The intellect, and the moral sense with its mundane didacticism, are inimical to poetry, and are admissible in a poem only if utterly subjected to the purposes of taste. Since poetry aims at "an elevating excitement of the soul," a spiritual or Uranian kind of love may be the truest of poetic themes; but as for passion, which is "an intoxication of the heart," Poe agrees with Coleridge that it degrades the soul and is discordant with poetry.

And yet, in "Israfel," we meet an angel whose very instrument is the heart, and whose song is all fire, fervor, and "burning measures." He causes the stars to be giddy, the enamored moon to totter and blush, the lightning to be red, and all of his celestial hearers to be mute with rapture. Why is Israfel's song not a degrading performance? We know that it cannot be, since the stars suspend their hymns to God in order to hear it. Most of the answers, however, are given by condensed and muffled implication in the fourth stanza:

> But the skies that angel trod,
>     Where deep thoughts are a duty—
> Where Love's a grown-up God—
>     Where the Houri glances are
> Imbued with all the beauty
>     Which we worship in a star.

Israfel's condition in heaven is here described in terms of the triad of faculties which I have just mentioned. *Deep thoughts* have to do with the intellect, *duty* pertains to the moral sense, and *beauty* to the aesthetic sense, or taste. An angelic soul, it seems, has the same constituents as a human soul, but the difference is that Israfel is an inhabitant of the skies. Throughout his early work, from "Al Aaraaf" onward, Poe argues that intellectual knowledge is not fit for man in the earthly condition of his soul, and that it wars with that sense of beauty which is our sole means of approaching the divine; but for the angel Israfel, who dwells "in the high Heaven of pure knowledge," there is no conflict between intellect and taste, and these faculties are in turn perfectly attuned to the moral sense. Israfel has an intact and harmonious soul, as the poet of Earth does not.

Often, when Poe wishes to evoke supernal beauty, he will do so by combining erotic words or images with inhibitory ideas. When Nesace, the spirit of Beauty, arrives at her palace in the second part of "Al Aaraaf," we are given this picture: "From the wild energy of wanton haste / Her cheeks were flushing and her lips apart; / The zone that clung about her gentle waist / Had burst beneath the heaving of her heart." Wantonness, flushing, parted lips and a burst zone are all very libidinous, but these effects are countered by the fact that she is a heavenly spirit whom we have just seen praying to God, and that she is here frozen into immobility like a statue—a statue perhaps by Canova, that sculptor whom Mario Praz once aptly dubbed "The Erotic Refrigerator." The same effect of chastened passion is achieved in two words in the poem "Evening Star," where Poe extols the "distant fire" of Venus. The dark-eyed Houri glances in "Israfel" may for a moment suggest mere voluptuousness, but then we are told that they are "Imbued with all the beauty / Which we worship in a star"—that they are objects of distanced and spiritual devotion. Having chastened his Houris, Poe can then proceed in his following lines to Q.E.D.: "Therefore, thou are not wrong, / Israfeli, who despisest / An unimpassioned song. . . ." Owing to his psychic wholeness and his heavenly environment, Israfel's song can be both passionate and pure; he can handle the erotic; he can intoxicate his heart without risking his spiritual balance; whereas the poet of Earth, a divided soul in a degraded environment, must forever be wary of falling into "The napthalene river of passion accurst."

The first version of "Israfel" is even more concentrated on the theme of passion in poetry than the later and more familiar one, but the second contains a parenthetical addition which once seemed to me decorative at best, but now strikes me as thoroughly pertinent. I refer to the lines in which we are told how "the red levin / (With the rapid Pleiads even, / Which were seven,) / Pauses in Heaven." The Pleiades are rapid because, when they were nymphs on Earth, they were pursued by the enamored hunter Orion; translated to Heaven by Zeus, they are safe from Orion's lust, but are still in an attitude of flight from him. As for the reduction of their number from seven to six, one of the Pleiades (named Merope) forsook the skies, according to Ovid, because of her passion for a mortal. Poe's evocation of the Pleiades is thus a double proof that, in Israfel's poetic preserve, unruly earthly passion is not allowed. The fall of Merope resembles, of course, the fall of

Angelo and Ianthe in "Al Aaraaf," and means exactly the same thing. Let me add, incidentally, that Merope's fall is a felicitous touch because it affords a counter-movement to the upward yearning of the speaker of the poem.

Assuming that all these things are in "Israfel," why did it take me so long to see them? For one thing Poe is theoretically opposed to *thinking* in poetry, and there are very few of his poems—the sonnet to Mrs. Clemm would be one of them—which are forthrightly argumentative in nature. One does not therefore feel encouraged to read "Israfel" as an implicit discourse on the facultative and emotional basis of poetry in Heaven and Earth. On the contrary, a poem which offers the rhymes *wrong, song, belong* and *long* within a six-line stanza, and gives us *levin, even, seven* and *Heaven* in successive lines, seems chiefly musical rather than verbal in intention—a melodic tribute to the angel's song. The impression that music has priority is strengthened when one notes that, in a present-tense poem, the verb *tread* has been wrenched into the past tense so as to rhyme with *God*. Though there are handsome passages in "Israfel," some of the language seems thoughtless or casual. When Poe seeks to broaden the range of Israfel's passion by speaking of "Thy grief, thy joy, thy hate, thy love," he slips into nonsense; an angel who dwells in "perfect bliss" does not sing of grief and hate. To describe the instrumental use of heartstrings as "unusual" is bathetic, to say the least. In what I take to be the crucial stanza, the expression "deep thoughts" may sound too banal to be taken seriously, while "duty" and "beauty," though they intend to say a great deal, may in so musical a poem be passed over as mere facile rhyming. Finally, although Poe the critic contended that "every work of art should contain within itself all that is requisite for its own comprehension," "Israfel" does not, in my experience, yield all of its suggested ideas unless one brings a general familiarity with Poe to bear on it.

Some time ago, at a funeral, I heard a familiar passage from St. Paul and had a delayed insight into "Annabel Lee." I had meant to electrify you with the quotation tonight, but in preparing to write this paper I found that the passage is already cited in Professor Mabbott's notes to the poem. This gave me mixed feelings of disappointment and comfort; as Allen Tate once remarked, in interpreting Poe we often fear that we are mad, and it can be reassuring to find that one is not being wholly original. So far as I know, the implications of the passage in question have not been explored, and so I shall state them briefly. Poe's poem says that Annabel Lee and her lover are children, and are therefore close to heaven and unsullied by the world. Their love is "more than love"; it is not merely a strong affection but a kind of blessed communion which the very angels might wish to enjoy. Thus far, what we have is a restatement, in one of Poe's last poems, of some lines from "Tamerlane": "Love—as in infancy was mine— / "Twas such as angel minds above / Might envy. . . ." But now Poe turns that hyperbole into narrative, and most improbably has the envious angels cause the death of Annabel Lee; with whom, nonetheless, the lover continues somehow to be in unbroken communion: "And neither the angels in Heaven above / Nor the demons down under the sea / Can ever dissever my soul from the soul / Of the beautiful ANNABEL LEE. . . ." One of the lessons in the Episcopal *Order for the Burial of the Dead* is taken from the eighth chapter of St. Paul's *Epistle to the Romans*. I shall read to you only the words which are applicable here: "For I am persuaded, that neither death, nor life, nor angels, nor principalities, nor powers, nor things present, nor things to come, nor height, nor depth, nor any other creature, shall be able to separate us from the love of God. . . ." It seems clear to me that St. Paul has emboldened Poe to imagine his angels as seeking to separate love from love and man from God, and that Poe's adaptation of the passage from *Romans* has the inescapable effect of identifying Annabel Lee with "the love of God." Within the burial rite, St. Paul's words are a promise that the dead are safely united with their Maker, but the passage as used by Poe asserts that the soul of Annabel's lover shall never be severed from hers, or from the divine love and beauty which her soul communicates. Annabel Lee, then, is not only a kinswoman of the angels, but a mediatory spirit like Nesace or the Lady Ligeia. Her story, in fact, is the Ligeia-story without Rowena. In "Annabel Lee," the angelic mediatrix is physically lost, but never is she lost to her lover's spirit, which nightly communes with her soul and its message through the glory of the moon and the divine beauty and order of the stars.

If I ask why an Episcopalian took so long to find St. Paul in "Annabel Lee," the answer is once again in good part a matter of tone, or music. The poem might be described as the balladic heightened into the vatic. It begins with the language and movement of ballad—"It was many and many a year ago"—but instead of regular stanzas, a consecutive story, a refrain, and the expected variations of rhyme, we have a changeable stanza, elaborate and irregular repetitions, and a rapt, chanting insistence on such rhymes as *sea, Lee, me,* and *we.* The poem's rich sound, exultant anapests, and vatic repetitions assimilate everything to one powerful effect, salvaging all banalities about moonbeams and dreams, and quite overwhelming the accents of St. Paul. For someone of my generation, to think of the use of quotations in poetry is to think of T. S. Eliot and his *Waste Land.* Despite the fact that more than ten percent of Eliot's poem consists of echoes, and despite the continual irruption of various dramatic voices, there is at all times a recognizable ground voice, which is the voice of the poet. We know when Eliot is talking, and when we are hearing the Buddha. But the voice of Poe's poem does not yield the floor to any other, and if after many readings one notices a smothered reference to Romans: 8, one does not even then feel strongly prompted, as one would in Eliot, to ponder the logic of the allusion.

There are similar obstacles, in Poe's tales, to the taking of his suggested meaning, though this is not true of them all. It seems to me that the choice of the name Prospero, in "The Masque of the Red Death," is both brilliant and accessible; Poe's Prospero resembles Shakespeare's in that he is separated from his dominions, but a more important resemblance is that both are capable of summoning up imaginary revels. The name Prospero thus readies us to see what the tale makes plain, that the Prince's thousand companions are all creatures of dream. In writing "The Tell-Tale Heart," a year after "The Masque of the Red Death," Poe was again thinking of Shakespeare, and when a ray of the mad hero's dark-lantern is directed at the old man's vulture eye, falling precisely upon "the damned spot," few readers would fail to think of *Macbeth*. Yet in my experience, this echo does not work so promptly as the reference to Prospero, and may not even be entertained, by the reader, as a suggestion. I think this occurs in part because "The Masque of the Red Death" is told in a deliberate authorial voice capable of firm intimations, whereas "The Tell-Tale Heart" is the first-person narrative of a terror-prone madman who is breathless with the desire to boast of his cleverness, and also to confess. His choppy, nervous, repetitive and self-obsessed language is in itself superbly suggestive of a state of mind, but it is not a likely fabric in which to detect ponderable literary allusions.

Yet they are present. Hearing a small sound, Poe's old man springs up in bed and cries "Who's there?", which is also the cry of Macbeth in Duncan's bedchamber, hearing a spectral voice. Poe's narrator then tells how the old man, "ever since the first slight noise," has been lying awake and saying to himself: "It is nothing but the wind in the chimney—it is only a mouse crossing the floor. . . . it is only a cricket which has made a single chirp." Macbeth, descending from Duncan's chamber, asks: "Didst thou not hear a noise?", and his wife replies: "I heard the owl scream and the cricket cry." When Lady Macbeth says "Out, damned spot," she is washing her hands of imaginary blood, and Poe takes up the idea again when he has his narrator say, while burying his dismembered victim beneath the floorboards: "There was nothing to wash out—no stain of any kind—no blood-spot whatever." The madman's victim is referred to, throughout the story, simply as "the old man," and that may put one in mind of Lady Macbeth's saying: "Yet who would have thought the old man to have had so much blood in him?" In addition to such echoes faint or strong, there are patent resemblances in Poe's tale to the plot of *Macbeth*: we have the nocturnal murder of an old man in his bedchamber, we have a knocking at the gate (or the street door, if you will), and, as in the matter of Banquo's ghost, we have a killer unhinged by hallucinations of his victim. All of this, nevertheless is very slow to transpire, because it is largely screened by the narration and also, I suspect, because one may not at once divine its reason for being there.

Why does Poe introduce an undercurrent of *Macbeth* into his story? I think it is because, in his accounts of psychic division, Poe often conceived inner conflicts in terms of regicide, rebellion, or usurpation. Tamerlane says: "My passions, from that hapless hour / Usurp'd a tyranny..." William Wilson murderously rebels against the "inscrutable tyranny" of his conscience; in "The Haunted Palace," a ruler called "the monarch Thought" is dethroned in a palace revolution. If we take this indication—and there are many others—that on some level the killer and victim of "The Tell-Tale Heart" are one person, that they have one heart and one riven nature, what names shall we assign to these portions of a self? The old man's offending eye may be helpful: for one thing, it is a "pale blue eye, with a film over it." We know, from "The Man of the Crowd," that "when the film from the mental vision departs," a condition of preternatural insight ensues. It follows that a filmy eye like the old man's represents a cramped, mundane and unimaginative awareness of things, as opposed to that of the narrator, who can hear all things in heaven, earth, and hell. That the old man's eye is like that of a vulture, and that his look makes the narrator's blood run cold, must remind one further of the "Sonnet—To Science"; there the scientific spirit, which is likened to destroying time, alters all with its peering eyes, preys like a vulture upon the poet's heart, and turns all to "dull realities."

Given Poe's insistence, in "The Tell-Tale Heart," on time and heart and vulture eye, I take it for a dead certainty that the story is consciously recalling the "Sonnet—To Science." Did Poe expect his reader to do the same? I doubt it very much. Even when Poe was contemplating unified collections, as in the days of the Folio-Club project, I see no evidence that he meant his reader to elucidate one poem or story by reference to another. Yet for us, as we struggle to understand him, cross-reference is an indispensable tool, and that is one measure of his difficulty. When the hero of "The Pit and The Pendulum" swoons, the voices of his inquisitors merge into a "dreamy indeterminate hum" suggestive of "the burr of a mill-wheel." If we apply that to the Simoom of "MS. Found in a Bottle," which the narrator first hears as "a loud humming noise" like that caused by "the rapid revolution of a mill-wheel," we are confirmed in our sense that the narrator is swooning, that his mind is embarking on a dream. The devil, in "Bon-Bon," takes off his green spectacles and reveals that he has no eyes; his vision, he explains, is of the soul, and includes the power to read the thoughts of any creature. In "The Purloined Letter" and "The Mystery of Marie Roget," Dupin too wears green spectacles which, whatever their practical uses as camouflage, serve also to symbolize the fact that he, like the devil, is a mind-reader and a seer. But not all similarities in Poe signify the same thing. To return to the "Sonnet—To Science" and "The Tell-Tale Heart," the poem is strong in its advocacy of the oppressed and rebellious poet, and of his effort to "seek for beauty in some happier star." In "The Tell-Tale Heart," however, what we have is not advocacy of the afflicted imagination but a description of its predicament: the story seems to say that, if imagination rebels against everyday temporal consciousness and earthly attachments, the cost may be a self-destructive madness. Let me offer another example of dissimilar similarity. Poe's Monos and Una withdraw from the "infected" and "diseased" world about them and "wrap their spirits in dreams"; Prince Prospero, in a story written several months later, withdraws into *his* dreams from a world devastated by Pestilence. The situations sound identical, but they are not, and the difference is plain from the characters of the dreams in question. The mood in which Prospero forsakes the world is described by Poe in two brutal sentences: "The external world could take care of itself. In the meantime, it was folly to grieve, or to think." Prince Prospero thus fatally fragments himself: he does not subordinate his intellect to imagination, but attempts to nullify it; and as for the moral sense, which might move him to grieve for his abandoned subjects, he defies it just as William Wilson did, and with the same suicidal consequences. The dreams which his "guiding taste" creates, though in some respects they resemble happier visions elsewhere in Poe, are far from being aspirant and spiritual—they are, in fact, a kind of "freaking out," and Poe is at pains to tell us that they partake of the mad, the terrible, and the disgusting. Monos and Una, confronted likewise by the corruption of our planet and the running-out of earthly time, engage not in desperate fantasy but in eager visions of an Earth purified by fire and of a regenerate mankind in whom taste and intellect shall be reconciled once more. Their very different dreams have a different and heavenly issue.

Though Poe did not write one thing to explain another, and though similarities may deceive, certain tales do give us particularly clear and trustworthy keys to Poe's suggestive methods. It is not only "William Wilson" which lets us get a foot in the door. In "The Island of the Fay," we are made witnesses to the process by which deepening reverie may transform a landscape into a mirror of the psyche—changing the water-borne flakes of sycamore bark, for example, into the flickering images of the hypnagogic state; this demonstration of the interiorizing of nature can make it easier for us to enter and navigate the psychic scenery of such a piece as "The Domain of Arnheim." "The Pit and the Pendulum," by commencing with a cataract of apocalyptic echoes from scripture, gives fair warning that it is going to be two stories at once—the literal story of a tortured prisoner and the symbolic story of a soul in danger of damnation on Judgment Day. Therefore the narrative is full of expressions, like "deliverance," "hope," "despair," and "eternal night," which at once belong to a description of tormented captivity and by their overtones imply another tale in which a terrified spirit awaits God's final justice or mercy. This obvious and brilliant use of resonant words, in "The Pit and the Pendulum," helps one to recognize similar effects elsewhere—in "The Fall of the House of Usher," for example, where such a word as "trepidation" not only conveys the fear and trembling and tension which pervade Roderick's domain, but hint also that the very cosmos is falling into disorder and will soon collapse toward its original state of unity. "Ligeia" is a rich and difficult story, yet for the common reader it is a relatively clear introduction to Poe's use of alchemical symbolism. Ligeia's presence is golden, her absence is leaden, and what happens to Rowena is a transmutation. In order to register these things, the common reader need know no more of alchemy than he could get from Milton's "Il Penseroso," whose Goddess Melancholy is described in terms of gold and lead, and who, like the Lady Ligeia, sponsors the transmutation of earthly experience into spiritual knowledge. If he grasps this aspect of "Ligeia" by way of Milton, as was the case with me, the common reader may then be able to sense something of the more complex alchemical goings-on in Roderick Usher's house.

But now I arrive at the necessity of granting that Poe is an odd sort of symbolic writer who often enshrouds his mystic meanings as if they were secret doctrine, and who is given to puzzle-making and teasing. No amount of "Il Penseroso" will help us to dig up all the alchemical treasure of "The Gold Bug"; for that, we must either become hermetic adepts or consult Professor St. Armand's authoritative essay. Often, Poe will challenge or mystify us by cloaking his hints in an ancient or foreign language: to be quite certain that the comic tales "Loss of Breath" and "Bon-Bon" have serious implications of an anti-physical or anti-materialist nature, the reader must absorb a Latin footnote and a Greek pun. I have already noted elsewhere that in "The Murders in the Rue Morgue" Poe uses the French phrase *au troisième* as one indication that Dupin's fourth-floor apartment, and that of the murdered women, are in some ulterior sense the same dwelling. Let me mention another bit of linguistic coyness from the same story. As the narrator and Dupin walk home from inspecting the scene of the crime, we are given this strange sentence: "I have said that the whims of my friend were manifold, and that *Je les ménageais*—for this phrase there is no English equivalent." That is complete bunk, of course; Poe uses the same verb *ménager* as a past participle in "The System of Doctor Tarr and Professor Fether," and promptly translates it as "humored." Here, the supposedly untranslatable phrase means simply that the narrator humored Dupin, or fell in with his whims. Why should Poe seek to make a mystery of the word *ménager*? My guess is that he wants us to contemplate the word, and in the process think of the closely related words *ménage* and *ménagerie*; that he wants us to realize, with the aid of other promptings, that there are three similar *ménages* in the story— each secluded, each with two occupants—and that one of these households, because it contains an orangoutang, is also a menagerie. To arrive at those perceptions is to be on one's way perhaps to detecting an occult level of the story at which (as I've proposed elsewhere) all the ménages are one, all of the occupants are principles of one nature, and the theme is the need to recognize and control the beast in oneself. If Poe's monkey-business with the word *ménager* is meant to work in the way I have surmised, there may be a similar provocation in "The Fall of the House of Usher," when the valet who has answered the door is said to "usher" the narrator into the presence of Roderick. Poe is inviting us, I suspect, to brood upon "usher" both as word and as name. It has been noticed that the primary meaning of "usher" is "doorkeeper," which accords with the valet's function in answering Roderick's door. The English word "usher" derives from *ostiarius*, which is based upon *os*, the Latin word for mouth, and thus the word "usher" contains an etymological identification of door and mouth which is constant with the architectural symbolism of the story. Another meaning of "usher," which we encounter in "William Wilson," is "assistant schoolmaster," and I suppose that Roderick might be seen as instructing the half-comprehending narrator in the mysteries of spiritual regeneration. But what most appeals to me—and I find that my notion is shared by Professor Earl Wilcox—is the possibility that the name "Usher" is meant to evoke the sevententh-century Anglican archbishop James Ussher, whose chronology of the world, beginning with the creation in 4004 B.C., was to be found in many Bibles of Poe's day. Poe was well aware of Ussher's chronology, referring to it in several tales and in his preface to the projected *Tales of the Folio Club*. The action of "The Fall of the House of Usher" is the purification and reintegration of a soul, but in the background of the story is a similar development in the whole cosmos, a development which becomes explicit when the story's final sentence echoes *Revelation's* prophecy of the fall of Babylon. In the light of the story's apocalyptic close, Poe's title "The Fall of the House of Usher" could mean not only the collapse of Roderick's house but the end of Bishop Ussher's chronology, the uncreation of the world.

None of these hunches about the word (or name) "usher" is capable of firm proof, so far as I can see; but it is certain that Poe *provokes* us to such speculations, and not to attempt a response is not to read him fully. Let me now mention one more kind of teasing which we find in Poe—his use of absurdity and self-contradiction. In "The Purloined Letter," Dupin calls on the Minister D——, and finds him "at home, yawning, lounging, and dawdling, as usual, and pretending to be in the last extremity of ennui. He is"—Dupin goes on—"He is, perhaps, the most really energetic human being now alive—but that is only when nobody sees him." What Dupin says is preposterous, of course; how should he or anyone else know how the Minister D—— looks and behaves when alone? Dupin could possess such knowledge only if he *were* the Minister D——. Well, perhaps he is. In the first half of "The Purloined Letter," Dupin and the Minister seem quite distinct characters, the only connections between them being that both are poets, that both have names beginning with D, and that Dupin knows something of the Minister's intellectual style and political leanings. In the second half of the story, however, the reader is more and more incited to merge his conceptions of Dupin and the Minister, and to perceive that they are "doubles." We are told that the Minister has a brother, who like him has literary gifts. Dupin belatedly acknowledges that he knows the Minister well. Both men, we find, are poetic geniuses with a consequent built-in mastery of mathematics, and Dupin, because of this identity of intellects, can unerringly read the Minister's thoughts. Both men are lynx-eyed, especially when it comes to observing letters; both know the trick of replacing one letter with another; it turns out that the Minister is "well acquainted" with Dupin's handwriting; it develops that the two men, who are now contending over the honor of a queen, have been rivals before, in Vienna; and in Dupin's concluding quotation from Crébillon, the reader is invited to liken Dupin and the Minister to the royal brothers Atreus and Thyestes, whose bloody feud began with Thyestes' seduction of Atreus' queen Aerope. This barrage of suggestion forces one to divine a "mystic" dimension of the story in which, as at the close of "William Wilson," the good and evil sides of one person are in conflict over a woman's honor and what it symbolizes. The absurdity to which I called your attention—Dupin's assertion that he knows what the Minister looks like "when nobody sees him"—is not, then, a slip of the pen but one brilliant and challenging hint in a narrative full of pokes and nudges.

As James Gargano and I once remarked in conversation, there are a number of other Poe talks in which initially discrete characters are made to converge, and to betray a relationship more intimate than was at first described. The narrator of "The Assignation" begins by claiming only a "slight acquaintance" with the visionary hero, but in the latter part of the story the hero is called "my friend," and there is considerable evidence that narrator and hero are close indeed. Similarly, the narrator of "The Fall of the House of Usher" says in his second paragraph that "many years have elapsed" since his last meeting with Roderick; but by the eighth paragraph, confronting Roderick in his *studio*, the narrator marvels that his host's appearance should have changed so greatly "in so brief a period." These absurdities or inconsistencies can be explained, but I shall not try to do so now; suffice it to say that they are not mistakes but deliberate contradictions, intended (I think) to jar us into an awareness that the narrator has passed from one state of consciousness into another.

I have now been out on a limb for quite a while, saying the sort of thing which would madden Mr. Julian Symons, and I think it is time for me to climb down and sum up. Drawing on my own wrestlings with Poe, I have given a few examples of what may happen if one treats him as a readable author whose meanings can sometimes be arrived at. I've mentioned some, but certainly not all, of Poe's modes of suggestion, and given examples of how cross-reference can both help and mislead the reader. I've tried to describe, in particular cases, some of the ways in which Poe's poems and stories can insulate us from their content and delay our discovery of things which, once discovered, seem obvious. Finally, I have conceded to Poe's detractors that he is the most secretive and difficult of our great symbolic writers. How much of him will permanently elude us, how much we can figure out, we can only learn by trying.

# The Analytic of the Dash:
## Poe's *Eureka*                                    Joan Dayan*

A year before his death, bard on the verge of realms unknown, Poe recited "The Universe" at the New York Society Library. Six months later in July 1848 he published *Eureka* with two other titles added: "A Prose Poem" and "An Essay on the Material and Spiritual Universe." While claiming to design a cosmology, this self-announced "Edgar A. Poe, who has spent more time in analyzing the construction of our language than any living grammarian, critic, or essayist" (H.11:229),[1] is out to remake English prose. Poe's preface to *Eureka* ends with a surprising request: "it is a Poem only that I wish this work to be judged after I am dead." Why does Poe present as summation of his life's writing what remains in terms of his literary criticism a contradiction ("A 'long poem' is simply a flat contradiction in terms")? Why does he ask that his final experiment in prose be made a "paradox" and be judged "as a Poem only"? *Eureka*, Poe's boldly unreadable composite work, says more about poetic language than any poem Poe ever wrote.

*This essay is an abridged version of the original in *Genre* 16 (Winter 1983): 437–66, and is published here with the permission of the author and the journal.

In treating Poe's call to cosmological gnosis, I argue that his dash, the graphic counter that turns organic nature into an additive and deductive space, is prime mover in crossing prose and poem. It is this super-segmentalism, this concrete interleaving, to which I now turn. The dashes in the essay—those brute lead-ons—force his reader to purify, reduce and simplify, elevating prose into poem, or in Poe's terms, clearing the text of "the chaff of inconsistency." Roughly speaking, we might consider *Eureka* as a slow, labored dramatization of the conversion of the manifold into one—a guide to the poet who longs to carve a line out of the mass of matter.

Poe's dash demarcates and deflects, suspends and goads our journey along *"The beaten path"* of reflection. "The use of Language is in the promulgation of Thought" (H.11:252), Poe tells us, and he uses the dash to anatomize the mind's work at engendering. His composition centers on the act of segmentation; and his motive in using the dash instead of mere words to picture the intervening points of his discourse draws attention to the formal travail. In attacking an overly reverent attachment to any species of literary afflatus, Poe uses the dash to show what happens when a self-confessed "scribbler" attempts to lay bare his heart or release a thought "—however flippant—however silly—however trivial—still a thought indeed" (H.16:2). In using the dash to work up his *"Art-Product,"* while imbuing it with "the 'brain-scattering' humor of the moment" (H.16:3), Poe discloses his science of method, reducible to what he dispassionately calls, in anticipation of what remained a non-existent magazine article, "The Philosophy of Point" (H.16:130).

In both his critical writings and his often caustic reviews of other American prose-specimens, Poe stresses the importance of punctuation. Encouraging us to appreciate and ferret out the proper typographical effects, the measure resulting from a well-used point, he explains in his *Marginalia:*

> That punctuation is important all agree; but how few comprehend
> the extent of its importance! The writer who neglects punctuation,
> or mis-punctuates, is liable to be misunderstood. . . . It does not seem
> to be known that, even where the sense is perfectly clear, a sentence
> may be deprived of half its force—its spirit—its point—by improper
> punctuation. (H.16:130)

For Poe, always ready to pun, his theory of "point" means more than one thing; the idea of punctuation becomes synonymous with the "pre-determined effect," the desired end or "point" of anything written.

To demonstrate the limits of vision, ever avoiding the "cant of generality" that besets him, Poe favors the dash whose particular and often playful application conveys the vicissitudes of form. Faced with the unsayable, Poe a late-in-coming empiricist, chooses not to deny, but to define. Poe admits the "propensity of man to define the indefinable"

(M.2:609), and he does not exempt himself from that very human leaning. He does, however, deflate the ideal pursuit through these scattered "pencil-scratches" that add a certain "helter-skelteriness" to the diction of ultimates. In fact, his obsessive definition begins to engender digression, while prolixity turns into a form of precision. A recurrent schematization of doubt, the dash is employed to project a series of moments or possibilities, held before what cannot be schematized—the desired "indefinitiveness of effect...."

... The dash used by Poe becomes a peculiarity essential to his effect. In his review of Hawthorne's *Tales*, he remarks, "to be peculiar is to be original," and qualifies the "true or commendable originality" as not "the uniform, but the continuous peculiarity...a peculiarity springing...from the ever-present force of imagination, giving its own hue, its own character to everything it touches, and especially *self-impelled to touch everything*" (H.13:143). Through the dash, a continuous peculiarity, Poe stamps his presence on the world of phenomena, or more precisely, on his world of words. In cutting through or carving out a space in normative sequence, the dash becomes the analogue to what Poe describes in *Eureka* as the "*force* of irradiation," the necessary "repulsion of limited capacity—a separate *something*" (H.16:210). Poe's dash may well be his attempt to disturb and distort meaning, to leave his mark on everything with which his pen comes into contact. And as he discourses on that mysterious and ineffable "irradiation" and its companion, the "seemingly inseparable idea of agglomeration," Poe ruminates again upon the odd detail, and there disperses his favored "protuberance":

> Now, I have elsewhere observed that it is by just such difficulties as the one now in question—such roughnesses—such peculiarities— such protuberances above the plane of the ordinary—that Reason feels her way, if at all, in her search for the True. By the difficulty—the "peculiarity"—now presented, I leap at once to *the* secret—a secret which I might never have attained *but* for the peculiarity and the inferences which, in its *character of peculiarity*, it affords me.
> (p. 229)

Amplifying the praise of his point by italics, Poe allows the dash to wreak havoc on sequentiality or the usual logic of linear progression. Fragmenting the sentence, the dash articulates the words in repetition and intensifies the effect, jumping out, so to speak, at the reader, bold "*in its character of peculiarity*."

When Poe says he wants to "bring the Matter more distinctly before the eye of the Mind" (H.16:285), he means to use words so that they can be perceived and investigated as facts. As Newton endeavored to subject physical nature to mechanical law, Poe will inquire into the operations—both atomic and verbal—of his own composition. Once seen as particles of matter (an effect attained through a disintegration both graphic and semantic), the words of his essay can frame a system that conforms to the laws of nature. "The higher order of genius should and will combine the original with that which is *natural* . . . in the artistic sense, which has reference to the *general intention of nature*" (H.11:278–79). Poe's dash helps to build up a world in conformity with "nature's general intentions" (H.11:113), in accord with all "the analogies of nature" (H.13:129). Showing how a composite structure is literally put together with words as separable parts, this mark delimits to establish the materiality or thing-ness of words. But in the process they lose their coarseness to take on the rhythms of thought, caprice and imagination.

The most significant function the dash performs in *Eureka* is that of "emendation." Words once presented as elements to be analyzed can then be submitted to a process of alteration and correction. The writer of *Eureka* is first of all a corrector. Again I cite from the *Marginalia*:

> Without entering now into the *why*, let me observe that the printer may always ascertain when the dash of the MS is properly and when improperly employed, by bearing in mind that this point represents *a second thought—an emendation*. In using it just above I have exemplified its use. . . . Now, instead of erasing the phrase "a second thought," which is of *some* use—which *partially* conveys the idea intended—which advances me a *step toward* my purpose—I suffer it to remain, and merely put a dash between it and the phrase "an emendation." (H.16:131)

Both an invitation to and excuse for prolixity, this device renders emendation as verbal disjunction, or displacement. It atomizes the line, but then multiplies rather than limits possible meanings. The tentative progression of words compounds difficulty to prove that no word can be adequate to a thing. The mystery of the compound urges Poe on. "There is no greater mistake than the supposition that a true originality is a mere matter of impulse or inspiration. To originate is carefully, patiently, and understandingly to combine" (H.14:73). Central to Poe's attempt to reform language is an understood equivalence between "physical chemistry" and what he calls "this chemistry of the intellect," his delight in discovering that "the admixture of two elements will result in a something that shall have nothing of the quality of one of them— or even nothing of the qualities of either" (H.12:38–39).

Besides these combinatorial possibilities, the dash also engenders a space of proximate levels. Through enumeration Poe ostensibly intends to present a layered means toward distinctness. The dash "stands, in general, for these words—'or, *to make my meaning more distinct*.' This force *it has*—and this force no other point can have . . . Therefore, the dash *cannot* be disposed with" (H.16:121–32). In *Eureka* this punctuation makes a game or fiction of "clear and distinct" discourse.

The word corrected by the dash is not (nor could it be, given Poe's eighteenth-century bent) a thing, but a way of speaking about, or providing a series of *points* or *terminations*. "We deceive ourselves by the idea of infinitely rarified matter. Matter escapes the senses by degrees— a stone—a metal—a liquid—the atmosphere—a gas—the luminiferous ether. Beyond this there are other modifications more rare. But to all we attach the notion of a constitution of particles—atomic composition" (O.I:257). Through these gradations, instead of a simple trust in an abstract "idea," Poe proves his point: step by step the objects are diminished, purified, emended to enact the minute modifications of spirit that is actually nothing more than "infinitely rarified matter...."

   ... In his determination to avoid obscurity, Poe chooses to define; and he understands definition as did Locke, "a definition is best made by enumerating those simple ideas that are combined in the signification of the term defined."[2] Just as Locke chose to enumerate a series of ideas instead of relying on a facile but less clear general term, Poe excuses his discursiveness, arguing that "distinctness—intelligibility, at all points, is a primary feature in my general design. On important topics it is better to be a good deal prolix than even a very little obscure" (p. 199). Yet, this claim for distinctness ends up a ruse that permits an inconclusive luxuriance of meanings, where words once enchained might mean anything he desires. The sensory pile-up turns us round on our heels, producing the "mental gyration" Poe wants us to undergo as we attempt to comprehend his essay in its singularity. The *priority of the search* for correct expression (often appearing in the guise of a search for cosmic truth) determines the stylistic maneuvers adopted. The dash simulates the breathless pause on the verge, "on the awful threshold of *the Future*" (p. 269). Commanding the correct method equivalent to scientific inquiry, it endows thought with the qualification—and quantification—necessary for that "philosopher proper" to give the infinite "a very determinate turn" (p. 293). IIow a finite mind can "comprehend" that which is not comprehended by any limit ("A thousand [colossal atoms] would assemble here; a million there—perhaps here, again, even a billion—leaving, thus, immeasurable vacancies in space," p. 269) depends upon Poe's keeping "unbroken that chain of *graduated impression* by which alone the intellect of man can expect to encompass the grandeurs of which I speak" (p. 277). Before the *"utmost conceivable expanse of space,"* he marks out the points along the road to revelation: "here let the reader pause with me, for a moment, in contemplation of the miraculous—of the ineffable—of the altogether unimaginable...."

   ... In *Eureka*, Poe correlates cogitation with linguistic display. As observer at the very bounds of thought, before "—a shadowy and fluctuating domain, now shrinking, now swelling, in accordance with the vacillating energies of the imagination" (p. 204), he forces an equation between the writer's protraction of his own mental effort and the attainment of his aim, "between the settling down upon the ultimate point and the act of cessation in thinking" (p. 203). The effect or impression created "is in the ratio of the period during which we keep up the mental endeavor." To maintain the duration, to extend, often to the reader's dismay or impatience, the process of thought, Poe turns the dash into the instrument of what he calls "the law of periodicity."

> Guiding our imaginations by that omniprevalent law of laws, the law of periodicity, are we not, indeed more than justified in entertaining a belief—let us say, rather, in indulging a hope—that the processes we have here ventured to contemplate will be renewed forever, and forever, and forever. (p. 311)

Method, transit, periodicity, and emendation, these terms are tools for a proper analysis of his prose. Word after word presented to the reader, in themselves apparently simple, coalesce into a complex sequence that strains our imagination. The ability to trace his law of periodicity, the regular recurrence of the same phenomena, or units of words, coming round at certain intervals, gives us the duration Poe wants us to feel. This certainty of a recurrent rhythm, analogous to a cosmic process ("Let me term it a mental pendulous pulsation," says Monos, M.2:615) amplifies the movement forward. The dash might also be analyzed as the interval between the phases or phrases in sequence. The importance of this half-stop becomes clearer if we compare it to the final period, which literally figures the end of the sentence and represents for Poe a closing-down of possibility.

> But it is in the act of discontinuing the endeavor—of fulfilling (as we think) the idea—of putting the finishing stroke (as we suppose) to the conception—that we overthrow at once the whole fabric of our fancy by resting upon some ultimate and therefore definite point. (p. 203)

And thus Poe provides the reason for his prolixity, for his substitution of a promised definition by interminable periphrasis. "If then I seem to step somewhat too discursively from point to point of my topic, let me suggest that I do so in the hope of thus the better keeping unbroken that chain of *graduated impression*" (pp. 276–77). The dash ultimately becomes an analogue for digression—for the rhetoric of seeming inconsequence that characterizes Poe's unnerving narrators. *Eureka's* narrator stands before the "Universe of stars," and begins his task of definition. "An interminable succession of stars?" No, he argues: "This was the untenable idea of Pascal when making perhaps the most successful attempt ever made, at periphrasing the conception for which we struggle in the word 'Universe.'" He gives us Pascal's "sphere . . . of which the centre is everywhere, the circumference, nowhere," only to reject the definition as "*no* definition," but then turns around and accepts it "as a definition (rigorous enough for all practical purposes)," followed by an italicized repetition of the same definition: "*a sphere of which the centre is everywhere, the circumference nowhere*" (pp. 204–05). When we consider such redundancy, it becomes clear that Poe devises a graduated use of words to reveal a vagueness. Tautology, a fault in grammar, is penned as necessary to his end, yet another means of tricking the reader: " 'Limited sphere'—A sphere is *necessarily* limited. I prefer tautology to a chance for misconception" (his note, p. 242). His excuse for wordiness joins the hoax to the supposed plea for clarity and Truth. . . .

. . . The apparent contradiction between an essential coherence ("unity," the "perfect consistency") and its manifestation in incoherence remains crucial to Poe's exposition. He urges the reader to fix his attention on "the idea of the *utmost possible Relation* as the Omnipotent design, and on the precautions taken to accomplish it through difference of form." His own words are thus given the status of touchstones or proofs of divine mechanism. Fixing our thoughts on his idea, he uses the dash not only to articulate the deficiency of mere words, but to ensure that our journey into the stars will never quite leave the ground. He keeps us in the path of the particular, "pursuing *the beaten path of astronomical* reflection, in accounting for the immeasurable voids alluded to" (p. 290). While ostensibly keeping "everything within the limits of the accountable—of the real" (H.14:206), the dash hollows out the void in the verbal sequence.

Recall *Eureka's* first query, Poe's petition for words adequate to his matter: "What terms shall I find sufficiently simple in their sublimity—sufficiently sublime in their simplicity—for the mere enunciation of my theme?" (p. 185). Suitably de-compounded in anticipation of his own cosmic tale, the phrasing lays the groundwork for Poe's attempted redefinition of poetic language as an eternal law coincident with natural phenomena. In explaining the diffusion of atoms, in equidistance, each from each, he mimes the action in his syntax:

> In such arrangement, under such conditions, we most easily and immediately comprehend the subsequent most feasible carrying out to completion of any such design as that which I have suggested—the design of variety out of unity—diversity out of sameness—heterogeneity out of homogeneity—complexity out of simplicity—in a word, the utmost possible multiplicity of *relation* out of the emphatically irrelative *One*. (p. 208)

Whenever Poe refers to the mechanism of a universe in its present state of diffusion, he uses his dashes to the full. Throughout *Eureka* Poe speaks of these atoms, once irradiated out from a center, as ever longing for a return into one. His own phraseology embodies the dissatisfaction through the dash, the figure that in fragmenting across the page becomes that *"determinate irradiation"* (p. 230) in the cosmos.

In an essay on Macaulay in *Graham's Magazine*, 1841, Poe discusses his "nebular cosmogony."

> This cosmogony *demonstrates* that all existing bodies in the universe are formed of a nebular matter, a rare ethereal medium, pervading space; shows the mode and laws of formation and *proves* that all things are in a perpetual state of progress; that nothing in nature is *perfected*. (H.10:160)

This "rare ethereal medium" is both more material and more void; it is the force implied in the dash. That particular, *un*-informing force is Poe's favored medium for displacement and dispersal. First he describes this "ether" as "a subtle *influence* ... ever in attendance on matter, although becoming manifest only through matter's heterogeneity" (p. 305); then, with "a perfectly legitimate reciprocity," he gives us matter (or words) "solely to serve the objects of this spiritual Ether" (p. 309). Respectful of the rules of silence before the unknown, Poe talks around this influence "—without daring to touch it at all in any effort at explaining its awul *nature*" (p. 305). The "words of the prophetic Newton are felt to be true, and will be fulfilled" (H.14:191–92), Poe writes; and *Eureka's* method enacts the cryptic nature of Newton's "certain most subtle spirit."[3]

The way Poe uses the dash to construct a universe of effects in simulation of the divine volition is the most striking way that he relates his making to that of God. He asserts: "Now, the laws of irradiation are *known*. ... They belong to the class of *indisputable geometrical properties*. We say of them, 'they are true—they are evident'" (p. 225). And if there is any doubt that he can prove the existence of this *"diffusive power"*—without explaining its nature—Poe proceeds to demonstrate the laws in question in his next one-sentence paragraph that gives us a veritable histology of the dash: "But these laws—what do they declare? Irradiation—how—by what steps does it proceed outwardly from a centre?" (p. 225). The dash leads towards, compounds and turns in on itself. And like Newton, Poe becomes reticent when ruminating on this *spiritus subtilissimus*. Of all Poe's stylistic eccentricities, the dash most boldly performs its mimicry of the great mover:

> That the repulsive something actually exists, *we see*. Man neither employs, nor knows, a force sufficient to bring two atoms into contact. ... This is but the well-established proposition of the impenetrability of matter. All Experiment proves—all Philosophy admits it. The design of the repulsion—the necessity for its existence—I have endeavored to show; but from all attempt at investigating its nature have rigorously abstained. (pp. 211–12)

An experiment proposed, an idea realized; this is the plot of *Eureka*.

> *As* density proceeds—
> *as* the divine intentions are accomplished—
> *as* less and still less remains *to be* accomplished—
> so—
> in the same ratio—
> should we expect to find an acceleration of *The End*:—
> and thus the philosophical mind will easily comprehend that the
> Divine designs in constituting the stars, advance *mathematically* to
> their fulfillment,—
> and more: it will readily give the advance a mathematical expression
> (p. 291)[4]

In the rhythms of dispersal and convergence therein lies the law; the two mutually opposed forces of gravity and diffusion both originate in unity and are held equipoised until the final ingathering. All of matter can be described through the antitheses of the following lexicon:

| | |
|---|---|
| gravitation | electricity |
| attraction | repulsion |
| homogeneity | heterogeneity |
| simplicity | complexity |

And Poe explains:

> The former is the body; the latter the soul; the one is the material;
> the other the spiritual, principle of the Universe. *No other principles
> exist.* All phaenomena are referable to one, or the other, or to both
> combined . . . attraction and repulsion are the *sole* properties through
> which we perceive the Universe . . . we are fully justified in assum-
> ing that attraction and repulsion *are* matter:—there being no con
> ceivable case in which we may not employ the term "matter" and
> the terms "attraction" and "repulsion" taken together, as equivalent,
> and therefore, convertible, expressions in Logic. (pp. 213–14)

Equality is the general law. Poe arranges a system of counterbalancing effects to accord with the principles of gravitation and repulsion; the two seemingly opposed categories are maintained as reciprocal reflections.

Through the dash, Poe presents the celestial mechanics of Newton, driving a visual wedge in between the desire for unity and the facts of dispersal. The dash not only segments, but invites us to make the condensations necessary for the reification of "essential language. . . .

To proceed from matter to "matter no more" is equivalent to Poe's prose effort to make "the true poetical *effect*" out of a "multiform novelty of combination among the things and thoughts of Time" (H.11:72). The origin in one, the ideal state of "Simplicity" is both starting point and end, the sole assumption in the discourse Poe advances and the motive for his "more ample phraseology" (p. 221). Through his wordy amplifications he challenges the reader to resolve the many into one. To decipher the pattern in the apparent fragmentation of elements is to work through complexity to discover "Matter in its utmost conceivable state of——what?——of *Simplicity*" (p. 206). In fact, anxious to prove "the ruling idea" of his text, Poe carries out this process of elimination on his own prose, taking six lines, for example, reducing them to two, and then drawing "a simple corollary from all that has been here said" that amounts to only six words:

> All existing bodies, of course, are composed of these atoms in proxi-
> mate contact, and are therefore to be considered as mere assemblages
> of more or fewer differences; and the resistance made by the repul-
> sive spirit, on bringing together any two such assemblages, would be
> in the ratio of the two sums of the differences in each:—an expression
> which, when reduced, is equivalent to this:—
>
> *The amount of electricity developed on the approximation of two*
> *bodies, is proportional to the difference between the respective sums*
> *of the atoms of which the bodies are composed.*
>
> That *no* two bodies are absolutely alike, is a simple corollary from
> all that has been here said. (p. 213)

The idea behind such condensation (where once again he leaves the emendations intact) is most clearly stated in the following:

> He who, divesting himself of prejudice, shall have the rare courage
> to think absolutely for himself, cannot fail to arrive, in the end,
> at the condensation of *laws* into *Law*—cannot fail of reaching the
> *conclusion that each law of Nature is dependent at all points upon all*
> *other laws,* and that all are but consequences of one primary exer-
> cise of the Divine Volition. (p. 255)

Why does Poe allow the traces of the condensing process to remain? The excessive and irritating details, the endless and always observable quantifications of many passages in *Eureka* are aimed at preserving the pendulum effect; they simulate "an act for the preservation of the coun-terbalance" (p. 253) until the fold into oneness—or in Poe's words, the "condensation of *laws* into *Law*" takes place. Since this last day has not yet arrived, the moment when all matter will contract to a point, Poe the earthbound creator can only enact the process towards the end. The "possible attempt at an impossible conception" thus becomes a route constructed with the odd turns, stops and involutions so central to Poe's tales. The story of the inconceivable journey of a narrator into his own "phraseology" is dramatized in *Eureka*—and we may suppose with the same motive.

Ever allowing for the second thought, the dregs of an idea discarded, Poe avoids the too easy rendering of the infinite. In his words, "It is the excess of suggested meaning—it is the rendering this the upper instead of the undercurrent of the theme—which turns into prose . . . the so-called poetry of the transcendentalists" (H.14:207–08). One way that Poe keeps the oft-propounded unity, "the unthought-like thoughts," the "*Spirit in itself*" an undercurrent, is by refusing to achieve it. "Unity" becomes no more than a word; the act or fact of process itself remains Poe's real point. His skilled indirectness finally places the burden of interpretation on the reader who must try (if he cares to see beyond the Poe of "vulgarity" and "fudge") to justify the imperfections and infelicities of his expression. The upper surface of a typical Poe text, to stratify his method, determines, declares exactitude upon exactitude, makes promises that exaggerate generalities into particulars so minute as to seem pedestrian. Yet in the course of reading something else emerges. Words can be "ornamented into poetry," as we recall Poe recognized (H.12:68, H.16:27), and the dash enables him to put prose to the test. . . .

. . . To present *"the thought of a thought"* or *"thoughts of thought"* (pp. 200, 203) demands an expression that mimes the effort itself, to *show* how "the conception for which we struggle" in any God-term is far different from the mere word. When Poe "purposely" gives us two versions of a "truth," an indulgence in redundancy with the apparent intent of killing the reader's interest, Poe is really working to rewrite the normal discursive prose version (the "vulgar version of the law") and substitute his own.

> Let us now adopt a more philosophical phraseology:—*Every atom, of every body, attracts every other atom, and of every other body, with a force which varies inversely as the squares of the distances between the attracting and attracted atom.*—Here, indeed, a flood of suggestion bursts upon the mind. (p. 215)

He has amplified the straightforward and concise Newtonian law made at the beginning of the paragraph: "—That all bodies attract each other with forces proportional to their quantities of matter and inversely proportional to the squares of their distances" (p. 215). Poe always argues with the givens, with those other antecedent voices ringing in his ears; he must remake. What, then, qualifies the new language of "suggestion" erected on the firm ground of the already done? Words add up into units of rhythmic recurrence to build as a series of formulae, separable parts to be once disposed, then picked up, displaced and reconstructed in other parts of the essay. We can segment Poe's more emphatic sentence as follows:

> Every atom / of every body / attracts every other atom / both of its own and of every other body

Not two pages later, Poe repeats this definition of gravity, now however, with a slight, visible change.

Let me now repeat the definition of gravity:—*Every atom, of every body, attracts every other atom, both of its own and of every other body*, with a force which varies inversely as the squares of the distances of the attracting and attracted atom. (p. 217)

His change is no more than a reduction in the italicized words. Before, apparent augmentation, now minimalization: the italicized words end after the kernel of the citation ("the cluster" in Poe's terminology). The core of the "law" is thus compressed, singled out and elevated from the prose sequence. The point is made through an appeal to observation, yet another nod to the gradual attainment of empirical knowledge ("the making of certain truths to be perceived," as Locke claims).[5] On the next page, Poe continues the crisis of elimination:[6]

Here let the reader pause with me, for a moment, in contemplation of the miraculous—of the ineffable—of the altogether unimaginable complexity of relation involved in the fact that *each atom attracts every other atom*—involved *merely* in this fact of the attraction. . . .—involved merely in the fact that each atom attracts every other atom at *all*. (pp. 217–18)

The dash leads us forward in the process of delimiting; the italics make us see the words as ideas reified. The invariable return of key words purifies and forms the language of *mereness*. Value is defined by what has been omitted. The dash draws attention to the repeating and leads in the words Poe wants emphasized as symmetrical, for example, "—involved *merely*"; "—involved merely," finally subsuming the parts into the totalizing "*all*."

Through such alternating subtraction and addition, Poe replicates in his composition the tale of the universe, its attainment of unity out of difference. Note the following queries of convertibility: "Does not one extreme impel the reason to the other? Does not the infinitude of division refer to the utterness of individuality? Does not the entireness of the complex hint at the perfection of the simple?" (p. 219). The dash usually ushers in each restatement and draws attention to its position and alignments with other words in the whole. As Poe blocks out a form to represent the unlimited, he depends upon this conspicuous exchange of extremes. In quoting his attempt to begin his discourse on divine creation, I will divide the one-sentence paragraph, his hammering question, where the dashes occur:

By Him, however—now, at least the Incomprehensible—
by Him—assuming him as *Spirit*—
that is to say, as *not Matter*—
a distinction which, for all intelligible purposes, will stand well instead of a definition—

> by Him, then, existing, as Spirit, let us content ourselves, to-night,
> with supposing to have been *created*, or made out of Nothing, by
> dint of his Volition—
> at some point of Space which we will take as a centre—
> at some period into which we do not pretend to inquire, but at all
> events immensely remote—
> by Him, then again, let us suppose to have been created—*what?*
> *What* is it alone that we are justified—
> that alone we are justified in supposing to have been, primarily and
> solely, *created?* (pp. 205–06)

Again, Poe uses the dash in conjunction with italics to embody the ritual
of exclusion he wants the reader to join. Almost uniformly, each restatement begins with the same word, and is then broken up into a
pattern that attenuates difference. The dashes, by performing the sequence of approximations (those "second-thoughts" or "emendations"),
screen the fact that the paragraph is really no more than a series of static
states, or circlings around a single word leading to a final and unanswer-
able question. The procedures toward this end force another kind of
reading than what prose ordinarily demands.[7] This emphatic play of
inversion, rhyme and parallelism must be understood as a discourse on
form. Significantly, Poe's query can be resolved into a kind of cosmic
dialogue that ends in silence. Split into an interchange between two con-
tinguous, but apparently contradictory terms or voices (matter / Spirit,
fact / thought) we might finally reduce the rumination into "*He created
what?*" and the converse, "*What created?*"

The deliberately open-ended quality of this passage operates as
coda to that prolixity leading nowhere ("*what?*"). Similarly, Joyce will
later summarize that night of catechism and star-gazing in Eccles street,
"nought nowhere nothing was reached." What we have here is an effort
at attunement, a push toward final symmetry and equalization. Let us
look at another example of how Poe collapses words into nothing and
thereby *fulfills* the "sole" assumption of his discourse—a discourse that
like the universe itself remains "in a state of *progressive collapse*"
(p. 297).

> Let us now endeavor to conceive what Matter must be, when or if,
> in its absolute extreme of *Simplicity*. Here the Reason flies at once
> to Imparticularity—to a particle—to *one* particle—a particle of *one*
> kind—of *one* character—of *one* nature—of *one* size—of one form—a
> particle, therefore, '*without* form and void'—a particle positively a
> particle at all points—a particle absolutely unique, individual, undi-
> vided. . . . (p. 207)

Poe sets us modes of repetition and phonic reduplication to convey a
tone that once made is not distinguishable from but is a part of the

subject itself. Also, the experience of this passage becomes visual proof of an earlier intuition, made by the human artist himself: "—*In the Original Unity of the First Thing lies the Secondary Cause of All Things, with the Germ of their Inevitable Annihilation*" (p. 185).

Once written, the words are neutralized and difference eliminated to call up a non-material effect. More precisely, Poe demonstrates how he makes words not say. Crossing repetition over repetition, the dash erases distinction while appearing to define. The hypnotic effect of this prose turned into incantation results from Poe's determination to move our soul, to make our "mind . . . take in, as if from afar and at one glance, a distinct conception of the *individual* Universe" (p. 199). As insistently as a refrain, his creating forces us to see that one particle "of *one* kind—of *one* character—of *one* nature—of *one* size—of one form" has *no* form at all. . . .

. . . Poe equates the "sense of the symmetrical" with the "poetical essence of the universe." And as *Eureka* nears its conclusion, he tries to give us a reason for the studied constraints of his text. The criterion of inner truth is a formal consistency; connecting truth with the technical side of writing. Poe explains: "By truth . . . we mean that perfection which is the result only of the strictest proportion and adaptation in all the poetical requisites" (H.10:72–73). The syntactic structure alone, the armature of the poem, discloses an unspoken harmony:

> . . . through the attainment of a truth, we are led to perceive a harmony where none was apparent before, we experience, at once, the true poetical effect—but this effect is referable to the harmony alone, and not in the least degree to the truth which merely served to render the harmony manifest. (H.14:29)

A clear attack on the moral sense, content, and on words themselves as bearers of meaning, Poe puts forth form as the potential for harmony. On one side, Poe equates truth with the objective, formal order ("the truth which merely served to render the harmony manifest"); and on the other, he makes absolute harmony correspond to "the true poetical effect." The obvious form that leads to the less obvious "effect" subverts our *search* for abstract truth. The dual convergence, the fact that, as Dupin says in "The Purloined Letter": "The material world abounds with very strict analogies to the immaterial," makes everything seen a passage to the unseen, the conspicuous devices of metrical art a link to the unsounding harmony of the increate. Or in Dupin's world, to the solution of the apparently insoluble crime. "What is true of *relation*—of form and quantity—is often grossly false in regard to morals" (M.3:989, 987).

Within the internally self-consistent system of *Eureka*, Poe has extended the range of analogy. "And this is the foundation of all philosophy," as Newton declared following his discovery: "*The Qualities of bodies, which admit neither intensification nor remission of degrees, and which are found to belong to all bodies within the reach of our experiments, are to be esteemed the universal qualities of all bodies whatsoever.*"[8] The "radical assumptions of this Discourse" (p. 255) Poe knows to be the revelation of poetic method. He offers us the kernel of "truth" in the fabulous letter that begins *Eureka*:

> ... investigation has been taken out of the hands of the groundmoles, and given as a duty, rather than as a task, to the true—to the *only* true thinkers—to the generally-educated men of ardent imagination. These latter—our Keplers—our Laplaces—'speculate'—'theorize'—these are the terms—can you not fancy the shout of scorn with which they would be received by our progenitors, were it possible for them to be looking over my shoulders as I write? The Keplers, I repeat, speculate—theorize—and their theories are merely corrected—reduced —sifted—cleared, little by little, of their chaff of inconsistency—until at length there stands an unencumbered *Consistency*—a consistency which the most stolid admit—because it is a consistency—to be an absolute and unquestionable *Truth*. (p. 196)

Poe again gives us the terms to apply to his own prose, his own investigation, as he praises those scientific purifiers, those who slowly correct, reduce, sift and clear their theories "of their chaff of inconsistency" (and very possibly allow the scattered chaff to remain). The content of this passage matters less than its significance as exemplum; it reenacts how one might achieve the final symmetry toward which *Eureka* ever tends. And the possibility of a symmetry both cosmic and poetic is reified in a replay some one hundred pages later that concludes *Eureka* while turning us back to its origins in fable.

> The sense of the symmetrical is the poetical essence of the *Universe*— if the Universe which, in the supremeness of its symmetry, is but the most sublime of poems. Now symmetry and consistency are convertible terms:—thus Poetry and Truth are one. A thing is consistent in the ratio of its truth—true in the ratio of its consistency. *A perfect consistency, I repeat, can be nothing but an absolute truth*. (p. 302)

In both cases, Poe reiterates through inversion and boils down the phrase to its essence. As he eliminates all words unnecessary to the final effect, convertibility, he leaves us with a "how-to" manual for writing the "pure" or "true" poem. The chiasmus, "inconsistency—... *Consistency*—a consistency.... —because it is a consistency—to be an absolute and unquestionable *Truth*," is intensified in the next crossing, "consistent in the ratio of its truth—true in the ratio of its consistency," finally leaving us with *perfect consistency = absolute truth*. Through this double-crossing Poe has both proved a theory and, as in all correct science, has arrived at truth through the experience of phenomena. The poet is the mathematician, and the *highest* order of the imaginative intellect is always preeminately mathematical, and the converse" (H.11:147). For Poe the move from idea to realization or from thing to idea is subject to endless crossings and recrossings, concretizing the convertibility that remains a sure sign of God's skill. Poe has pared down his prose representation to the essentials to emend those many "roads to Truth" (p. 195) and lead us down "the broadest, the straightest and most available of all mere roads—the great thoroughfare—the majestic highway of the *Consistent*" (p. 196).

## Notes

1. H=*The Complete Works of Edgar Allan Poe*, ed., James A. Harrison (New York, 1902). M=*Collected Works of Edgar Allan Poe*, ed., Thomas Ollive Mabbott (Cambridge, MA, 1978). O=*The Letters of Edgar Allan Poe*, ed., John Ward Ostrom (rev. ed., New York, 1966). All references cited parenthetically in the text with volume and page number.

2. Locke, *An Essay Concerning Human Understanding* [1689], ed. A. C. Fraser (New York: Dover, 1959), 3.3.10, 20.

3. Newton, *Principia*, 3, 547. See the connection between this subtle spirit and Newton's alchemy in Betty Jo Teeter Dobb's substantial investigation, *The Foundations of Newton's Alchemy or "The Hunting of the Greene Lyon"* (Cambridge, 1975), pp. 204ff.

4. I have segmented this passage to demonstrate how Poe sets up prose patterns to resolve themselves into metrical schemes.

5. Locke, *Essay*, 1.1.5, 40.

6. Mallarmé praises this crisis of elimination in his "Tombeau d'Edgar Poe": "donner un sens plus pur aux mots de la tribu." Later, in "Little Gidding," Eliot will recall, "Since our concern was speech, and speech impelled us / To purify the dialect of the tribe." Poe's attempt to present "matter unparticled" leads more directly to Mallarmé's labor, ". . . je n'ai créé mon oeuvre que par élimination," a purifying destruction that advanced him further "dans la sensation des Ténèbres absolues."

7. In *Eureka* Poe demonstrates how truth can be seized materially by a language that mimes the two tendencies of matter—dispersal and convergence. These fluctuations within the text (scansion in time or projected timeless point) embody the opposition, as we now see it, between paradigmatic and syntagmatic. As Kristeva puts it (taking us from Freud and *"le déplacement* et *la condensation"* to R. Jacobson): "La *condensation* (la métaphore) résulte de la surdétermination, tandis que le *déplacement* (la métonymie) resulte d'une censure." See Julia Kristeva, *La Révolution du langage poétique* (Paris, 1974).

8. Newton, *Principia*, 3, Rule 3, 397.

# Psychoanalysis and Edgar Allan Poe: A Critique of the Bonaparte Thesis

Roger Forclaz*

The explanation of genius in terms of medical science is particularly tempting in Poe's case. Hereditary madness, epilepsy, dipsomania and degeneracy, sexual impotence, syphilis, drug addiction, sadonecrophilia: more explanations of genius have certainly been propounded for Poe than for any other writer. Among the numerous "scientific" interpretations drawing on psychoanalysis, two deserve particular mention, those of Joseph W. Krutch[1] and of Marie Bonaparte,[2] the second being by far the more significant. Whereas Krutch merely seeks to locate the source of Poe's genius in sexual impotence and construes creative activity as a compensatory mechanism for a being who was sexually inhibited and haunted by the threat of insanity, Marie Bonaparte goes much further: she attempts to explain art with the aid of Freudian theories and to interpret Poe's work in the light of psychoanalysis; she purports to elucidate deep-seated sources of Poe's genius and of creative imagination in general, showing how a literary work is rooted in the depths of a writer's personality. The detailed demonstration of a coherent thesis (apparently at least) seems so convincing that it has led many readers to believe that psychoanalysis provides the key to Poe's personality and work. In 1933 the distinguished man of letters Edmund Jaloux went so far as to hail Marie Bonaparte's book as "the most important critical work which has been written in France on Poe."[3] The fact that it has been translated not only into English but into German and into Italian as well seems to confirm this view.[4]

According to Bonaparte, Poe's art is the product of neurosis: Poe was a "repressed sado-masochist and necrophilist" (299); art was a "safety-valve" for his repressed instincts; if he had not possessed the literary genius which enabled him to sublimate his dangerous impulses in art, he might conceivably have spent part of his life in prison or the madhouse (209). He claimed to write horror tales because it was the fashion of the day, but he was actually a madman dominated by a cruel psyche, and dark forces ruled his inspiration (96). Because his work reflects the phantasies of his unconscious, its only interest lies in its autobiographical significance. "Metzengerstein," a retelling of the legend of the Wild Huntsman, becomes a phantasy of reunion with the mother

*This essay, especially prepared for this volume and published here for the first time, is a condensed adaptation of a two-part essay in French that appeared in *Revue des langues vivantes / Tijdschrift voor levende talen* 36, no. 3 (1970):272–88; 36, no. 4:375–89.

in death (280). Tales as different as "MS. Found in a Bottle"—based on the legend of the Flying Dutchman—"A Descent into the Maelström," "The Unparalleled Adventure of One Hans Pfaall," and "The Pit and the Pendulum" are actually phantasies of a return to the womb (352, 369, 584–86).

But Marie Bonaparte's study proceeds less from a true scientific spirit than from an exaggerated confidence in science and from a desire to explain everything "scientifically." A system that pretends to explain literature only by means of the unconscious and of early childhood, without taking into account literary movements or the intellectual climate of an era or of a country, can hardly be called scientific. According to Bonaparte, Elizabeth Arnold's death in 1811 was the leading influence on Poe's genius; neurosis and the Oedipus complex are sufficient to account for it. It is no accident, however, that Poe's tales deal with themes similar to the dramatic roles played by his mother thirty years earlier; both were influenced by the public taste and the romantic atmosphere. It is obviously impossible to account for the creative activity of an artist solely by reference to sexuality and the Oedipus complex. Since Marie Bonaparte's book, scientists have recognized that the reduction of art to neurosis does not stand on safe ground. William Phillips, for instance, states that "any total approach to art that sees the creative gift or process as a form of neurosis is bound to produce a lopsided and absurd theory."[5]

Marie Bonaparte is unable, in fact, to explain the nature of genius and the mechanism of creative activity: she confesses her helplessness when she speaks of a "mysterious gift" escaping the investigation of the psychoanalyst (664). She nevertheless attributes the same function to the work of art and to dreams, that of a safety valve for repressed instincts, even though she admits that there is a fundamental difference between them: the work of art is distinguished from the dream by its social value. Art has a cathartic function: the artists are among the elect because their function is "to bring about, in others, the *catharsis* of their repressed instincts"; thanks to a mysterious gift, certain men have the power to clothe these daydreams and fictive instinctual gratifications in forms which allow others, too, to dream their dreams with them (664, 697). The work of art is thus simply a "wish-phantasy" which is subject to the same prohibitions as the dream, because the secret desires expressed are not only externally thwarted, but also condemned by conscience: Poe would never, in fact, be able to gratify the murderous, sadistic urges he expresses in "The Black Cat" (667). Literary creation was for him a fictive gratification of instincts which cannot be satisfied in real life. This theory of the cathartic function of art is obviously at variance with Bonaparte's fundamental thesis, which considers Poe's work as the product of neurosis: Poe would have been a criminal if he had not been able to sublimate his dangerous impulses in his tales. Is the key to Poe's genius his abnormality or is it rather that "mysterious gift" which enables the artist to give expression to sadistic or other instincts lying dormant in man's heart?

In likening the creative process to dreaming, Marie Bonaparte completely overlooks the role of conscious thought in creation. She holds that Poe, like all writers, wrote what his unconscious dictated (135). But this theory is contradicted by Poe's frequent use of sources. Is it legitimate to speak of "psychic determination" when such borrowings occur for three-fourths of Poe's fictional work? Bonaparte thus attributes a symbolic value to such a detail as the hermetically closed room in "The Murders in the Rue Morgue": it is a symbol of woman and of her sexual organs (454, 656). But Poe found this detail in a story of Sheridan Le Fanu,[6] and it is one of the conventions of detective novels, from Gaston Leroux's *Mystery of the Yellow Chamber* to Ellery Queen's *A Room to Die In*. The internal necessities of the tale—the creation of a problem apparently insoluble—are in fact quite sufficient to account for Poe's choice of setting.

The negation of the role of conscious thought is particularly hard to maintain in the case of Poe, who was, more than most writers, a conscious artist. According to Bonaparte, Poe's esthetic theories are a rationalization *a posteriori*; the *Preface* of 1840 reveals Poe's deliberately literary attitude toward his "gloom": he pretends to be able to choose his subjects at will, but this was what he was never able to do (96). The following year, however, Poe approached two new genres, quite unlike those he had previously cultivated, the detective story and the "landscape sketch." The tales he published in 1841—"The Murders in the Rue Morgue," "A Descent into the Maelström," "The Colloquy of Monos and Una," "The Island of the Fay," "Never Bet the Devil Your Head" and "Eleonora"—are totally different from one another as well as from those he had written before, thus corroborating his defense, in the *Preface* of 1840, against the accusation of "Germanism": "Tomorrow I may be anything but German, as yesterday I was everything else."[7] Bonaparte invokes Poe's famous words about the "terror of the soul" in support of her theory; she interprets them as being a confession slipping from the writer's pen. Needless to say, Poe's real meaning is quite different: he contrasts the stories creating a pseudo-horror, including all the paraphernalia of the Gothic novel, with those in which terror is deduced from its "legitimate sources" and urged to its "legitimate results"; with a single exception—which is obviously "Metzengerstein"—his tales belong to the latter category.[8]

Marie Bonaparte's thesis is also contradicted by the fact that, far from obeying an imperious necessity, Poe began his career as a tale-writer by writing parodies of the fiction then in vogue, which he planned to publish in book form under the title "Tales of the Folio Club." Nor does her thesis take into account the numerous revisions of the tales. A case in point is "Loss of Breath," which is read by her as a confession of Poe's sexual impotence; the suppression of the hanging episode in the last version is attributed to the fact that it revealed the latent meaning of the tale (373 ff., 401). But the first version had actually been written in 1832, and the hanging episode was added in 1835, when Poe expanded his tale in order to make of it a satire of the "extravagancies" of *Blackwood's*, as he pointed out in a letter to Kennedy.[9] The version of 1835 was thus not the first one, a fact which contradicts the theory of the "first draft" as revealing Poe's unconscious.

The most outstanding example of distortion of reality occurs in Marie Bonaparte's interpretation of "The Mystery of Marie Roget," a tale in which Poe tried to unravel the enigma of the murder of Mary Rogers. According to her, the tale was inspired by Virginia's hemorrhages and by Poe's "fugue" to New York City, where Mary Starr, his former sweetheart, lived. She completely disregards the writer's references to the murder of Mary Rogers in the tale and in the footnotes, and she even takes the trouble of propounding a far-fetched interpretation of the epigraph—where a parallel is drawn between the real murder and the fictitious one—in support of her theory. According to her, the nightmare of rape and murder must have been dreamed by Poe during his half-crazed wanderings in the woods surrounding Jersey City (448–51). Why, then, did Poe write such a rambling, inconclusive story, so utterly unlike his masterpieces and unworthy of his genius? Reality is quite different from Marie Bonaparte's thesis: the trip to New York City actually took place at the end of June 1842, whereas the tale was finished a month before, as we learn from two letters Poe wrote to Roberts and to Snodgrass, to whom he offered his story, telling them he was convinced he had discovered the truth (*Letters*, 1:200–2).

One of the main defects of this allegedly scientific method is the use of Poe's work as the primary source of information about the writer. Bonaparte starts from the preconceived notion that the writing is the product of the abnormality of the author. It is begging the question to use Poe's work, as she does, in order to demonstrate a thesis which should have been established in the first place; it is the only source for many of the psychoanalyst's "facts": its testimony is adduced as a proof of Poe's necrophilia, sexual impotence, and sadism. Bonaparte's argument is not free from contradictions, however: the purity of Poe's works is for her an incontrovertible proof of the author's impotence (373); but elsewhere we are told that all his works show that Poe was a potential sadonecrophilist (103). This testimony is, however, not so convincing after all, as we are also told that those who commended the purity of his works did not suspect that Poe's own total chastity was doubtless all that held Poe back from enacting the tragic events described in "The Black Cat" (87).

In view of such contradictions, is it possible to take seriously the psychoanalyst's theories? The same contradictions occur in the interpretation of *Eureka*: this work is presented as "the flight from and, repudiation of, woman" (596) and a "cosmic homosexual phantasy" (636), but also as a "Poesque phantasy of reunion with the lost Mother in death" (631) and a "womb-phantasy" (634). We are told that in extreme deference to the fiats of morality, Poe avoided the Mother—and Woman—and ended his literary career on that "cosmic, homosexual phantasy" (636); but the psychoanalyst has obviously forgotten "Annabel Lee," written a year later, which she considers as "a true necrophilist phantasy" (130).

The explanation proposed for Poe's personality is characterized by the same contradictions: Marie Bonaparte simultaneously assumes a deficient adherence to the Oedipus complex—necrophilia—and a too strong adherence to it—sadomasochism—which is impossible since it contradicts the distinction established between the two types of fixation (685 ff.). But she proposes another formula in her interpretation of *Eureka*, thanatophilia, and identifies Poe's "repulsion" with libido; to Poe's unconscious, union with the loved object would have been equated with death, and repulsion should be interpreted as the avoidance of women and all love-objects (625–26). Such a theory is hard to reconcile with what he are told about Poe's "dire sado-necrophilist sexuality": alcohol was for him a means of flight from the temptations aroused by his dire sexuality; not without reason did he flee in horror from all sexual commerce with women; unconsciously, he sensed the danger that the sex act would release his sadonecrophilia (87–88). Elsewhere, "The Pit and the Pendulum" is presented as a testimony of the bisexuality of Poe, who "always flung back from his ecstatic attraction towards women to libidinal subjection to the male," against which "the male in him constantly rebelled" (592).

From this point of view, Poe's sexuality may take any possible form: sadonecrophilia, mother-fixation, erotic aggression, revolt against the father, passivity towards the father, and even father-fixation caused by a reversal of libido towards the father when an erotic Oedipal impulse is thwarted. This phenomenon is explained by "our inherent primary bisexuality" (634), held to be particularly strong in Poe's case; his sexual instinct is thus seen as both intense and congenitally unstable (636).

The "scientific" value of this explanation of Poe's personality is indeed questionable; the fomulas presented to us are irreconcilable and cancel one another. If Poe was sexually impotent, he could not at the same time have been a sadonecrophilist, or at least his sadonecrophilist sexuality was repressed and did not attempt to rise to the surface. How could a man inhibited by the castration threat—a threat alleged to be the source of his recoil from sexuality—still need art as a safety valve? If his sexuality was inhibited, as Bonaparte claims, how could Poe still be obliged to flee the temptations and dangerous impulses arising from it?

The most characteristic feature of Marie Bonaparte's study lies in the method used to prove her thesis and to decipher the hidden meaning of Poe's work. According to her, a literary work is a kind of "two-part song," with a manifestly coherent story on the surface and, intertwined with it, another and secret story which is the secret theme and which does not obey the rules of logic (352, 584, 654). No explanation is given for the passage from one to the other; the psychoanalyst merely speaks of "secondary elaboration" by which the dream is subjected to the censorship of logic and criticism (663). This process sometimes occurs at a later stage: when Poe revised his tales, he occasionally eliminated passages revealing their latent meaning (274). Bonaparte cares neither for the artistic value of a story nor for its obvious contents, nor for the chronological order in which the tales were written; her only concern is to penetrate the "hidden meaning" of Poe's work. But the chief characteristic of her method is that it enables her to claim any proof she wants to claim. There are so many possibilities, either for the representation of an idea or for the expression of logical relationships, that it would be difficult indeed for Marie Bonaparte not to be able to demonstrate her thesis; for the hopeless cases, she can always resort to the "missing link"! Where symbolic figuration is concerned, the possible representations are endlessly various. Thus, the mother can be represented by an animal, by the elements, by buildings or parts of buildings, and so forth. It even happens, thanks to the process of splitting, that a person is represented by several symbols, as in "The Black Cat," where the mother is represented by the narrator's wife, the two cats, the house and the basement; in *The Narrative of Arthur Gordon Pym* we even find her "split up on every page and attached to all objects in nature" (650–52). Conversely, through the process of condensation, the same symbol may express different things; the strange character described in "The Angel of the Odd" is simultaneously mother and father (649)!

This diversity also occurs for the expression of logical relationships: as contradictions never disturb the unconscious, the universe of *Eureka* can be both the son and the mother. Likewise, the fact that negation does not exist for the unconscious permits the suppression of the concept of contraries; a symbol can thus express two opposite ideas: in "Loss of Breath" and in "The Black Cat," the theme of hanging simultaneously represents virility and its negation (629, 656–57). Conversely, one and the same thing can be expressed in two opposite ways: the desire for the father's death is expressed directly in "The Tell-Tale Heart," but elsewhere by its opposite, as in "The Man of the Crowd," where the father is condemned to wander eternally instead of being condemned to death, or in "The Facts in the Case of M. Valdemar," where, through "hypocrisy in the unconscious," this desire masks itself as its contrary, the desire to keep the father perpetually alive (425, 570, 658). A wish-phantasy can likewise be expressed by a real situation being inverted to its opposite: in "Valdemar," the father is represented as subject to the son, a situation reflecting Poe's desire that his passivity towards his father in real life should be reversed; in this case, the tale openly expresses its unconscious intent and the son keeps his father alive the better to kill him (658). What then becomes of the hypocrisy in the unconscious?

The possibilities for the application of the process of reversal are thus so varied that Marie Bonaparte herself becomes lost among them; she so frequently resorts to this device that it is not surprising to see so many demonstrations brought to a successful conclusion: the variations are so numerous that the decision is won beforehand, regardless of the contents of the tale. Something can thus be represented by its opposite, as in "The Man of the Crowd," where the solitude of the primitive "crime" is replaced by the crowd and the multiplicity of women; elsewhere, a "turning inside out" occurs, with the contents substituted for the receptacle: in "The Murders in the Rue Morgue," the woman is represented as inside that which, in effect, is inside her (425, 656). But we must not forget the reversal of affect: sometimes a tragic affect is transformed into a comic one, as in "Loss of Breath," where Poe's impotence is expressed by the loss of breath and by the motif of hanging; sometimes a phantasy is expressed by the negative sign of anxiety, as in "The Black Cat," where the memory of hours spent in early childhood in the mother's bed returns in the form of anxiety when the narrator awakens with the cat upon his chest, or in "The Pit and the Pendulum," where the wish-phantasy to possess the mother in intracloacal fashion and the passive wish-phantasy towards the father are expressed by the negative sign of anxiety (476–77, 661–62). Once they have been repressed, the mighty and primal wish-affects, we are told, cannot again emerge save as painfully charged anxiety, and the overwhelming anxiety with which all Poe's greatest tales are charged issues exclusively from this source (662–63).

But there are, according to Marie Bonaparte, other sources of anxiety in Poe's tales: the unsatisfied libido of the infant brought about by the barrier of incest—a libido which has been converted into that anxiety from which Poe's tales draw their sustenance and which inspires the convulsions of the "incestuous" Metzengerstein (282)—or the castration fear, which is the central theme of "The Black Cat" and of "The Pit and the Pendulum." In the first, all the primitive anxieties of the child seem to be gathered, as though to express the utmost extreme of anxiety, those of birth, separation, castration, conscience and death ((481–82), whereas

the second "faithfully and biographically records Poe's bisexual oscilla-
tions between his male and his female trends," trends which always
encounter the castration threat as an insurmountable obstacle (592).
These interpretations are at variance with the thesis about the surging of
wish-affects with the negative sign of anxiety.

The principle of suppression of contradictions is indeed one of the
cardinal principles of Marie Bonaparte's book; otherwise, many ingenious
interpretations would not have been possible. Yet one can hardly claim
that Freudianism provides the key to Poe's personality and work when
so many contradictory theories and conflicting interpretations are proposed. Poe's work does have a psychological dimension that can be
explored and clarified by means of Jungian depth psychology, but Bonaparte's use of Freudian theories has created a mythical image of Poe
that does not at all correspond with reality, and her use of "science" has
not explained Poe's genius. Like those of other pseudo-scientific critics
before her, Marie Bonaparte's enterprise can best be summed up in
Rousseau's words quoted by Poe: *"de nier ce qui est et d'expliquer ce qui-
n'est pas"* (to negate that which is and to explain that which is not).[10]


## Notes

1. *Edgar Allan Poe: A Study in Genius* (New York: Alfred A. Knopf, 1926).

2. *Edgar Poe: Sa vie—son oeuvre: Etude analytique* (Paris: Denoël & Steele,
1933). New edition: Paris: Presses Universitaires de France, 1958.

3. *Nouvelles Littéraires* 571 (23 September 1933):3.

4. *Edgar Poe: Eine psychoanalytische Studie.* Uebersetzung aus dem Franzö-
sischen von Fritz Lehner. (Wien: Internationaler Psychoanalytischer Verlage, 1934).
*The Life and Works of Edgar Allan Poe: A Psycho-Analytic Interpretation*, trans.
John Rodker (London: Imago Publishing Co., 1949). London: The Hogarth Press,
1949. Reprint: New York: Humanities Press, 1971; *Edgar Allan Poe: Studio psican-
alitico* (Roma: Newton Compton Editori, 1976); References in the text are to the
London 1949 edition.

5. William Phillips, ed., *Art and Psychoanalysis: Studies in the Application of
Psychoanalytical Theory to the Creative Process* (Cleveland and New York: Meridian
Books World Publishing Corp., 1963), xvi.

6. Cf. Patrick Diskin, "Poe, Le Fanu, and the Sealed Room Mystery," *Notes
and Queries* 13, no. 9 (1966):337–39.

7. *Tales of the Grotesque and Arabesque* (Philadelphia: Lea & Blanchard,
1840), 6.

8. "With a single exception, there is no one of these stories in which the
scholar should recognise the distinctive features of that species of pseudo-horror
which we are taught to call Germanic.... If in many of my productions terror
has been the thesis, I maintain that terror is not of Germany, but of the soul,—
that I have deduced this terror only from its legitimate sources, and urged it only
to its legitimate results," ibid.

9. Cf. J. W. Ostrom, ed., *The Letters of Edgar Allan Poe* vol. 1 (Cambridge, Mass.: Harvard University Press, 1948), 84.

10. T. O. Mabbott, ed., *Collected Works of Edgar Allan Poe*, vol. 2 (Cambridge, Mass.: Belknap Press of Harvard University Press, 1969–1978), 568. Edgar Allan Poe, *Essays and Reviews* (New York: The Library of America, 1984), 357, 1303. The phrase comes from Part 6, Letter xi (second footnote) of Rousseau's *La Nouvelle Héloïse.*

# The Heart of Poe and the Rhythmics of the Poems
### Claude Richard*

When the individual heart has stopped beating, when the obsessive *cadence*[1] which haunts both the conscious and the narrative prose of characters and narrators in the "Tell-Tale Heart" or "The Fall of the House of Usher" has been silenced, when "the pulses [are] still,"[2] Monos begins to perceive "a feeling [which] took no root in the pulseless heart" (4:209).

That feeling, however, and the "purely sensual pleasure" into which it dissolves announce the progressive perception of another kind of *rhythm*—essential or cosmic—which no longer has reference to the senses and the perceptions of the body—even the dead body. The emergence of this rhythm is allowed by the fading away of the bodily cadence ("no artery throbbed"), leaving room for another inconceivable or unutterable kind of "pulsation": "But there seemed to have sprung up in the brain, *that* of which no words could convey to the merely human intelligence even an indistinct conception. Let me term it a mental pendulous pulsation" (all 4:209).

Those two pulsations—the throbbing of the heart and the essential, cosmic rhythm—contend for supremacy in Poe's work, in a metaphysical conflict of forces seeking to establish hegemony not on the subject as psychological entity but on his poetic utterance, therefore seeking to found the legitimacy of poetry on a rhythmical concept.

The beating heart is the individual heart, the physical organ (of emotion) often neurotically projected as an externality (Madeline, the old man). The heart of the hallucinatory other beating audibly in an externalized space spells the cadence of horror and madness: "here! here! it is the beating of his hideous heart!" (5:94) shrieks the narrator of the "Tell-Tale Heart." Usher, in his madness, has never ceased hearing "the heavy and horrible beat of [Madeline's] heart" (3:296).

*This essay was written specifically for this volume and is published here for the first time by permission of the author.

Thus the specific cadence of a heart beating in a phantasmagorically externalized space (in the vault, under the planks) incarnates in sounds the threat of madness, while the silent pulsation of God's heart cannot, in essence, be perceived by the senses.

Since the beating of God's heart is creative of Time (which the poetic consciousness inhabits), it cannot be perceived sensually as a cadence by an external ear and thus it belongs to the Platonic realm of the intelligible or, in Poe's metaphysical mythology, to the progressive awareness of the dead body which, in some tales such as "Mesmeric Revelation," is metamorphosed or rarefied into what may be called a metaphysical subject. This soundless essential rhythm is thus assimilated to the *silent* "music of the spheres" ("Al Aaraaf," I, 125)—whether Platonic (16:163) or Keplerian (*Eureka*), a *"mousikē"* which constitutes "an all-sufficient education for the soul!" (4:204).

Thus two voices can be heard in Poe's poetry: on the one hand the voice of the angel Israfel, which—since it proceeds from a fleshless, incorporeal body—is in rhythmical coincidence with the harmonious pulsations of the cosmos; on the other hand, the human voice uttering "a mortal melody," a melody under the sway of the vital cadence of the heart which can sing nothing but paltry mortality.

## "THE HELLISH TATTOO"

### The Organic Heart

Tamerlane, Poe's first hero, sings the raving complaint of him who has been vanquished by the *tyranny of the heart*: "O yearning heart" (15), "O craving heart" (21). The oral confession is a rhetorical means of understanding the devastation brought by the passionate heart. In Poe's early work, passion almost always results in a fall. Passion "withers" (16). Loss—of woman (Ada), of innocence and of the type of knowledge it allows—comes from the passions of the heart. In a "Halo of Hell" (19), the heart deprives the grown-up child of the Platonic understanding of essences through memory (*Eureka*, 16:312).

Passion grows with life, shrinking the space of poetic knowledge, and favoring the "tyranny" (66) of a strange adult voice that "swells . . . the battle cry of victory . . ." ("Tamerlane," 51–54). The tyranny of the heart, signified by the overbearing presence of its pulse, progressively destroys the feeling of Love ("as in infancy was mine," 87–88) which leads man to the recognition of "the Beautiful" (*"to kalon,"* 11:71). Emotional cadences and the rhythms of "supernal Loveliness" (14:274) exclude each other: the desire for beauty, the thirst for "the beam of loveliness," that is, poetry as tendency or "thirst" (14:273) is what makes the nature of angels (the earthly poet is a bastardized angel).

Poe has repeatedly, poignantly, argued that "poetry and passion are

discordant" (11:285) or, to use different vehicles for the central metaphor of his theory of poetry that "poetry has nothing to do [...] with
*the heart*" (13:131). As late as 1846 he was desperately pleading for the
exclusion of passion from the realm of poetry—a necessary exclusion
which had been one of the major themes of his "grand" and "impover-
ished" poetry.[3] "Grand" because "impoverished"? By a disciplinarian of
purity? A purity he conceived in phonological terms and which he often
turned into the self-reflective topic of his poetry.

"Stanzas" strives to express in terms of the personal myth of Poe's
epistemological poetry the havoc played by the heart in the realm of
poetic imagination: questioned "in youth" by the spirit, "the Earth"
yields a reply which leads to communion ("secret communing," 2). With
age, however, the ontological status of "that object" changes: it becomes
a mere "symbol [or] token" (24) and its function in the cognitive dialogue between the poetic mind and "outer reality" has changed from
an epiphanic, revelatory potentiality to a negative or perhaps simply
dissuasive role: "giv'n . . . to those who *otherwise* would fall . . . *Drawn
by their Heart's passion*" (27–28. Italics mine).

The sign—or the symbol-as-presence—can no longer herald another
presence to come. It can at best perform—in adulthood—a negative function of protection against the onslaught of the heart and its blinding,
deafening passions.

The dissuasive sign or symbol, the left-over token of a lost fusion
of subject and object, can do no more than *prevent* damnation, postpone
the inevitable Fall—the Fall of the poetic spirit in the bogs of the Babylon of the heart (the scarlet beast by the tarn offering "the wine of her
impure passion" [Revelation 18:3]). Abandon—the despised "Shelleyan
abandon"—is mainly abandon of the poet to his heart. For Poe, poetic
discipline has to do mainly with keeping emotionality in check.

When God's voice is heard in "Al Aaraaf" (I, 132–50), his message,
entrusted to Nesace, the word-bearer—is primarily inhibitive. "Be," orders
the God of Poetry to Nesace, "To ev'ry heart a barrier and a ban" (I,
149–50). Nesace's voice raises an interdiction—like the sign or the symbol
—in order to counteract the destructive effects of "the heart." Angelo and
Ianthe, lovers not even in the flesh, cannot hear the voice of Nesace
embodied in Ligeia's song. They will be damned: "Heaven no grace
imparts to those who hear not for their beating hearts" (II, 176–77).
The cause of the Fall ("They fell," II, 263) is not so much "passionate
love" (II, 230) as the actual deafening sound ("them . . . who hear not")
of "the beating of their hearts" (II, 264).

What is crucial to grasp is that the damnation is not a metaphysical
damnation of "passionate" man but the downfall of the artist: "I have
imagined some well known characters of the age of the stars' appearance, as transferred to Al Aaraaf—viz Michael Angelo...."[4] The wages

of the heart's passion are the loss of *poetic* grace, that is, the definitive blurring of the glorious vistas opening up on a perpetually desired and perpetually lost "Eden." The cadence of a living heart deafens the poet who can no longer perceive the sublime "echoes" which are the soul of true poetry (*infra*).

"Waking life" ("Dreams") is hauntingly scanned by the "chaos" of the cadence of "deep passion" (6–9). The conflict now is between chaotic living cadences, such as "the hellish tatoo" of the old man's heart and a cognitive dream ("The summer dream beneath the tamarind tree," in "Sonnet to Science," 14) always dispelled by the sonorous insistence of the organic cadence of life.

The irreducible signifier of the presence of life, the "tattoo" of blood, implies, in Poe's intricate narrative strategies, that the language of madmen, perverts, and fetishists (often his narrators) beats according to the clock-like cadence of a heart. This alienating power of the cadence of emotional hallucination Poe that theorized with astonishing insight under the name of "the force of monotone" ("The Philosophy of Composition," 14:199).

*"The Force of Monotone"*

"The Raven" is, first and foremost, a narrative. To the plot of his poem, Poe applies the devices of first-person narrative successfully used in "The Gold Bug"[5] and "The Tell-Tale Heart." The poem rests on a twofold effect of monotony which is primarily evocative of the state of the narrator's mind: the monotony of semantic repetition (refrain) and the monotony of prosodic repetition (cadence). The "effect" produced—and there is no need to recall here Poe's theory of "effect"—is primarily an effect of inescapable *sameness*, the function of which is better understood through the narrative situation which imposes as a structuring device "a monotone of sound" (14:199). The narrating narrator of "The Raven" is primarily "a student" (14:206–7), steeped in "curious forgotten lore." In the midst of his speculative reading he receives a non-verbalized message ("a tapping"), a "noise" ("rapping") which allows all interpretations as to its origin ("visitor," "phantom"). When, in the course of the "dialogue," the noise assumes verbal shape ("Nevermore," stanza 8), the question the narrator fatally raises is the question of sense: "its answer little *meaning* . . . bore" (st. 8) (emphasis mine).

At once the story becomes the story *of the meaning of a word* for a specified individual and the student progressively moves from an amused skepticism as to the possibility of meaning to a vaguely worried suspicion that sense might be lurking behind the word: "what this bird . . . *meant* in croaking 'Nevermore'" (st. 12). This psychodrama of reading therefore consists in the ways through which the addressee will grant meaning to the signifier.

"The Raven" therefore illustrates, in a way which should be familiar to readers of the staccato prose of the narrator of "The Tell-Tale Heart," the fettering of poetic language by the repetitive cadence of the primitive emotion of blood stirring: the narrator qua narrator can now only deplore mechanically the loss of the inspiring poetic object (Lenore) and thus is deprived by his own tongue of the thirst for and aspiration towards supernal beauty.

One must therefore assert finally that there is in Poe, a spontaneous hate for the *sounds* of life, mainly, as could be expected, for the sounds of the body (for Poe, there are, obviously sounds of the soul, however muffled, if sonorous at all). The vital cadence of the body perturbs the superior values Poe looks up to—"the ideal," "beauty," "poesy."

The destructive violence of the cadence of life has to do with the silencing of the secret rhythms perceived in the tomb—the rhythm of "deathness"—so that two main types of enunciative situations determine the quality of Poe's poems: on the one hand narrative poems told by a living voice dominated by the living cadence of the heart ("these were days when my heart was volcanic," "Ulalume," 13) and thus unable to suggest the spiritual harmony of pure poetry; on the other hand, poems in which, though these may also be narrative, *incorporeal* voices (properly speaking, ethereal, see *infra*) strive towards the expression of *mousiké*—a rhythmical presence which is not necessarily musical.

The obstacle to the spiritualisation of poetry is "the hellish tattoo" of the heart, the insistence of the palpitating body whose haunting recurrent beat dispels the elusive harmony of "etherealized" (both rarefied and celestial) bodies and keeps the vibrations of the strings of the lute from being heard.

## THE "LUTE'S WELL-TUNED LAW"

### From Drums to Lyre

In "Romance," Poe celebrates the myth of the education of a poet: the child who received his first lessons from the spirit of romance ("taught me my alphabet") has been granted a language ("my earliest word"). "Of late," however, the years of adulthood prey ("condor years") on the poetic soul; its capacity for vision and expression shrinks to few "hour[s] with calmer wings." They are the rare moments when the heart and the primary poetic rhythm vibrate coincidentally in a harmony generated by the vibration (as opposed to a beat) of stringed instruments: the lyre of "Romance"; the lute of "The Haunted Palace," "Israfel," the epigraph of "The Fall of the House of Usher," and the harp of "The Poetic Principle."

In those privileged moments ("that little time with lyre," 18), the human poet is similar to the Koranic angel, "whose heart-*strings* are a lute" ("Israfel," italics mine). The coincidental vibrations of the heart and the strings produce a *rhythmics of truth* which it would be aesthetic sin to abandon in favor of any other pretendedly artistic activity: "My heart would feel to be a crime / Unless it trembled *with* the strings" ("Romance").

True poetry is generated by a vibration of strings, of fibers, that is, by a movement of the heart which is foreign to its beating. Or, to follow Poe's paradoxical imagination, poetry should be the product of a bodiless, fleshless heart, a heart reduced to its undulatory waves of being.

But the fact is that this almost abstract (in the sense that a wave is bodiless) vibration assumes revelatory value in Poe's poetry: it is, properly speaking, a rhythm, that is, a constantly displaced co-occurrence of subject and object through expectation, prevision, and surprise (Paul Valéry in *Cahiers, passim*). This mute rhythm allows a type of nonverbal communication with the intimate nature of things (with matter, pulsing through eternal time) and with the "secret" dynamic nature of the cosmos.

The nature of this bodiless heart is made explicit in "Mesmeric Revelation" in a passage describing the poetic essence of a nonorganic theory of knowledge.

> V. Yes; organs are contrivances by which the individual is brought into sensible relation with particular classes and forms of matter, to the exclusion of other classes and forms. . . . A luminous body imparts vibrations to the luminiferous ether. The vibrations generate similar ones to the optic nerve. The nerve conveys similar ones to the brain; the brain also, similar ones to the unparticled matter which permeates it. The motion of this latter is thought, of which perception is the first undulation. But in the ultimate, unorganized life, the external world reaches the whole body, (which is of a substance having affinity to brain, as I have said,) with no other intervention than that of an infinitely rarer ether than even the luminiferous; and to this ether—in unison with it—the whole body vibrates, setting in motion the unparticled matter which permeates it. (5:251)

Thus a hierarchy of vibrations, from the (most revelatory) vibrations issued by "the luminous body" to the vibrations of unparticled matter (a striking epistemological oxymoron), allows communication by coincidence of tempo between the self as vibrating subject and the world as vibrating object. What stands between man and knowledge is "organic" life and "it is to the absence of idiosyncratic organs, therefore, that we must attribute the nearly unlimited perception of the ultimate life" (5:251). Poetic "effect" is achieved in the rhythmical emergence of this vibratory coincidence.

The vibration of Israfel's heart, a nonphysical organ, expresses the uncanny joy of this coincidental vibration: the strings of his angelic heart are nonmaterial (or made of unparticled matter). They are vibratory thought, immaterial but manifest, like a voice (coming from the body but bodiless): "whose *heart strings* are a lute *and* has the sweetest *voice*" (epigraph; emphasis mine). This voice has magical effect ("the spell of this voice"), an effect which does not belong to rational or verbal communication. It harmonizes the cosmic choir of things. The stars, the moon, the Pleiads—including the "Lost Pleiad" ("which were seven,"), restored to life by the spell of the voice—are organized into a "starry choir" as they "listen" to "the trembling wire" which is the true life of poetry: "the trembling *living* wire" (3rd st.; italics mine).

That is the pure poetic passion—the vibration of the heart of angelic beings—because their nature bears no trace of palpitating humanity. The passion of the angelic voice is the poetic "law of the lute" nostalgically referred to by Roderick Usher.

"The Haunted Palace" is Usher's work and must be studied within the frame of the narrative situation where it originates. As a specimen of Usher's art it exhibits both his madness ("a full consciousness . . . of the tottering of his lofty reason upon her throne," [3:284]) and his perverted conception of art: thus "The Haunted Palace" tells, in heavy *allegorical* terms, of the ending of "the lute's well-tuned law." "Once . . . in the olden time long ago," the mind and the body of man "moved musically" (st. 3) in harmony with the law of the lute. Then poetry—the sound of stringed instruments—produced "a troop of Echoes" (st. 4)— "the august and soul-exalting echo" (10:66) Poe is looking for in the highest spiritual art of Shelley and de la Motte Fouqué. Those echoes of supernal beauty "sing in voices of surpassing beauty . . ." (32). Literally "surpassing": the beauty of the vibrating voice consists exclusively in its capacity to pass beyond "mortal melody" ("Israfel," 49). Usher's madness—the madness of the artist—is here expressed by the rise of a "melody" in the very heart of an echo-producing harmony: "now . . . vast forms . . . move fantastically to a discordant *melody*" (43–44). The "lute's well-tuned law" appears now as the law of a tone, of a pitch, of a nonverbalized signifier while the discordance of melody betrays itself by the abundance of words: "a hideous throng rush out" (47) through his pale lips.

Thus the true presence of "poesy" in sounds is implicitly associated with the reduction of vocalising effects and the rise of what Poe has named, with underestimated accuracy, "the rhythmical creation of Beauty."

### "The Rhythmical Creation of Beauty"

The creation of beauty is the only explicit aim of Poe's poetry: it requires, for the poet, a state of mind and body which can perhaps be best described as an arduously obtained detachment from the fetters of life.

"For Annie" evokes that privileged poetic state. It comes to being after "the fever called 'Living'" has subsided; the narrator, in a state resembling death ("any beholder might fancy me dead," 15–16), is no longer inhabited by the sounds and cadences that deafened man: "The moaning and groaning, / The sighing and sobbing are quieted now." The poet may reach this ephemeral poetic state only when all passion has been spent, when "that torture the worst has abated—the terrible torture of thirst / For the naphtaline river of Passion accurst."

Then, but then only, can the poet hope to quench his thirst: from stanza 10 ("For *now*....") to stanza 15 ("But my *heart*....") the poem blossoms into sensorial correspondences which purify the subject-object relationships by erasing all traces of passion. "The holier odor" (62) and dream emerge as the true epistemological approaches to the truth ("the dream of truth," 69). Freed from the fetters of passionate cadence, the poetic body whose flesh has been quieted or dispelled is now literally lit up:

"But my heart is *brighter*. . . .
For it *sparkles* with Annie
It glows with the *light*
        Of the love of my Annie" (95–100, italics mine).

The poetic heart, the "heart of hearts" of "To My Mother," is this disincarnate organ capable of absorbing light. To be imbued with light in the very texture of the material fibers of being, to be affected by the signifier of the *rhythm of light*, bears witness to the rise of that state in which the poet may be traversed by a kind of truth not susceptible of being enclosed or expressed by signs:

And *rays of truth* you *cannot see*
Are flashing thro' Eternity—
        ("Tamerlane," 228–29. Italics mine.)
And rays from God shot down that meteor chain
And hallowed all the beauty twice again
        ("Al Aaraaf," II, 25).

Light—the nonsemantic signifier, the pure message containing the totality of language, the transparent cipher of truth—brings into Poe's poetry a grace beyond meaning which may be regarded as the essence of poetic grace. Poe's poetry exhibits this invisible light, those rays without material origin as a poetic *Fiat Lux*: the grace-granting woman whispers, "Let there be light" ("To M.L.S.," 10). The light issuing from Annie's eyes transforms the heart and body of the poet on whom it falls. Equivocal is the role of woman in this poetry: maleficent if her body obtrudes, woman as luminescence (especially in death where the materiality of woman is rarefied and spiritualized),[7] becomes a benevolent messenger like Helen with her agate *lamp*) who softens and quiets down the maddening heart-beats, thus promising the perception of the subdued *rhythms* of pure poetry.

This "circumscribed Eden of the poet's dream," an "Eden of bland repose" created by luminous woman, is explicitly associated, in "To F——," with a locus whose magic would precisely be conjured up by beatlessness:

> . . . thy memory is to me
> Like some enchanted far-off isle
> In some tumultuous sea—
> Some ocean throbbing far and free. . . .

The island-woman is a rhythmical haven ("en- *chant* -ed") surrounded by the frightening *throbbing* of an ocean: above this island, in the narrow space of verticality, reigns the light of "serenest skies" (*serenus*). Those skies are the skies of dream inhabited by a mute rhythm—an *anima*, like a breath or a soundless harmony.

Despite its iambic cadence "The Sleeper" rhythmically suggests general drowsiness, a subduing of the prosodic beat; that sleepiness comes from a muffled music which conveys, beyond words and cadences, the rise of the poetic spirit—or sentiment. This "effect" cannot be analysed as the product of a semantic or phonic presence but as a *passage* (a vaporisation or etherealisation) towards another state:

> An opiate vapour. . . .
> Steals drowsily and musically
> Into the universal valley (3, 7–8).

As it comes in the flow of iambic tetrameters, the second line breaks up the cadence: no prosody founded on alternance or monotony can account for its effect. The line itself achieves the progressive metamorphosis of reality into an opiate incense. The hazy penetration of music into the matter of the world (the universal valley), the spiritualisation through music of the body of things generates a rarefaction of solid matter which always announces the dawn of the poetic sentiment. Poetry, in other words, is always assimilated to a rhythmical *dissolution* of reality.

Irene "with her destinies": the poetic body in harmony with the universal rhythm, with the vibrations of the cosmic lyre. Where "all Beauty sleeps" (16), a rhythm prevails—a pure rhythm never embodied in signs, implying the rise (*Aufgang*) of pure Beauty as a state-to-come in a territory once claimed by the palpitating body. Irene then imposes her "strange" appearance and "solemn silentness" (35–36). The throbbing body has been rhythmically conquered by a disquieting strangeness: an elusive poetic state as ephemeral as the "moment" of death. Irene the sleeper thus stands as a figure of death ultimately perceived by the poet as an entry into the poetic structure organized by God into "the most sublime of poems" (*Eureka*, 16:302). Like dream or sleep, and perhaps poetry, death creates the conditions for a co-pulsation, both corpuscular and undulatory, of the metaphysical subject and matter. The "lands" of Dream ("Dreamland") offer, in spite of apparent horrors, peacefulness to "the heart whose woes are legion" (39).

That "Eldorado" of the heart dimly perceived by the traveler, that "Holy-Land" he craves is unlocated even though it glimmers beyond the dark forests: "No spot of ground / That looked like Eldorado" ("Eldorado," 12–13). It is a *limen*—a magic locus one can only traverse and be thus temporarily cured of corporal cadences. The poetic locus of Poe's imagination is an immaterial place, a bodiless space where women, deprived of their corporality by a monstrous and sublime poetic act, help the poet sense, through the rhythmical etherealisation of their material being, the pulsional rhythmics of poetic truth.

"To Helen" (1848) and "Eulalie," among later poems, endeavor to convey the properly poetic value of the dissolution of human matter. The poetic Word therefore tends towards spiritualisation—in both the chemical and mystical senses—and thus metamorphoses the flesh-as-presence into a rhythmical movement of evaporation.

The woman as flower "gives out" her "odorous soul in an ecstatic death" ("To Helen," 12–14). We learned from "Al Aaraaf" that the flowers when their "odorous heart burst[s]" (I, 72), "bear" to Heaven "in odors, the Goddess' song" (I, 80–8)). The incorporeal woman, imbued with light, evaporates like "a soul, soaring" ("To Helen," 4) in the enchanted garden. Woman expires: as breath, she inspires a poetry of immaterial exchange. Poetry becomes an immaterial circulation (like a look) of ethereal matter between two bodies—a rhythmical exchange of identities between the nourishing body and the nourished word, a movement of dissolution saving only the eyes ("all expired . . . save only the divine light in thine eyes," 37–38). Poe's rhythmics is a rhythmics of light, an irradiation from "a *luminous* center" (*Eureka*, 16:225).

When reduced to her eyes, and their light ("only thine eyes remained," 51) woman recovers her primary poetic function: "they fill my soul with Beauty" (61).

A "rhythmical creation of beauty" by the evocation of a speechless voice in nature—a voice without a phonic presence—Poe's poetry creates mute rhythmic effects which might be described as luminous utterance. Those immaterial voices are the voices of the Angel, of the Messenger or even the "silent voice of God" which assert nothing but the reality of rhythm as unreachable essence of Truth.

### The Voices of Poetry

If cadence is a presence, rhythm is an "effect," a circulation of "ethereal" bodies—an energy. The strings of the lute produce "the sweetest voice" of Israfel—a nonvocalized voice, a voice without a content or message which can only be compared to light and the effects of light described in "Al Aaraaf." That voice transforms the stellar world into "a starry choir." Harmony—which has no signifier proper—is incarnate in a voice which is itself devoid of signifiers since it is the transcendental signifier of poetry. Israfel's voice teaches a lesson which is never included in his song or conveyed by it: his voice "bears" the vibratory, undulatory nature of reality made up of isolated particles attracted by the power of "loveliness" towards the nothingness of oneness. Ether— the locus of rarefied matter—is therefore the space where the primary movement of dissolution prophesies ultimate unity (*Eureka*).

No sensuousness remains in this almost fleshless *desire*: the glance of the Houri herself is spiritualised, "imbued with all the beauty / which we worship in a star" (25–28).

Thus "the fervour" of the Angelic "lute" or of God's eye ("Al Aaraaf," I, 120) supersedes the "fever" of life ("brought to a fever by the moonbeam," in "Spirits of the Dead"). The voice of the angel conveys an essential "loveliness," an unincarnate principle of love which "appertains to eternity alone" ("The Poetic Principle," 14:274).

Bodiless desire, the pure tendency of immaterial matter for the incorporeal other, the abstract pattern of relations also named Harmony is what Nesace sings, the Messenger who evokes Ligeia, "the Melodious," in the pure lyric of the second part of "Al Aaraaf" (II, 68–155). Those voices are pure insofar as they say nothing but "I am the voice" ("A voice was there," I, 122): the "harshest idea" of Ligeia "will to melody run" (II, 100–4). The pure melody of voice—Nesace's "embassy"—brings about the epiphanic death of angels: the seraphs of the Empyrean die a death described as "sweet error . . . sweet was their death" (II, 162 and 168). Death-as-ecstasy comes to be in the bosom of a "light that fell . . . from eye of God" (II, 159–60). A lethal voice, an epiphanic voice, a soundless music ("the music of the spheres"), the true poetic voice sings the co-presence of contraries from which Poe's poetry draws its rhythmic energy: God's voice is "a sound of silence" (I, 124).

Ligeia's voice therefore—directly derived from God's musical silence— plays, once again, a noncreative, almost dissuasive function: it only "keeps watch on the harmony" (II, 110–11), it "keeps vigilance" (II, 119) over the fragile essential harmony, thus allowing by her embassy the promise of the rise of rhythms.

Those rhythms are essential; they have nothing in common with "natural rhythms." The latter exist: "the sound of rain . . . the rhythm of the shower" (II, 120–23), "the murmur that springs from the growing grass" (II, 124–25)—create "a music of things" (II, 126) which could be mistaken for an "essential" harmony. But those rhythms "are modell'd, alas" (II, 126). They are not originary. Those imitative rhythms that *reproduce* or represent the unheard "model," those natural rhythms cannot provide the foundation of poetic music. They incarcerate poetry in repetition: "And just as the lily is repeated in the lake, or the eyes of Amaryllis in the mirror, so is the mere oral or written repetition of these forms, and sounds, and colours, and odours, and sentiments, a duplicate source of delight. But *this mere repetition is not poetry*" (14:273; italics mine).

The ultimate aim of Poe's poetry is to try to make the reader over-hear the *echo* of something else—an unrefracted ray, an unheard rhythm, a pregnant silence, an unperceived harmony to provoke "a thirst un-quenchable" (273). The "ecstatic prescience" of poetry is the promise of a light (*"glories* beyond the grave," 14:273–74), which will be per-ceived as rhythm in death or in dream. "Go!" says Nesace to Ligeia, "breathe on their slumber / . . . The musical number / They slumber'd to hear" (II, 144–47). The sacred *number,* the *numerous* (rhythm) of Being, transforms dream into a musical epiphany.

Poe's poetry aims at the creation of this poetic *state* through the hypnotic architectures of language. To be in the poetic state allows man to dream the presence of the soundless ontological rhythm, that is, to perceive Being as rhythm.

## Notes

1. *Cadence* (from *cadere,* to fall—like a foot on the ground, or a stress on the expected syllable) will be used, throughout this article, as defined in *Webster's New Universal Unabridged Dictionary*: "any regularity and uniformity of beat or measure, as in marching or dancing." The difference from "rhythm" (used in a sense not entirely free of influence by Heidegger) will be explored in the article and become, I hope, self-evident.

2. All references to Poe's prose works in parentheses are to J. Harrison, ed., *The Complete Works of Edgar Allan Poe* (New York: T. Y. Crowell, 1902). All references to his poetry are by line number, from Floyd Stovall, ed., *The Poems of Edgar Allan Poe* (Charlottesville: University Press of Virginia, 1965).

3. "There has never been a grander conception of poetry, nor a more impover-ished one." Richard Wilbur, Introduction to *Poe: Complete Poems* (New York: Dell, 1959) 39.

4. John W. Ostrom, ed., *The Letters of Edgar Allan Poe* (New York: Gordian Press, 1966), 1:19.

5. " 'The Raven' has had a great 'run,' Thomas—but I wrote it for the express purpose of running—just as I did the 'Gold-Bug,' you know. The bird beat the bug, though, all hollow." *Letters* 1:287.

6. *Letters* 1:78.

7. See, Claude Richard, "Le Corps de Lénore," *Prévue* 28 (Fall 1985).

# Frames of Reference for
# Poe's Symbolic Language
Eric W. Carlson*

Some twenty years ago at an MLA seminar on "Poe's Symbology," the discussion centered on this question: "Do not Poe's tales and poems need a closer reading for symbolic overtones and interrelationships within the context of Poe's views on life and art?" At that time a number of new approaches to Poe had been added to the earlier bio- graphical, Gothic, Romantic, Freudian, social (i.e., Southern), and tran- scendental or Platonic interpretations. Richard Wilbur's hypnagogic reading was widely known and accepted. The neogothic interpretations by Stephen Mooney, Allen Tate, and Leslie Fiedler also had commanded attention. Then in the 1960s and 70s Poe was presented as a psycho- moral allegorist, an existentialist, a "psychal transcendentalist," a Ger- man "Romantic Ironist and Absurdist"; and more recently he has been read in other new contexts: phenomenology, Jungian psychology, al- chemy, Gnosticism, "indeterminacy," "duplicity" and "hoaxing" as au- thorial intentions, "autobiographical cryptograms," the structuralist view of fiction as an allegory for the writing process, the American Romance, and the American apocalypse. Even though each of these has con- tributed some special insight, the sheer proliferation of such incom- patible approaches and contradictory findings has become a matter of special concern to some Poe critics. In 1981, for instance, Frederick S. Frank, after a survey of over one hundred critiques of *Pym*, concluded that *Pym* scholarship had been fractured into the work of formalists, archetypalists, folk-lorists, mythographers, etc.[1] Similarly, in 1982 Douglas Robinson classified the kinds of *Pym* criticism into a half dozen ap- proaches, stating a preference for the "visionary" reading as "methodo- logically the most fruitful and descriptively the most accurate." In other words, "by seeking to understand Poe as the author of *Pym* and his entire oeuvre, and *Pym* as the intended creation of Poe, the visionary critics aspire to a higher level of understanding at which synthesis becomes possible."[2]

At this juncture in the history of Poe criticism, two axioms of modern functional aesthetics might profitably be restated as follows:

1. An author's symbolism reflects his theory of literature,

2. His theory of literature reflects his outlook on life.

In other words, a symbolic system is the function of a writer's artistic perspective, that is, his symbology or theory of literature; and his symbology reflects his philosophic perspective or general outlook on life. That these fundamental principles are all but forgotten in our

*This essay, published here for the first time, is an amplified version of a paper read at the Poe Studies Association in New York, December 1983.

critical climate today is evident not only among many Poe critics but also among proponents of the "new theory." In a lecture entitled "What Happened to Structuralism?" Peter Caws, professor of philosophy at George Washington University, observed that structuralism today sorely lacks a phenomenology and an ontology.[3] Alexander Hammond reached a similar conclusion regarding Poe criticism from a survey of Poe biographies, old and new, when he asked for a modern literary biography that penetrates to the inside narrative—Poe's intellectual and aesthetic concerns. Carl Weber was quoted as maintaining that "emphasis must be placed upon those facts which determine his [the author's] emotional personality, for from them emerge his writings. . . . One must penetrate into the inner life of man, learn what he read and what he thought, inspect his secret desires and ambitions, and study his rebuffs and disappointments. The literary biographer's task is not so much to appraise the pearl as to explain why the oyster grew it."[4]

In short, sooner or later every serious student of Poe must study out Poe's Philosophic Perspective, his Artistic Perspective (including his symbology), and his Psychology of Realization (or epistemology). Poe passages and selections defining these perspectives constitute a frame of reference or base line from which, by the method of *literary parallax*, the sensitized reader can discover definite meanings in otherwise ambiguous writings. Among such passages are the opening and closing pages of *Eureka*, the 1844 letter to Lowell on matter and spirit, the colloquies, "Mesmeric Revelation," "The Poetic Principle," and the *Marginalia* passage on psychal fancies.

The most significant critical essays on Poe's frame of reference are Allen Tate's "The Angelic Imagination," Richard Wilbur's "The House of Poe" and his long introduction to the Poe section in *Major Writers in America*, Robert Jacobs's *Poe: Journalist and Critic*, especially the last two chapters, Eric Carlson's "Poe's Vision of Man" in *Papers on Poe* (ed. Richard P. Veler), and essays or chapters by Geoffrey Rans, Edward Davidson, Ottavio Casale, David Halliburton, Barton St. Armand, John Lynen, Maurice Beebe, and Douglas Robinson, among others. An exemplary interpretation using this approach is Richard D. Finholt's "The Vision at the Brink of the Abyss: 'The Descent into the Maelstrom' in the Light of Poe's Cosmology," which defines *Eureka* and "Mesmeric Revelation" as a base line by which to measure the narrator's achieved lucidity of vision, his reunification with God, the organic Unity of all life.[5]

The first tenet of the "perspective" approach is that in all creative art theme emerges out of the artist's or author's deep realizations about life. As Willa Cather remarked of her novel *My Antonia*, "practically everything beside the central purpose or the central feeling comes spontaneously and unexpectedly, though they all grow out of the main theme and *out of the feeling and experience that made me choose that theme*" [italics added].[6] This angle of vision is not to be confused with the "intentional fallacy," however. If a work has a conscious theme but no perspective behind it, it is the product of "rational" manipulation, as in programmatic and applied art. It is written "off the top of the head," as we say. Writing mainly to fascinate or to deceive or to hoax the reader is not truly creative; it has no depth of subconscious inspiration—only skill in technique, if that. A valid artistic purpose emerges only out of a mature philosophic perspective. Then the author "writes better than he knows,"—and his deepest revelations will take the form of "insight symbols"—as Allen Tate called Poe's—rather than irony, satire, and parody.

The organic relationship between Poe's symbolism and his outlook on life was clarified by Allen Tate in his classic essay, "The Angelic Imagination" (1952), in which he sought to define what he called the "philosophic perspective" of *Eureka* and the three angelic colloquies as clues to the meaning of Poe's symbols:

> Poe's symbols refer to a known tradition of thought, an intelligible order, apart from what he was as a man, and not merely the index to a compulsive neurosis; and, secondly . . . the symbols, cast into the framework of the three faculties, point towards this larger philosophical dimension, implicit in the serious stories, but very much at the surface in certain of Poe's works that have been almost completely ignored.

As his primary source, Tate quoted the three paragraphs from *Monos and Una* on "man's general condition at this epoch," which passage, he said, "adumbrates a philosophy of impressive extent and depth." He added that "Poe's flash of unsustained insight, in *The Colloquy of Monos and Una*, has, I submit, a greater dignity, a deeper philosophical perspective, and a tougher intellectual fibre, than the academic exercises of either Arnold or Mr. Richards." From the 1841 colloquy Tate proceeded to *The Power of Words*, "the full angelic vision of 1845," and then to *Eureka* as Poe's major essay on "the angelism of the intellect," with particular attention to the theme of hypertrophied intellect overpowering both feeling and will.[7]

Most Poe critics—among them Davidson, Wilbur, and Jacobs—follow Tate's view of Poe's symbols as "cast into the framework of the three faculties," as pointing toward Poe's perspective. My title phrase "Poe's Symbolic Language" refers to Poe's use of certain words and phrases that are stretched well beyond their denotative and usual metaphoric meanings until they function as motifs and symbols, as in "To Helen" and "Ligeia." A recent count of such expressions in the critical writings came to seventy. That a fair number of them occur also in the poems and tales suggests that a unifying pattern of ideas and language underlies Poe's work as a whole.

Within Poe's universe of artistic language there is an "inside" dimension that includes the speaker's mind or consciousness, his "voice" or tonal imagination, and sets of symbols or "metaphors" that reveal the "deep emotional self," the "shadowy" recesses of the unconscious. In his 1847 review of Hawthorne's tales, Poe linked this subliminal realm with "legitimate originality." "True originality," he wrote, "is that which, in bringing out the half-formed, the reluctant, or the unexpressed fancies of mankind, or in exciting the more delicate pulses of the heart's passion, or in giving birth to some universal sentiment or instinct in embryo, thus combines with the pleasurable effect of *apparent* novelty, a real egoistic delight." It is not surprising that Poe found acceptable only the allegory that is "properly handled, judiciously subdued, seen only as a shadow or by suggestive glimpses...."[8] Such expressions of intuitive sensibility to the shadowy depths of the psyche bring to mind Poe's use of the terms *mystic* and *moral* to signify an "under or *suggestive*" current of meaning: "the *moral* of any sentiment," he wrote, "is its mystic or secondary expression. It has the vast force of an accompaniment in music. This vivifies the air; that spiritualizes the *fanciful* conception, and lifts it into the *ideal*." After a set of examples, he continued his analogy to music: "With each note of the lyre is heard a ghostly, and not always a distinct, but an august and soul-exalting *echo*. In every glimpse of beauty presented, we catch, through long and wild vistas, dim bewildering visions of far more ethereal beauty beyond." A concluding reference to "the according tones of the accompaniment" completes the analogy as a way of clarifying the function of sound-impressionism in poetry.[9] The artistic hypnosis produced by these rich and resonant overtones is described as an "elevating excitement of the soul"— at its highest pitch a psychedelic state of mind associated with the arabesque in art and with vorticism in literature. David Ketterer defines Poe's arabesque both as a fluid, intuitive perception (method) and as an "ideal" or psychal reality (theme) that transcends the rational and the mundane to disclose "the ultimate life." Although Ketterer rightly concludes that "Poe belongs primarily with the Transcendentalists" and though he touches on Poe's arabesque fluidity—the hypnotic use of sound in rime, repetition, and refrain—the arabesque dimension is exhaustively documented only as a visual and symbolic design.[10]

But it is Poe's tonalism that, along with his arabesque design, reflects the subliminal as a value in the new interaction of music and literature during the Romantic movement. For Poe the power of lyric poetry and song lay not in voice volume and stress so much as in the quantitative "flow" of the line. Among his contemporaries, Sarah Helen Whitman, John Esten Cooke, and Thomas Wenthworth Higginson testified to this musical quality in Poe's recitations. Of Poe's reading of "Al Aaraaf" in Boston in 1845, Higginson wrote: "his voice seemed attenuated to the finest thread; the audience became hushed, and, as it were, breathless;

there seemed no life in the hall but his; and every syllable was accentuated with such delicacy, and sustained with such sweetness as I never
heard equaled by other lips.... The melody did not belong, in this case,
to the poet's voice alone; it was already in the words."[11] The power of
Poe's poetry lies in these undertones and overtones, reenforced by
rhythms of the deeper swells and ebbings of sound, as much as in the
theme, symbolism, and visual imagery. Both tone and symbol are part
of that "harmony of elements" which, through a "suggestive indefinitiveness of meaning" enables the poet to create a "definitiveness of vague
and therefore of spiritual *effect*."[12]

This symbology, this theory of the Vague, as it has been called, is
supported both by an epistemology and an ontology. In his 1842 review
of Longfellow's *Ballads*, as well as in "The Poetic Principle," Poe defined "the world of mind" as made up of intellect, taste, and moral sense,
conceiving taste to occupy naturally a middle position between pure
intellect and moral sense, thus serving to unify the tripartite self.[13]
When, in "Monos and Una," Poe remarked that "the pure contemplative
spirit and majestic intuition of Plato" were "entirely forgotten or despised," he had in mind the same faculty of "taste" or "poetic intellect,"
the neglect of which contributed to the cultural crisis of 1841. The following pages described how Monos was "born again" into a life of
heightened intuitive consciousness, beginning with a stage of synesthesia
"extravagant" both in precision and sensibility, and ending with the
power of "enduring *love*" and the "immortality" of "nothingness."[14]

This view of man's psychic potential and cosmic destiny was expanded in the climactic dozen paragraphs of *Eureka* that follow the
otherwise seeming finality of the paragraph on Nothingness or Material
Nihility. Allen Tate and the Romantic Ironist stop at that paragraph
and conclude that for Poe, God is zero; the universe and the life of
man are Absurd. "But," asks Poe, "are we here to pause?" "Not so," he
replies, and goes on to talk about the Divine Will and the law of
periodicity whereby the Universe will swell into existence at every throb
of the Heart Divine forever, and forever, and forever (Harrison 17:311).
In the final paragraph two identities are distinguished: the consciousness of "a proper identity" and "an identity with God...all is Life—
Life—Life within Life—the less within the greater, and all within the
*Spirit Divine*." So ends *Eureka*, with a rather direct statement of Poe's
ontology and transcendental cosmogony.[15]

These major documents express a deep faith in the poetic intellect
as indispensable to man's sanity and salvation; and an equally strong
belief in the universe as an ongoing process to infinity under the power
of Divine Will, a Will embodied in man's instinctive aspiration to Beauty,
to full self-realization, and to identity with God, knowable only as "Life
within Life." In these documents, among others, Poe's universe of dis-

course relies heavily on certain key terms: *soul, psychal, excites, elevating, intense, taste, poetic intellect, dim, indeterminate, intuition, Beauty, spiritual, ethereal, Nature, Life, identity, Divine Will, moral sense.* In another cluster of terms, *moral sense* is joined by *energy, moral* and *moral energy, vitality,* and *will.* This latter group becomes the semantic core of Poe's ontology, as *taste, poetic intellect, intuition,* and *psychal fancies* represent the semantic core of his epistemology, the two groups functioning in organic relationship.

*Moral, moral sense,* and *moral energy* play a crucial role in several tales. In "William Wilson" the narrator speaks of his alter ego's "moral sense" as being far keener than his own. This first, literal, and only use of the term in this tale is preceded and followed by incidents and language suggestive of a deeper psychic identity: the strange student's dignity, singular whisper, sudden appearances and departures in semi-darkness, and the narrator's fanciful recollection of "dim visions of my earliest infancy—wild, confused and thronging memories of a time when memory herself was yet unborn," as if he had been acquainted with this being "at some epoch long ago...."

This kind of Jungian memory occurs also in "The Fall of the House of Usher" where the narrator tells us that Roderick "had been one of my boon companions in boyhood.... Although, as boys, we had been even intimate associates, yet I really knew little of my friend. His reserve had been always excessive and habitual"—another suggestion of some shared or complementary psychic identity, now lost. The narrator, viewing Roderick's chamber, remarks that "many books and musical instruments lay scattered about, but failed to give any vitality to the scene." This lack of vitality is said to reflect Roderick's "want of moral energy." Despite this deficiency and his cadaverous complexion, however, Roderick is described in a way that transforms his other facial features into symbols of sensibility and poetic intellect—his "large, luminous, and liquid eye, his delicate Hebrew nose, finely moulded chin, and silken hair." According to Poe's definition of "true genius" the faculties must be in "absolute proportion," which is a product of "sensibility, together with that intense vitality...implied when we speak of 'Energy' or 'Passion.'"[16] The Usher family had long been noted for "a peculiar sensibility of temperament" expressed in many works of high art, of charity, and devotion to musical science. And even now Roderick still speaks occasionally with "energetic concision—that abrupt, weighty, unhurried, and hollow-sounding enunciation—that leaden, self-balanced, and perfectly modulated guttural utterance, which may be observed in the lost drunkard, or the irreclaimable eater of opium, during the periods of his most intense excitement." Here the allusion to opium, along with the adjectives *hollow sounding, leaden,* and *guttural,* may cause the reader to overlook the two adjectives *energetic* and *abrupt,* which imply vitality, and the words *concision, weighty, unhurried, self-balanced,* and *perfectly modulated,* which suggest disciplined control. Later, Roderick's disintegration is symbolized by "the more ghastly hue" of countenance, the no longer *luminous* eye, the lost *huskiness* of voice, replaced by a *tremulous quaver.* The narrator also remarks that in "The Mad Trist" of Canning "there is little in its uncouth and unimaginative prolixity which could have had interest for the lofty and spiritual ideality of my friend," implying that Roderick has not wholly lost his transcendental genius. And if Madeline represents Roderick's ailing, dormant, and suppressed vitality and will, without which he cannot function as artist (poet, painter, and creative musician), she reappears in symbolic guise and manner at the threshold (of consciousness): as the huge doors slowly opened, "there *did* stand the lofty and enshrouded figure of the lady Madeline of Usher," with "blood on her robes, and the evidence of some bitter struggle upon every portion of her emaciated frame."

Poe's use of *moral energy* and *vitality* is clarified by Howard Mumford Jones in his essay on "The Raven": "Premising the discussion by the fact that in Poe's day the word 'moral' (as in Wordsworth's 'all my moral being') was interchangeably used for 'ethical' or 'psychological' (sometimes it simultaneously meant both), we note Poe's insistence that the point of his poem is 'to seek a moral' in what is narrated; i.e. to try to comprehend the ethico-psychic statement of 'The Raven,' or, more simply, to understand that here is an exercise in the psychology of the Anonymous Young Man."[17]

In the next example, metaphor transforms into symbol. In his fiction, especially, Poe's fondness for the terms *wild* and *wildly,* is unmistakable. In a paper on "Poe's Critical Vocabulary," Robert Jacobs once pointed out that *wild* in Thoreau's usage denotes untamed, savage—its literal sense—and in Poe's criticism implies extravagant or uncontrolled by reason or caution.[18] Sherman Paul has noted that Thoreau traced this word to the past participle of *to will,* hence *self-willed,* which derivation Thoreau found in an 1852 volume entitled *The Study of Words* by Richard Trench.[19] That a similar connection occurred to Poe is suggested by the frequent use of *wild* in "Ligeia," his story on the power of the will. The epigraph reads in part: "For God is but a great will pervading all things by nature of its intentness." This concept, central to Poe's metaphysics, is again hinted at in "Morella"—in the reference to "the wild Pantheism of Fichte" as an example of "theological morality." Pollin's *Word Index to Poe's Fiction* lists *wild* as appearing 137 times.[20] Among the most significant are the uses of *wild* as a synonym for psychal, as in "the wild ideas of the land of dreams" (in "Berenice"); and in "the wilder visions of that land of real dreams" beyond this life, and "wild, full, liquid eyes" of the hero in ("The Assignation").

One line in 'Israfel'—"He might not sing so wildly well"—brings to mind a passage in Emerson's "The Poet" that must have struck a responsive chord in the synesthetic Poe:

> Like the metamorphosis of things into higher organic forms is their change into melodies. Over everything stands its daemon or soul, and, as the form of the thing is reflected by the eye, so the soul of the thing is reflected by a melody. The sea, the mountain-ridge, Niagara, and every ᵗflower-bed, pre-exist, or super-exist, in pre-cantations, which sail like odors in the air, and when any man goes by with an ear sufficiently fine, he overhears them and endeavors to write down the notes without diluting or depraving them.

And, Emerson added, "the poet knows that he speaks adequately then only when he speaks somewhat wildly, or 'with the flower of the mind,' " with "the intellect inebriated by nectar."[21] In "Al Aaraaf," lines 42–81, Poe's own precantations sailed like "perfume" in the air "To bear the Goddess' song, in odors, up to Heaven." Two lines in this passage—"and thy most lovely purple perfume, Zante! / Isola d'oro—Fior di Levante!"—anticipate "Sonnet—To Zante" and line 3 in "To Helen": "That gently, o'er a perfumed sea." Like Emerson, Poe associated fragrances and nectar, as sensory equivalents, with Love and Beauty in the experience of poetry.

Another revealing source for Poe's use of *wild* is his brief essay on George P. Morris, a song-writer. Here Poe wrote of "a certain wild license and *indefinitiveness*... that quality of the indefinite, which imparts to all songs, richly conceived, that free, affluent, and hearty manner, little scrupulous about niceties of phrase," as caught in the French word *Abandonnement*.[22] Such a "wild license" was felt by the narrator when he heard "the wild improvisations" of his [Usher's] speaking guitar." And in the next paragraph: "His long improvised dirges will ring forever in my ears," especially "a certain singular perversion and amplification of the wild air of the last waltz of Von Weber." If one listens to that waltz and concludes that its melody is *not* "wild," as Burton Pollin once demonstrated, one must attribute that adjective to the "singular perversion and amplification" that was the product of Usher's "excited and highly distempered ideality." In these examples, the word *wild* connotes a highly imaginative, extravagant, or eccentric quality—an *abandonnement* of conventional standards to the point of excess or at least artistic distortion; it also implies energy and intensity, but without a guiding focus or sense of direction and purpose.

In "Ligeia," Poe's composite portrait of Ligeia is also made up of partial symbols—facial features, eyes, teeth, and voice, hand, gait, height. The *wild* motif occurs eleven times, far more than in any other of the tales. The symbolic value of this word seems to increase as the context is enlarged, as for example, "the ceiling, of gloomy-looking oak, was excessively lofty, vaulted, and elaborately fretted with the wildest and most grotesque specimens of a semi-Gothic, semi-Druidic device." In this passage, *wildest* implies arabesque, which is coupled with *grotesque,* that favorite pair in Poe's aesthetic, in turn extended to equate with the fusion of Gothic and Druidic stimuli (or traditions) inherent in Ligeia's "transcendentalism." Other examples are simpler and less contextual: *wild words, wild change, wild eagerness,* whereas the theme of Ligeia's "gigantic volition" resounds in her "wild desire for life" and in her "so wildly earnest a desire for the life which was now fleeting so rapidly away" and, in the next sentence, by "this wild longing—it is this eager vehemence of desire for life—*but* for life—that I have no power to portray...." Several of the narrator's visions, opium-induced, are termed "wild" but after he reports that "my soul was awakened within me" the visions become "passionate waking visions of Ligeia," in which *waking* suggests deeply felt self-realizations, not random dreaming. In the final sentence, the climactic image is that of "the full, and the black, and the wild eyes—of my lost love—of the lady— of the LADY LIGEIA." Here *wild eyes* carries the cumulative weight of the earlier symbolic allusions.

Of course, this kind of analysis of one artistic element cannot do justice to the gestalt that is "Ligeia," an impressionistic and symbolic "tale of effect," with its Gothic overplot, its narrator (his "mind" or consciousness), its Ligeia and Rowena as symbolic figures, and its tone and style—in short, a work of art that really works through its multiple dimensions and its "totality of impression." Given its rich, intricate pattern of figurative and symbolic language, one can understand why Poe regarded this story as his best.

In the existentialist fables, too, this language appears within the larger context of "psycho-epistemology," to borrow a term from Brandon.[23] When the Poe hero suffers overt defeat or death or confesses his crime days or years later, he is driven by his moral energy to a "mad" (psychal) self-awareness. In the visionary tales of 1835–39 and the visionary poems of 1845–49, death is less a finality than a "metamorphosis" that leads to a sense of "proper identity" and an "identity with God" through a spiritual rebirth of "psychal" power.

For the past nearly seventy years this transcendental-symbolic reading of Poe has gradually emerged and been reaffirmed, partially or wholly, by the mainstream of Poe biographers, critics, scholars, and creative writers—among them, Baudelaire, Sarah Helen Whitman, Hansson, Forrest, Stovall, Margaret Alterton, T. O. Mabbott, A. H. Quinn, J. E. Reilly, Beebe, Davidson, P. Quinn, Wilbur, Rans, Finholt, Casale, Gargano, Moldenhauer, Lynen, Jacobs, Broussard, St. Armand, Levine (1972), Stauffer, Carlson, Griffith (1972), Halliburton, Ketterer, Irwin, Ljungquist (1975), Forclaz, Richard, Bickman, Pitcher, Frank, E. Arthur Robinson, Douglas Robinson, G. R. Thompson (1983), Harold Bloom, Joan Dayan. In the confusion of rival and conflicting interpretations it is not always evident how much consensus of competence exists under the surface of current controversy. But the history of Poe criticism from

1829 to the present clearly manifests a persistent preference for the "visionary" (sometimes Gnostic) interpretation of Poe's major poems and tales when read in the context of his philosophic and artistic perspectives. That consensus, tested by time and only slightly qualified by the few legitimate claims of irony, hoaxing, parody, and "undecidability," remains as a solid baseline from which new triangulations can be made.[24]

## Notes

1. Frederick S. Frank, "Polarized Gothic: An Annotated Bibliography of Poe's *Narrative of Arthur Gordon Pym*," *Bulletin of Bibliography* 38 (1981): 117–27.

2. Douglas Robinson, "Reading Poe's Novel: A Speculative Review of *Pym* Criticism, 1950–1980," *Poe Studies* 15 (1982):47–52.

3. Peter Caws, a lecture at the University of Connecticut, 13 November 1983.

4. Alexander Hammond, "On Poe Biography: A Review Essay," *ESQ* 28 (3rd Quarter 1982): 197–211.

5. "Allen Tate's ... Robinson": these essays are identified in the Introduction to this volume. Richard Finholt, "The Vision at the Brink of the Abyss," *Georgia Review* 27 (1973): 356–66.

6. Robert H. Footman, "The Genius of Willa Cather," *AL* 10 (May 1938): 138, n. 60.

7. Allen Tate, "The Angelic Imagination," *Kenyon Review* 14 (Summer 1952): 455–75; repr. in Eric. W. Carlson, ed., *The Recognition of Edgar Allan Poe* (Ann Arbor: University of Michigan Press, 1966), 254. Hereafter *REAP*.

8. Edgar Allan Poe, "Tale-Writing: Nathaniel Hawthorne" (1847), in James A. Harrison, ed., *The Complete Works of Edgar Allan Poe*, vol. 13 (New York: Thomas Y. Crowell, 1902), 146, 148.

9. Edgar Allan Poe, "Alciphron: A Poem. By Thomas Moore," *Burton's Gentleman's Magazine* 6 (January 1840): 53–56. Harrison, *Complete Works* 10: 60–71.

10. David Ketterer, *The Rationale of Deception in Poe* (Baton Rouge: Louisiana State University Press, 1979), 35–43, 151–61, 206–11, 222, ch. 6, ch. 7.

11. Thomas Wentworth Higginson, "Edgar Allan Poe," *Literary World* 10 (15 March 1879): 89–90; reprinted in *REAP*, 67–75.

12. "Marginalia," *Democratic Review* 15 (December 1844):580. Harrison, *Complete Works* 16:28.

13. Poe's review of Longfellow's *Ballads and Other Poems*, *Graham's Magazine* 20 (April 1842):248–49; Harrison, *Complete Works* 11:70.

14. Poe, "Colloquy of Monos and Una," *Graham's Magazine* 19 (August 1841): 52–55; Harrison, *Complete Works* 4:200–12; *Collected Works of Edgar Allan Poe*, ed. Thomas O. Mabbott (Cambridge: Harvard University Press, 1978), vol. 2, 607–19.

15. *Eureka: A Prose Poem* (New York: George P. Putnam, 1848); Harrison, *Complete Works* 16:179–315, 311, 337.

16. "Fifty Suggestions," *Graham's Magazine* 34, no 23 (May 1849): 317–19. Reprinted in Burton R. Pollin, ed., *Collected Writings of Edgar Allan Poe* (New York: Gordian Press, 1985), 2:xxix, 489–91.

17. Howard Mumford Jones, "Poe, 'The Raven,' and the Anonymous Young Man," *Western Humanities Review* 9 (1955):127–38.

18. Robert D. Jacobs, "Poe's Critical Vocabulary," Poe Studies Association, N.Y. Historical Society, December 1972.

19. Sherman Paul, *The Shores of America: Thoreau's Inward Exploration* (Urbana: University of Illinois Press, 1958), 412.

20. Burton R. Pollin, *Word Index to Poe's Fiction* (New York: Gordian Press, 1982).

21. Ralph Waldo Emerson, "The Poet," *The Complete Works of Ralph Waldo Emerson*, ed. Edward Waldo Emerson, vol. 3 (Cambridge: Houghton Mifflin, 1903), 25, 27.

22. Poe, "George P. Morris," *Burton's Gentleman's Magazine* 5 (December 1839):332–33. Cf. Harrison, *Complete Works* 10:41–45 and Pollin, *Collected Writings*, 2: 337–43.

23. Nathaniel Brandon, *The Disowned Self* (Los Angeles: Nash Publishing Co., 1971), 102.

24. For an excellent account of Poe's transcendentalism, literary and philosophic, with special attention to *Eureka*, and a survey of studies by Pochmann, Campbell, Conner, Davidson, Smithline, Casale, Holman, Ramakrishna, and others, see Ottavio M. Casale, "Edgar Allan Poe," in Joel Myerson, ed., *The Transcendentalists: A Review of Research and Criticism* (New York: Modern Language Association, 1984), 362–71. Casale's earlier "Poe on Transcendentalism," *ESQ* 50 (First Quarter 1968): 85–97, remains the best essay on the subject.

# INDEX